P9-CDD-549

Bind, Torture, Kill

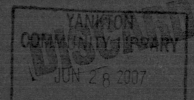

Bind, Torture, Kill

The Inside Story of the Serial Killer Next Door

Roy Wenzl, Tim Potter, L. Kelly, and Hurst Laviana

HC

An Imprint of HarperCollins*Publishers*

PHOTOGRAPHY CREDITS: pages 2, 4, 19, 21, 35, 37, 40, 41, 42, 48, 58, 80, 93, 94, 97, 99, 120, 123, 124, 231, 235, 239, 265, 273, 276, 277, 278, 279, courtesy of the Sedgwick County District Attorney's Office; 5, 72, courtesy of Cindy Landwehr; 17, 34, courtesy of the Wichita Police Department; 9, 30, 44, 63, 69, 165, 167, 168, 187, 242, 258, 291, 299, *The Wichita Eagle*; 43, Dave Williams/*The Wichita Eagle*; 87, 170, Jaime Oppenheimer/*The Wichita Eagle*; 91, 117, 298, courtesy of the Sedgwick County Sheriff's Office; 111, Mike Hutmacher/*The Wichita Eagle*; 150, 151, courtesy of Danny Saville; 179, courtesy of Janet Johnson; 196, courtesy of KAKE-TV; 248, 288, 289, 319, Jeff Tuttle/*The Wichita Eagle*; 313, 314, 315, 316, 317, 318, Bo Rader/*The Wichita Eagle*; 330, courtesy of the Kansas Department of Corrections.

HarperCollins books may be purchased for educational, business, or sales promotional use. For information please write: Special Markets Department, HarperCollins Publishers, 10 East 53rd Street, New York, NY 10022.

FIRST EDITION

Designed by Kris Tobiassen

Library of Congress Cataloging-in-Publication Data has been applied for.

ISBN: 978-0-06-124650-0
ISBN-10: 0-06-124650-6

07 08 09 10 11   DIX/RRD   10 9 8 7 6 5 4 3 2 1

Contents

A few words about the dialogue:

We have reconstructed many conversations through the recollections of those involved, quotes in news coverage, and our own notes. To the best of our knowledge, remarks presented within quotation marks reflect what was said at the time.

In cases where dialogue could not be reconstructed but the essence was available, we did not use quotation marks; we used phrasing to indicate that these words are substantially similar to what was said—or in the case of BTK talking to his victims, the conversations as he recalled them.

Italicized phrases reflect participants' recollections of their thoughts.

Introduction

The Wichita Eagle has covered the BTK serial killer since he first struck in January 1974. From 2004 to 2006 alone, the *Eagle* published roughly eight hundred pieces about BTK's reemergence, the intensive investigation, the resolution, and how the case affected our community. The paper spent thousands of dollars on transcripts of court proceedings, then posted them online for everyone to read. The newspaper's expansive and in-depth coverage earned us awards and accolades. Some might think that there'd be little new to say—especially considering the 24/7 attention BTK got from cable news shows.

But we've got the inside scoop. It's not only that we know more about the BTK story than anyone else, we've lived it—in my case, grown up with it. We have drawn on the *Eagle*'s thirty-two-year archive—including original reporters' notes, internal memos, and photographs.

Over the course of three decades, BTK, the *Wichita Eagle*, and the Wichita police developed complicated relationships. It was through the *Eagle* that BTK sent his first message in 1974. It was to the *Eagle* a few years later that the Wichita police chief desperately turned for help in trapping the killer. It was in a macabre letter to the *Eagle*—delivered to the police by reporter Hurst Laviana—that the killer announced his reemergence in 2004. And it was through the *Eagle*'s classifieds that the head of the investigation tricked BTK into making a mistake that led to his capture in 2005.

And when BTK—family man and church president Dennis Rader—was finally in his prison cell, it was to us, for this book, that Police Lt. Ken Landwehr and his key investigators told their side of the story in intimate detail.

Landwehr and the detectives were unhappy with the rampant errors in other books about this case; they knew we cared about this chapter of our community's history just as much as they did, and they trusted us to get the facts right. Laviana has covered crime in Wichita for more than twenty years. Tim Potter has been nicknamed "Columbo" by the cops for his habit of calling back to double-check facts in his notes. Roy Wenzl has two brothers in law enforcement. My father was a Wichita homicide detective.

But this is not a "just the facts, ma'am" recitation of the case. The people who stopped BTK are real cops—and real characters. They've lowered their shields to let us take you along with them on stakeouts and shoot-outs and into their homes and hearts. In the past, talking to us for newspaper stories, they've been guarded. Landwehr's public face has always been stoic. He has never sought publicity, never played games, never answered questions about himself. He is witty in person, but not easy to know.

Starting work with him on this book, Wenzl told Landwehr that we wanted to portray him accurately, not as "a plaster saint, all sweetness and success. . . . I want to know your flaws. I want to ask your wife about your flaws."

Wenzl, who had covered cops for years, could not imagine any police supervisor saying yes to this. It required daring.

Landwehr shrugged, pulled out his cell phone, and dialed Cindy Landwehr.

"Hey," he said. "Do ya wanna talk to these guys?"

Then Landwehr looked at Wenzl.

"Once you get her started about that, she might not ever stop."

The portraits of Rader and Landwehr that we have been able to draw for this book are mirror images—both men are native sons of the heartland of America, products of churchgoing middle-class families, Boy Scouts who grew up to marry and have children of their own. Yet one became a sexual deviant who killed for his personal pleasure while the other became a cop who dedicated himself to protecting the lives of others. The choices they made destined Rader and Landwehr to become opponents in a deadly game of cat and mouse.

In writing this book, we had a choice to make as well. Others have focused on portraying the evil; we wanted to give equal time to the people who stopped it.

L. KELLY

1

January 15, 1974, 8:20 AM

The Oteros

Her name was Josie Otero. She was eleven years old and wore glasses and wrote poetry and drew pictures and worried about her looks. She had started wearing a bra and growing her hair out; it fell so thick around her head and throat that the man with the gun would soon have a hard time tying the cloth to keep the gag stuffed in her mouth.

As Josie woke up that morning, the man with the gun crept to her back door and saw something that made him sweat: a paw print in the snowy backyard. He had not expected a dog.

He whistled softly; no dog. Still, he pulled a Colt Woodsman .22 from his waistband and slunk to the garage wall to think.

In the house, Josie had pulled on a blue T-shirt and walked from her room to the kitchen. It was a short walk; it was a small house. Her mom, Julie, was in the kitchen, wearing her blue housecoat. She had set the table, putting out cereal and milk for breakfast and tins of potted meat for school-lunch sandwiches. Joe, Josie's dad, was eating canned pears.

At five feet four, Josie was already an inch taller than her mom and as tall as her dad. But she worried the worries of a child.

"You don't love me as much as you love the rest of them," she had blurted one day to her brother Charlie. At fifteen he was the oldest of the five Otero kids.

"That's not true," he said. "I love you as much as I love any of them."

She felt better; she loved them all, Mom and Dad and Charlie, and Joey, who was nine, and Danny, fourteen, and Carmen, thirteen. She loved the way Joey studied his brothers and tried to be tough like them. He was so cute; the girls at Adams Elementary School adored his brown eyes. This morning he had dressed to draw attention: a long-sleeved shirt pulled over a yellow T-shirt and white undershirt, and purplish trousers with white pockets and white stripes down the back.

It was Tuesday. They would play with the dog, help Mom pack lunches, then Dad would drive Josie and Joey to school as he had done already for Charlie, Danny, and Carmen. Mom had laid their coats on a chair.

Outside, the man hesitated.

In the pockets of his parka he carried rope, venetian blind cord, gags, white adhesive tape, a knife, and plastic bags.

The Oteros had lived in Camden, New Jersey, and then the Panama Canal Zone for seven years, and then their native Puerto Rico with relatives for a few months. They had bought their house in Wichita only ten weeks earlier and were still getting their bearings. Wichita was a big airplane manufacturing center, and this spelled opportunity for Joe. He had retired as a technical sergeant after twenty years in the U.S. Air Force and now worked on airplanes and taught flying at Cook Field, a few miles outside Wichita, the Air Capital of the World. Boeing, Cessna, Beech, and Learjet all had big factories there; the city that once sent

Charlie, Danny, Joey, Carmen, Josie, Julie, and Joe Otero.

sixteen-hundred B-29 Superfortress bombers to war now supplied airlines and movie stars with jets. Julie had taken a job at Coleman, the camping equipment factory, but was laid off a few weeks later in a downsizing.

They now lived among the 260,000 people of Wichita, many of whom were ex-farm kids who cherished the trust they felt for their neighbors and left their doors unlocked. The airplane manufacturers had come to Wichita decades earlier in part because they were able to hire young people who had grown up on neighboring farms, learning how to fix tractor engines and carburetors from early childhood, and these workers and their families had brought their farm sensibilities with them to the city. People still left the keys in their cars at night and took casseroles to sick neighbors. This was a culture the Oteros liked, but Joe and Julie had more of a New York attitude about safety. Joe had acquired the dog, Lucky, who hated strangers. Joe had street smarts, and at age thirty-eight he was still wiry and strong. He'd been a champion boxer in Spanish Harlem. Julie, thirty-four, practiced judo and taught it to the children.

Joe was streetwise but playful. At work among Anglo strangers, he made people laugh by mocking his own Puerto Rican accent. He made shopping fun, once dragging the kids around a store on a sled as they laughed. When Joe signed the mortgage for the house (six rooms and an unfinished basement), he joked to the broker, "I hope I'm still alive when this lien is paid off."

Two months later the Oteros were still unpacking boxes.

One night Joe and Charlie had watched the movie *In Cold Blood*, the story of two losers who in 1959 murdered four members of the Clutter family in Holcomb, Kansas.

How could anybody do that? Charlie asked.

"Be glad nothing like that has ever happened to you," Joe said.

Dennis Rader had seen the woman and the girl one day while driving his wife to work at the Veterans Administration; his wife didn't like driving in snow. On Edgemoor Drive, he saw two dark-skinned females in a station wagon backing onto Murdock Avenue.

After that, he stalked them for weeks and took notes. He followed

Julie several times as she drove Josie and Joey to school. He knew that they left about 8:45 and that it took Julie seven minutes to get back home. He knew the husband left for work around 8:00 AM. He did not want to confront the husband, so he timed his own arrival for about 8:20. The husband would be gone. The boy would be there, but he was incidental to the plan. He would kill the boy, but he did not want him. He wanted the girl.

He did not know that the Oteros were down to one car.

Joe had wrecked the other one a few days before, breaking some ribs. To get Carmen, Danny, and Charlie to school before 8:00, Joe had taken the station wagon that Julie usually drove. Charlie had started to close the garage door, but Joe told him to leave it up because he would come back. With his injury, Joe wasn't able to work.

It was twenty degrees outside, and snow lay frozen on the hard ground.

Rader was twenty-eight; he had dark hair and green eyes that had lately spent a lot of time looking deep into the dark. He liked to look at pornography; he liked to daydream. He had nicknamed his penis Sparky. He fancied himself a secret agent, an assassin, a shadow.

Rader had risen in the dark this morning, packed his coat pockets, parked several blocks from the target house, then walked. The house sat on the northwest corner of Murdock Avenue and Edgemoor Drive

Dennis Rader, while he was in the air force in the 1960s.

in east Wichita. He had arrived as the dim light of dawn obscured the comet Kohoutek that for weeks had hung like a ghost above the southern horizon.

He thought of the girl with long, dark hair and glasses. She looked like she was made for SBT, his abbreviation for "Sparky Big Time."

But now, in the backyard, he hesitated.

Where was the dog?

Over the next thirty-one years, Rader would write many words about this day, some lies, some true:

He selected the family because Hispanic women turned him on.

He fantasized about sex, trained himself how to kill. He tied nooses, and hanged dogs and cats in barns. As a teen and then later in the air force, he peered through blinds to watch women undress. He broke into homes to steal panties.

He stalked women as they shopped alone in grocery stores. He planned to hide in the backseat of their cars and kidnap them at gunpoint. He would take them to places where he and Sparky could play: bind, torture, kill.

He had always chickened out.

But not this time.

He crept from the garage to the back door.

He reached out to open it.

Locked.

He pulled a hunting knife and severed the telephone line, which was tacked to the white clapboard wall.

He suddenly heard the back door opening. He pulled his gun and found himself staring into the face of the little boy. And finally he saw the dog, standing beside the boy. The dog began to bark.

Quickly now, as the sweat began to flow, Rader hustled the child into the kitchen—and came face-to-face with another surprise. The man was home.

The dog barked and barked.

Rader towered seven inches over the smaller man, but he felt quaking fear now. He pointed his gun.

This is a stickup, he said.

The girl began to cry.

Don't be alarmed, he told them.

Across town several miles to the west lived a college kid who had no clue how the events of this day would shape his life.

He was something of a character, or so his mother thought. He could never sit still; he always had to be doing something with his hands. He was a smart aleck. As a little boy playing cops and robbers, he always played the cop. When the other boys pressed him to be the bad guy, he walked away.

He seemed the straight arrow, but he was not. He got into fights, like a lot of other boys growing up on the rough blue-collar west side of Wichita, but learned to avoid them. He won debate championships in high school but hid his partying from his mother. He played the beagle Snoopy in a high school production of *You're a Good Man, Charlie Brown*. He made Eagle Scout in 1971, the year before he graduated, but drank to excess on Fridays. He liked school. He liked mysteries, especially the stories about Sherlock Holmes.

Kenny Landwehr was still a teenager, not yet a deeply reflective soul, but he knew why he liked those stories: Holmes solved murders, the hardest crime to solve because the best possible witness was dead.

Kenny Landwehr, Eagle Scout.

2

All Tied Up

The afternoon paper landed on Wichita's porches between 3:00 and 4:00 PM, with the headline TAPE ERASED, JUDGE TOLD on the front page. Judge John Sirica in Washington, D.C., was furious about an eighteen-minute gap in a recording of one of President Nixon's private conversations about the Watergate burglary. That was the national news at the moment Carmen and Danny Otero arrived home, walking up Murdock Avenue from Robinson Junior High.

They saw several odd things: the station wagon was gone, the garage door up. The back door was locked. Lucky was staring at them from the backyard. That got their attention, because their parents never left him out—he barked at strangers. When they got the front door open, they found their mother's purse on the living room floor, its contents scattered.

They saw Josie's little white purse in the kitchen and their father's wallet with its cards and papers strewn across the stove top. Potted meat containers and a package of bread, still open, sat on the table.

Danny and Carmen ran for their parents' room. There they found them, their hands tied behind their backs, their bodies stiff and cold.

Charlie at that moment was walking home along Edgemoor, still keyed up from final-exam day at Southeast High. On the street, he picked up a religious pamphlet off the sidewalk.

"You need God for your life," it said. He dropped it. Mom had taught them about God.

When Charlie saw Lucky standing outside, when he saw the garage door up, he decided he would tease his mom for being forgetful. Then he walked inside and heard Danny and Carmen yelling from his parents' room.

What he saw there sent him running for the kitchen, where he grabbed a knife. "Whoever is in this house, you're dead!" he yelled. No one answered.

He picked up a yardstick and whacked it around until it shattered.

The phone was dead. Charlie ran outside and banged on a neighbor's door.

Officers Robert Bulla and Jim Lindeburg reached 803 North Edgemoor at 3:42 PM. A teenage boy ran to them, looking wild and unstrung. He said his name was Charlie. He told the officers what they would find in the house.

Stay outside, they told Charlie and the two children with him. Bulla and Lindeburg walked in, saw the purse, walked deeper inside the house, and pushed on the door to the master bedroom. A man lay tied up on the floor; a woman lay on the bed, bare legs bent and hanging over the edge, her faced streaked with dried blood from her nose. The rope around her neck had been cut. The cops learned later that Carmen had nipped at it with toenail clippers, trying frantically to revive her mother.

Bulla felt for pulses, then radioed dispatchers: two possible homicide victims.

Lindeburg and Bulla walked out of the house to the children, who looked frantic. There are two more children, the teens said. They have not come home yet. We can't let them see this. The family station wagon was missing, they said: a brown 1966 Oldsmobile Vista Cruiser. The officers made a note.

More officers arrived, then detectives.

Officers questioned the children.

"You think your father could have done this?"

Charlie kept telling the cops to stop Josie and Joey from coming home.

Officers told the children to move away from the house. Detective Ray Floyd pulled Charlie aside.

They had found the two kids in the house, Floyd told him.

They were dead.

• • •

The phone on Jack Bruce's desk rang minutes later.

"We've got four dead people in a house on Edgemoor," the emergency dispatcher said.

"What?"

"Four dead people. On Edgemoor."

"What do you mean, four *dead* people?"

"They're dead, and all four are all tied up."

Bruce, a tall commander with a confident manner, was a lieutenant colonel supervising vice and homicide detectives. He heard other phones ring on other desks now, and he watched detectives bolt out the door. Within minutes, Bruce was talking on two phones at once, trying to keep people from bumping into each other. He made assignments, sent lab people, coordinated shifts. The entire police department mobilized.

Sgt. Joe Thomas arrived minutes after the first call and secured the scene, which meant keeping people from messing up evidence before detectives took charge. Thomas took a quick tour, looking into each room just long enough to get angry. Within minutes, the place filled: detectives, lab people, police brass. Like Thomas, they were shaken by what they saw.

Danny and Carmen Otero enter the roped-off crime scene to talk to police.

Detective Gary Caldwell walked down into the dark basement. He did not have a flashlight. Caldwell felt his way, turned a corner, groped for a switch, and brushed against something hanging from the ceiling.

He found the switch and saw a dead girl, nearly naked, hanging by a rough hemp noose from a sewer pipe. Her dark hair was draped across one cheek, and her tongue protruded past a gag.

Maj. Bill Cornwell ran the homicide unit; he took over. He and Bernie Drowatzky, a craggy-faced veteran detective, noticed that whoever had done this had used a variety of knots to tie wrists, ankles, and throats. They suspected the killer had run out of cord: some of the victims' wrists had been taped.

The boy had died beside his bunk bed. In the boy's room, Cornwell saw something that stayed with him for life: chair imprints on the carpet. They looked fresh. Cornwell thought he knew what that meant: the killer, after he tied the boy's wrists, after he pulled two T-shirts and a plastic bag over the boy's head, after he pulled the clothesline tight around the boy's neck, had placed a chair beside the child so he could watch him suffocate.

There were so many ligature marks on the throats of the other Oteros it looked as though the killer had strangled them more than once, letting them have some air, then finishing them.

Keith Sanborn, the crew-cut district attorney for Sedgwick County, took a grim house tour. The detectives told him they had found dried fluid on the girl's naked thigh, and spots of the same stuff on the floor. Looks like he masturbated on her, they said.

Cornwell's boss, Lt. Col. Bruce, went in after the bodies were taken away that night, walking past reporters and photographers stamping outside in the cold. They had shot pictures of the surviving children being hustled under the crime scene tape; they had filmed bodies being removed. *This will shake up the city,* Bruce thought.

"Get some rest," Bruce told his detectives. "Get a night's sleep so you can come back." No one listened.

Caldwell and Drowatzky volunteered to stay in the house all night. If the killer came back, they would greet him. Caldwell called his wife and told her; she got upset. Then he and Drowatzky settled in. Sometimes they peeked out the windows; all they saw were photographers and a parade of gawkers.

Back at his office, Cornwell pondered conflicting reports. A neighbor said he had seen a tall white man with a slender build wearing a dark coat outside the Otero house at about 8:45 AM. Other witnesses described a much shorter man—perhaps just five feet two. They said he had bushy black hair and a dark complexion. Police Chief Floyd Hannon told reporters the suspect might be Middle Eastern. But in the sketch artist's composite drawing, the man looked Hispanic. In fact, the man looked a lot like Joe Otero with a thin mustache. Someone else said he had seen a dark-haired man driving the Oteros' station wagon at about 10:30 that morning.

A detective had found the Oteros' car parked at the Dillons grocery store at Central and Oliver, a half mile away. The position of the seat showed that the driver might be short.

Cornwell stayed in his office all night, taking calls, pitching ideas, taking catnaps in a chair. He and other detectives did not go home for three days; they had sandwiches brought in. For ten days, seventy-five officers and detectives worked eighteen hours a day.

The killer had tied a dizzying variety of knots: clove hitches, half hitches, slipknots, square knots, overhand knots, blood knots. There were so many knots that one detective photocopied the names, drawings, and descriptions of knots from an encyclopedia published by the Naval Institute Press. Maybe the killer was a sailor, Bruce thought.

Detectives studied the autopsy reports. The coroner found bruising on Julie's face; she had been beaten before she died. There were deep indentations around Joe's wrists; he had fought to break his bonds. There were ligature marks and broken capillaries on Joey's neck and face; he had died of strangulation and suffocation.

The autopsy showed that Josie had weighed only 115 pounds and that she had died in a hangman's noose with her hands tied behind her back. She was bound at the ankles and knees with cord that snaked up to her waist. The killer had cut her bra in the front and pulled her cotton panties down to her ankles.

The lab people had scraped dried fluid from her thigh. When they put the scrapings under a microscope, they saw sperm.

At the end of the first week, sleep-deprived detectives began to run out of energy and ideas.

They tried one nutty idea: Caldwell and Drowatzky stayed all night in the house again, this time with a psychic. She claimed that she had once helped solve a crime by leading police to a body in a trunk. The two cops sat in silence as the psychic scribbled her impressions. Nothing came of it.

There had been one major foul-up. Someone lost most of the autopsy photos and several crime scene photos. The chief blew his stack.

Still, there was a pile of photographs to study. Among them was a curiosity—a picture of an ice tray in the kitchen with ice still in it. The killer had struck before 9:00 AM and turned up the heat before leaving the house. Witnesses saw the Oteros' Vista Cruiser on the street at about 10:30 AM. The crime scene photographer arrived six hours later. And the photo showed ice. It didn't take a Sherlock Holmes to figure this out: Someone from the police who had surveyed the dead then opened the Oteros' freezer and made himself something to drink.

Chief Hannon held press conferences at least twice a day, disclosing specifics, speculating about motives and suspects. The morning *Wichita Eagle* and afternoon *Beacon* covered every development. Readers learned that Josie and Joey were model students; that Joe and Julie Otero had taken out a $16,850 mortgage on their "junior ranch" home, that the killings indicated "some kind of fetish." The coverage included a forensics photo of a knotted cord that the killer had used, front-page diagrams by newspaper cartoonist Jerry Bittle showing where in the home the bodies were found, and a sketch of Josie hanging from the pipe.

None of this made a lasting impression on Kenny Landwehr, the west-side kid. The Otero murders occurred on the east side. Wichita in 1974 was a socially divided city, the boundary clearly drawn by the Arkansas and Little Arkansas rivers that converge downtown. These were broad stereotypes, but the west side was more blue-collar, the east side more elite. Landwehr's parents, Lee and Irene, read about the killings with dismay, but their son paid scant attention, even though he'd day-dreamed about joining the FBI.

The inspiration for this was Irene's brother, Ernie Halsig, an FBI agent. "If you apply to the FBI, they'll want you to have some account-ing," Uncle Ernie said. So Landwehr, majoring in history at Wichita State University, added accounting to his schedule.

To make a little money, he worked as a salesman at Beuttel's Clothing Company in Wichita's industrial north end.

He did not feel strongly about the FBI. He had other preoccupa-tions: girls, golf, beer—sometimes a lot of beer. He played pool and foos-ball at a west-side lounge called the Old English Pub.

He didn't dwell on the Otero murders; the Pub seemed dangerous enough. There was this guy who hung out there . . . Bell . . . James Eddy Bell. He was an asshole, a big and ugly bully. In the Pub, Landwehr gave Bell plenty of space and spoke politely around him.

That was hard. Landwehr had a smart mouth.

3

January–April 1974

Fear and Possibilities

The Oteros were buried in Puerto Rico. The surviving children left Wichita for good; they found a home with a family in Albuquerque.

Charlie Otero's future would include depression, anger, a rift with his siblings, and prison time for domestic assault. He would forsake God, as he believed God had forsaken his family. He had no answers for the questions that troubled him:

Why had someone attacked his family?

How did he get past the dog? How could he talk a boxer like Dad into putting his fists behind his back?

There must have been more than one killer, Charlie thought.

Charlie wanted to kill them all.

Police started with four possibilities:

1. **Was the killer somebody within the family?** They quickly ruled out that idea.

2. **Was there a drug connection?** In the air force, Joseph Otero had served in Latin America. After his discharge, Joe took a job that gave him access to private airplanes. This intrigued detectives. Maybe a big overseas drug deal had gone sour, and Joe lost his life and family in a revenge killing.

   Cornwell and Hannon flew to Panama and Puerto Rico to chase this idea. Bruce was dubious—the cops had not found so much as a single aspirin in the house, let alone illegal drugs.

3. **Was someone out to get Julie?** She had worked at Coleman. Did she have a jealous boyfriend there? Her former supervisor had

been shot and wounded just days before she died. Was there a connection?

4. **Was the killer a thief who killed to cover his tracks?** Detectives looked at known burglars, though the only things missing were Joe's watch, Joey's radio, and a set of keys.

Four ideas, four wild goose chases.

Dennis Rader had spent two hours with the Oteros, then he had slid into their Vista Cruiser and driven to the Dillons grocery store. He just made it—the Oteros had run the tank nearly dry. On the way, he kept the hood of his parka up to hide his face. Before he got out, he adjusted the seat forward to disguise his height. He walked to his own car, a white 1962 Impala coupe. There he took an inventory of everything he had brought that morning, then realized, with a sick feeling, that he had left his knife at the Otero house.

He drove back to the house on North Edgemoor, pulled into the garage, walked to the back door, and picked up the knife. Then he drove home, his head pounding. He took two Tylenol, then drove to some woods he'd played in as a boy, along the Little Arkansas River north of Wichita. There he burned sketches he had made during the planning, along with things he had used to kill the family. He hurried. His wife would be getting off work, and he wanted to be home.

After the murders, Wichitans who had never locked their doors did so. Some bought guns and alarm systems. Kids like Steve and Rebecca Macy came home from high school every day with a new routine: Rebecca would sit in the car. Steve would carry a baseball bat into the house and check every room and closet—and the phone—before letting his sister in.

Younger children like Tim Relph, a seventh grader, lived with fear for years, wondering whether their families might be attacked. The route his parents drove to get him and his siblings to school took them along the same streets the Oteros used.

Homicide captain Charlie Stewart began to sleep near his front door.

Lindy Kelly, a former homicide detective, was so angry about what he'd heard from his best friend, Sgt. Joe Thomas, that he violated his rule about never scaring his children with stories about work. He told his thir-teen-year-old daughter, Laura, about the chair imprints in the carpet. The guy had sat and watched the little boy struggle, Kelly said.

Thomas began a routine that would last the rest of his life. Every morning when he picked up the *Eagle*, he carried a doorstop, a heavy metal bar that would come in handy for beating the Oteros' killer to pieces if he decided one day to pay him a visit.

Rader slipped back into the comforts of home. He had been married nearly three years and still opened doors for his wife, helped her put on her coat. They attended church with their parents; he helped with the youth group. But he made the rules and liked things neat, orderly, and on time. She complied.

He liked to study crime novels, detective magazines, and pornogra-phy. He liked to masturbate while playing with handcuffs. In their snug home—only 960 square feet—he hid small trophies. On his wrist he wore Joe Otero's watch. It ran well and got him to school on time. Wichita State University had started spring classes, and he had chosen a major—administration of justice—that let him study police officers closely and learn more about his new pursuit. He enjoyed the irony.

He began to write about what he had done; he told his wife he had a lot of typing to do for school. He wrote that Joe Otero had thought in the first moments that his intrusion was a practical joke. He wrote what Josie had said just before he hanged her. He wrote it all down, finished it on February 3, 1974, and filed it in a binder so he could read it whenever he pleased. He signed the document "B.T.K." Bind, torture, kill.

He knew he had done things that could have got him caught: he had left his knife behind. He had let himself be seen. He had not anticipated the dog. He had assumed the father had left. He had walked into a place with too many people.

He decided to do better next time. And there must be a next time.

He had enjoyed his time with the girl.

April 4, 1974

Kathryn Bright

The safe thing would be to never kill again, especially after the way he'd botched so many details of the Otero murders. But Rader had Factor X, as he called it, or the Monster Within, his other name for whatever impelled him. He was inventing new abbreviations and names now: BTK for who he now was, Sparky for his penis, trolling for what he did, which was hunt women. He called his female targets projects—PJs for short. In his writings, he called Josie Otero "Little Mex."

Rader went trolling again a few weeks after he killed the Oteros—after he came down from the high the murders gave him.

He was trolling every day now, spying on women, following them to work and back home, writing notes on each. He had to keep track—he spied on multiple projects, breaking off if one did not look safe. He peeped in windows, walked alleys, and hunted females living alone.

Kathy Bright's high school yearbook photo.

In the spring of 1974 he settled on a woman he called Project Lights Out.

Kathryn Bright had lived in the little house at 3217 East Thirteenth Street for only a year. She was twenty-one. One semester at the University of Kansas in Lawrence had left her missing her family, so she had come home and worked at Coleman, where Julie Otero had worked for about a month.

By family she meant cousins too: counting the five Bright kids, there were eighteen. They were all tight; they often went to see their grandparents on a farm outside Valley Center. They would hook a cart to a donkey named Candy and ride for hours. When Kathryn was six, a newspaper photographer shot their picture. Kathryn stood smiling in the middle. "Youngsters Find Donkey Pal," the headline said.

At nine she learned the ukulele and played with a kids' group dressed in Hawaiian outfits.

Sometimes the Bright kids would go to a cousin's farm in nearby Butler County, make mud pies, and drive a car around a cow pasture, their legs too short to reach the brake pedal. They'd stick it in first gear, hope for the best, and laugh.

In church Kathryn sang in a trio with a sister and a cousin. They liked the hymn "In the Garden."

And He walks with me,
And He talks with me,
And He tells me I am his own,
And the joy we share as we tarry there,
None other has ever known.

Rader saw her one day while on his way to take his wife to lunch. A pretty good figure, as he said later. Other things caught his eye: long blond hair, a jeans jacket, an old beaded purse. The first time he saw her, she was collecting her mail.

He treated his wife to lunch that day, but as they ate, he daydreamed. He went back and spied on the woman for weeks. This might work, he decided; she looked like a college girl, living alone, no man around, no children, no dog.

Rader squeezed rubber balls to strengthen his hands. It had freaked him out how long it had taken to strangle the Oteros; his hands had gone numb. He wanted to be ready this time.

He made a plan. In normal life, he was a Wichita State University student; he would carry books to her door and tell her he needed a quiet place to study. Then he would force his way in.

Before he knocked, he pulled on his rubber gloves.

His plan went to pieces immediately.

No one answered his knock.

On impulse, he smashed through the glass of the back door, and then panicked a little. He realized she might come home, see the glass, and run. He cleaned it up as best he could, hid in a bedroom, and pulled out his Colt .22 to take the safety off. And—*bang!*—the gun went off. That scared him; he thought she might smell the gunpowder when she arrived. As his heart pounded, the front door opened. He heard her talking to someone.

It was a man. Rader began to sweat again.

He could hear them laughing. He had no place to run. But he had the .22, and a .357 Magnum in a shoulder holster, so he stepped toward them.

Hold it right there, he said.

Kevin Bright.

I'm wanted in California, Rader told them. They've got wanted posters out on me. I need a car. I need money. I just need to get to New York. I need to tie you up. But I don't want to hurt you.

That's when Rader realized he'd made another mistake.

He had brought no rope; he had assumed she would be alone, easy to control. He had planned to tie her with panty hose or whatever she had, so that when the cops found her body they would see a method different from the Otero murders. But now here he stood, Mr. Bind, Torture, and Kill, with nothing to bind them.

He marched them to a bedroom, went through her dressers, found bandannas, belts, nylons, T-shirts.

Rader would learn later the man's name was Kevin. Tie her hands, he told Kevin. Kevin did so. He walked them to the bedroom by the front door and told Kevin to lie down. He tied his hands together and tied his feet to a bedpost.

So far, so good.

Do you have any money? he asked.

Kevin gave up three dollars from his right front shirt pocket. He had eight more in his wallet, but he didn't tell the robber about that.

Rader marched the girl back to the other bedroom. He sat her in a chair, tied her to it with nylon stockings, and bound her ankles. Rummaging through the house, he found another ten dollars. He called out that he had found the money. He wanted them to think that this was just a robbery, that they would survive if they behaved. *Calm them*, he thought. He got them to tell him where to find their car keys. He would need transportation after he finished.

Time for a little music. He turned on her stereo, turned up the volume. He knew now, from Project Little Mex, that there would be strangling sounds, so he wanted to kill them in separate bedrooms. He did not want one of them to hear gagging noises and start thrashing. He decided to kill the man first, to put down the bigger threat. He had done the same in January. He looped a nylon around Kevin's throat, and began to pull.

And that's when Project Lights Out fell apart. Kevin broke his leg bindings, jumped up, and charged, his hands still tied behind him.

Rader pulled his .22 and shot Kevin in the head. He fell, and blood poured onto the floor. Rader stood amazed.

He ran to the next room. The girl was struggling and screaming. "What have you done to my brother?"

So that's who the guy was.

It's all right, Rader told her. He was trying to fight, so I had to shoot him, but I think he'll be all right. When I get out of here, I'll call the police and tell them to come untie both of you.

She kept struggling. Rader ran to the other bedroom and kicked Kevin to make sure he was dead. He wasn't. Kevin leaped up, charged again, broke the bindings on his wrists, and grabbed at the gun. For a few moments, Rader thought he would die right there: Kevin got his hand on the trigger and tried to pull it. They fought, grunting and straining, until Rader broke free and shot Kevin in the face, dropping him again.

Rader ran back to the woman. She was thrashing like a snared bird. He picked up a piece of cloth, looped it around her throat, and began to pull. She broke free from the chair. He wished he had brought his own rope.

He felt terrified now. He punched her in the face, on the head, on the shoulders. She tried to fight, tried to get away.

Someone probably heard those shots, he thought.

He pulled a knife; she fought like a wild animal. Like a hellcat, he'd

The chair in which Rader tied Kathy Bright with panty hose.
She was stabbed eleven times. Note the bloody smears on the wall, at left.

say later. He stabbed her in the back, once, twice, again, then spun her around and stabbed her in the gut, and still she fought. *God,* he thought, *how much stabbing does it take?* In the detective magazines they said to go up for the kidneys and lungs. He stabbed as they lunged around the room, smearing her blood on the walls. At last she went down.

And he heard a sound . . . from the next room.

Shit! he thought.

Rader ran to where he had left the brother. The brother was gone.

He ran to the front door; it was open.

I'm dead meat, he thought. He stepped out, blood covering his hands and clothes, soaking into his suede shoes.

He saw the brother running up the street.

The game is up, Rader thought. *I'm done for.*

He ran back to the woman.

She lay groaning, blood coming out of eleven wounds. Should he shoot her? *What difference did it make now?* The brother was alive and loose and could identify him. *Get out of here.*

5

April–July 1974

Lessons to Learn

Kevin Bright ran to two neighbors, William Williams and Edward Bell. He told them the man who had shot him was still at his sister's house. "He's in there now, doing a number on my sister," Bright said. "Please help me."

They called police, then drove Bright to Wesley Medical Center. It was 2:05 PM. Dispatchers radioed "residence robbery in progress." Officer Dennis Landon went to the back door. No one answered his knock. Officer Raymond Fletcher went in the front, his .357 drawn. They found a woman bleeding on the living room floor, a phone in her hand. She had crawled out of the bedroom. Her skin felt clammy. Her breathing was shallow, her face gray.

"Hang on," Fletcher told her. "We've got help on the way."

Landon turned her over.

"What happened?" he asked.

She pulled up her blouse. Landon saw knife wounds, at least three.

"Do you know who did this?"

She shook her head no.

"What is your name?"

"Kathryn Bright." Her voice was weak.

"How old are you?"

"Twenty-one."

They pressed cloth from the kitchen against her wounds and elevated her legs to get what blood she had to her head. Landon saw nylon stockings tied to her wrists. There was a blue scarf and a cord tied around her throat. Her right hand clutched a white rag, and her ankles were bound with a nylon stocking.

"I can't breathe," she told Landon. "Please untie my ankles."

Landon pulled a pocket knife and cut the nylon. She was covered in blood: face, hair, hands, stomach. She was bleeding from her left nostril and her face was badly bruised. She was losing consciousness.

They told her an ambulance was on the way, and that she would be all right. But then her face began to turn blue.

She grabbed Fletcher's arm.

"I can't breathe," she said.

"Help me."

BTK's strangling cord was still tied around Kevin's throat when he arrived at Wesley. Kathryn arrived in an ambulance minutes later. Officer Ronald Davenport watched as the medical people turned her over to look at her back. More stab wounds.

"Help me," she said.

She was too weak to say more. Davenport and other officers asked Kevin what had happened. He tried to talk, but choked up blood. The bullet that hit his upper jaw had knocked out two teeth; officers later found them in his sister's house. He had powder burns on his face. The other bullet had grazed his forehead. Doctors sent him to intensive care.

Kathryn died four hours later.

Kevin told police later that he lived in Valley Center but had stayed at his sister's house the night before because it had snowed, and he had not wanted to drive home.

For a small guy, Kevin had put up a big fight. Kevin was nineteen, stood only five feet six, and weighed only 115 pounds, the same as Josie Otero. He'd taken two shots to the head, yet had fought gallantly. Kevin said the killer was much bigger: five feet eleven, about 180 pounds, maybe twenty-eight years old, light complexion, a mustache, dark hair. He wore a black and yellow stocking cap—the colors of Wichita State University—gloves, a windbreaker, and an army coat with fur around the hood. There had been a silver wristwatch on his left arm, an expansion band on the watch.

"And he sweated a lot," Kevin told them.

The cops worked hard on the case but got nowhere. And with Kevin giving conflicting answers at times, they weren't sure his description of the attacker was all that solid.

It occurred to some of them that Kathryn Bright's murder was related to the Oteros'. Kathy and Kevin had worked at Coleman—as had Julie Otero.

But other cops said no. They still believed there was a Latin American drug connection with the Oteros. And there were differences—the Oteros had been strangled and suffocated; the Brights had been strangled, shot, and stabbed.

Rader ran several blocks to his car in his bloodstained shoes. He drove to his parents' house; they lived near him. In their shed, in an old wooden box filled with sawdust, he hid his weapons. He stripped off his clothes and the bloody shoes, putting them in the chicken coop; he would burn them later. He cleaned up, went home to his wife, and pretended that nothing unusual had happened.

He was sure he would be arrested. But a day passed, then another. He watched television and read the paper. The cops had not figured it out.

He began to write a long document, "An April Death," he called it; seven pages, single-spaced.

He clipped Kathryn's picture out of the newspaper. He wondered if he might be too smart to be caught. That gave him another idea.

Why not have some fun with the newspaper? Why not flaunt himself a bit?

On the evening of July 7, 1974, six months after the Otero murders, four people in their early twenties were killed after a dispute over $27.50. Three of the victims died in a duplex at 1117 Dayton Street on the west side of Wichita. The killer and his accomplice drove the fourth victim, a twenty-one-year-old named Beth Kuschnereit, to a rural spot in neighboring Butler County.

The man with the .38 was James Eddy Bell, the big guy with the menacing temper who worried Kenny Landwehr and the other beer drinkers at the Old English Pub.

Kuschnereit pleaded with Bell. He gave her two minutes to pray, then he shot her in the face. As he put it later, he "blew her head off."

Bell and his accomplice were picked up, tried, and convicted.

It was the second quadruple homicide that year, and it shook up everybody in town. Only seventeen people had been murdered in Wichita the year before, and the cops solved all seventeen.

Landwehr was more disturbed about the Dayton Street killings than he had been about the Oteros. He had known the Dayton Street people, and when he walked to the Pub, which was frequently, his route took him past the duplex where three of them had died. He was still thinking about trying for the FBI after college, but now it didn't seem as important. The FBI didn't have a homicide unit.

6

October 1974

The Monster as Muse

Several months after the Otero murders, three talkative men in jail began to imply that they knew details about the crimes. Detectives quickly realized they were blowing smoke, but not before the story got into the *Eagle*.

That story upset the one man who knew the truth. And he wanted credit.

A few days after the story appeared, *Eagle* columnist Don Granger got a phone call.

"Listen and listen good," a harsh voice said. "I'm only gonna say this once." The man sounded Midwestern, his tone hard and aggressive, as though he liked giving orders. "There is a letter about the Otero case in a book in the public library," he said. He told Granger which book, then hung up.

Granger knew why the call came to him. Months earlier, the *Eagle* had offered five thousand dollars to anyone providing useful information about the Otero case. Granger had volunteered to take the calls.

This caller had not asked for a reward, though.

The *Eagle* had made an arrangement with the cops that reflected what editors thought was best for the community at the time: it would set up a "Secret Witness" program to solicit and pass along information it received about the Oteros' killer. Abiding by that agreement, Granger called the cops right after he took that strange call. Years later, some reporters and editors would grouse about this, saying Granger should have found the letter first and copied it for the newspaper, but in the 1970s the

Eagle's management thought helping the cops catch the killer was more important than getting a scoop—or challenging the investigative tactics.

Bernie Drowatzky found the letter right where the caller had told Granger it would be, inside the book *Applied Engineering Mechanics*. Drowatzky took the letter to Chief Hannon. The letter contained so many misspellings that some cops thought the writer had a disability or was disguising his writing voice.

I write this letter to you for the sake of the tax payer as well as your time. Those three dude you have in custody are just talking to get publicity for the Otero murders. They know nothing at all. I did it by myself and with no oneshelp. There has been no talk either.

Let's put it straight. . . . .

The letter then accurately described the positions of all four Otero bodies and named the rope, cord, and knots that bound them. The letter's notations about Josie Otero, for example, read:

Josephine:

Position: Hanging by the neck in the northwest part of the basement. Dryer or freezer north of her body.

Bondage: Hand tie ith blind cord. Feet and lower knees, upper knees and waist with clothes line cord. All one lenght.

Garrotte: Rough hemp rope ¼ dia., noose with four or five turns. New.

Clothes: Dark, bra cut in the middle, sock.

Death: Strangulation once, hung.

Comments: Rest of her clothes t the bottom of the stairs, green pants, and panties. Her glasses in the southwest bedroom.

The letter contained details only cops and the killer knew. The writer seemed to confirm Cornwell's suspicion that the killer had tortured the Oteros: He said he strangled Julie Otero twice.

I'm sorry this happen to the society. They are the ones who suffer the most. It hard to control myself. You probably call me "psychotic with sexual perversion hang-up." Where this monster enter my brain I will never know. But, it here to stay. How does one cure himself? If you ask for help, that you have killed four people, they will laugh or hit the panic button and call the cops.

I can't stop it so, the monster goes on, and hurt me as wall as society. Society can be thankfull that there are ways for people like me to relieve myself at time by day dreams of some victim being tortore and being mine. It a big compicated game my friend of the monster play putting victims number down, follow them, checking up on them waiting in the dark, waiting, waiting . . . . . the pressure is great and somt-times he run the game to his liking. Maybe you can stop him. I can't.

He has areadly chosen his next victim or victims I don't know who they are yet. The next day after I read the paper, I will Know, but it to late. Good luck hunting.

YOURS, TRULY GUILTILY

The letter gave detectives a sick feeling. They had failed to catch the killer for nine months, and now he said he would kill again. He was even giving himself a name, as though he were another Boston Strangler or Jack the Ripper.

P.S. Since sex criminals do not change their M.O. or by nature cannot do so, I will not change mine. The code words for me will be . . . bind them, toture them, kill them, B.T.K., you see he at it again. They will be on the next victim.

The letter was a lead, but Hannon—who had talked to reporters twice a day with updates on the case in January— kept it secret for now. He thought publicizing the letter might panic people and provide details for copycats. And he worried that publicity would prompt BTK to kill again.

Some cops suggested BTK's evident ego could be turned against him. They called editors at the *Eagle*.

A few days later, the *Eagle* began running a personal ad:

B.T.K.

Help is available.

The ad provided a phone number—and for the sake of convenience asked that BTK call before 10:00 PM.

The cops also talked to Granger.

A few days later, on Halloween morning, the *Eagle* ran a column by Granger, buried back on page 8D, which became the first mention in the news of "BTK." In it, Granger did not mention that he had received a call or that police had a letter. The newspaper knew more about this case than it let on, but it kept the police department's secret, a decision later reporters would criticize. Granger merely asked BTK to call him:

For the past week Wichita police have tried to get in touch with a man who has important information on the Otero murder case—a man who needs help badly.

You may have noticed the classified ad that ran at the top of our "Personal" column Friday, Saturday, Sunday, Monday and Tuesday . . .

There really is a "B.T.K." Police can't say how they know, but they're convinced B.T.K. has information about the murder of Joseph Otero, his wife and two of his children . . .

Granger said the phone number in the ad was being monitored "by officers ready to help B.T.K."

There was an alternative, Granger noted. The columnist was willing to talk with BTK himself, and he helpfully provided his office and home phone numbers.

This may expose me to a certain amount of crank, prank calls, but the nuisance is worth the trouble if we can only provide help for a troubled man.

BTK did not respond. Rader was busier than ever. A few days after Granger's column ran, BTK went to work for the security alarm company ADT.

After the Otero and Bright murders, ADT had done booming business installing alarms in homes. The new job put BTK inside homes as an installer.

Rader enjoyed the irony.

Eagle **columnist Don Granger received the first phone call from BTK.**

December 1974–March 1977

A Scoop

The *Eagle* had kept BTK's claim about the Oteros secret because the cops said publicity might prompt him to kill again. But there was another newspaper in town then, the weekly *Wichita Sun,* and it employed a reporter named Cathy Henkel who thought otherwise. On December 11, 1974, two months after the cops found BTK's message in the library, the *Sun* published a story in which Henkel revealed that she had received a copy of the BTK letter from an anonymous source. She reported that BTK stood for "bind, torture, and kill," and that the murderer had threatened to strike again.

The story frightened people, as Hannon feared, but it also prompted them to take precautions. Henkel had written the story in part because she thought people had a right to know someone was stalking them. She had consulted private-sector psychologists before she published. Although the cops had worried that *revealing* the secret might encourage BTK to kill again, the psychologists argued the opposite: because BTK probably craved publicity, *keeping* the secret might prompt him to kill.

By the time the *Sun* broke the story, police had already interviewed more than fifteen hundred people about the Otero murders. Now the tip lines lit up. People suspected their neighbors and coworkers. Some turned in their own fathers or sons. None of the tips panned out.

The one-year anniversary of the Otero killings passed.

Floyd Hannon retired as police chief on May 31, 1976. He regarded his failure to catch BTK as a stain on his career.

The city manager, Gene Denton, replaced Hannon with Richard LaMunyon, the captain of the vice unit. LaMunyon looked even younger than his thirty-six years. The choice startled longtime commanders. They had advanced by seniority before; there were a lot of older men at the top.

In contrast, LaMunyon's nickname became "The Boy Chief." Denton regarded his youth as an asset: he wanted a chief who thought differently.

LaMunyon, at his first staff meeting, took his place at the head of the table and broke the ice with a joke: "Well, boys, what do we do now?" In the following months he quickly set a new tone and began to replace older men with younger men. Soon, people still in their twenties became field patrol supervisors or detectives.

LaMunyon made a big deal about officer education. He had a master's degree in administration, but he was no mere pencil pusher. In 1966, ten years earlier, LaMunyon and two other officers survived a fight that nearly took their lives. Their attacker had knocked one officer senseless and tossed LaMunyon over the hood of a patrol car. LaMunyon's service revolver fell to the ground. The attacker snatched it up and stuck it in the throat of a third officer.

LaMunyon grabbed the man's gun hand. The gun fired, blowing off the middle, ring, and pinkie fingers of LaMunyon's right hand. LaMunyon drew his nightstick with his left hand and beat the attacker senseless. Doctors reattached Lamunyon's fingers, but they remained stiff for life.

One of the first things the new chief did was study the BTK files. The case had to be a top priority, he decided.

He never got the sight of Josie Otero out of his head.

March 1977 arrived with the birds and buds of spring. There had been no letters from BTK since the message in October 1974, when he threatened to kill again. But he had not killed.

Rader was installing home alarms for ADT and attending WSU. He was intensely busy at home. His wife had given birth to a son about nine months after he wrote the letter about killing the Oteros. They named him Brian.

Rader had married in 1971, two years and eight months before he killed the Oteros, and while he was taking classes at Butler Community College twenty-five miles away in El Dorado. His bride, Paula Dietz, worked then as a secretary for the American Legion. For the ceremony at Christ Lutheran Church, two of his three younger brothers stood up with him.

He appeared to adore Paula; people noticed that his voice and posture grew softer when he spoke of her.

Years later, in a self-regarding tone, Rader would complain that family got in the way: I had a wife, I had to work, you know, I can't go out. When you live at home with a wife, you can't go out and prowl around till three or four in the morning without your wife being suspicious.

He had never stopped trolling and stalking, though.

8

March 17, 1977

Toys for the Kids

It was Saint Patrick's Day. Rader would later recall there was a parade downtown. His wife was at work; he was on spring break from Wichita State.

He put on dress shoes, nice slacks, and a tweed sports jacket. He thought he looked spiffy, like James Bond. He carried a briefcase with his tools—tape, cord, gun, plastic bags. He also carried a photograph. It was a tool too—he would show it to make people think he was a detective searching for a lost boy.

He had trolled, picked out targets, then backed off. Serial killing was like fishing, he would later confide: sometimes you're unlucky. Or you get tangled up with chores, work, school.

His primary target this day lived at 1207 South Greenwood. If that target didn't work out, he had a backup just a block to the east at 1243 South Hydraulic. There was an alley behind that address, a place to hide.

Shirley Vian.

And if those targets didn't work out, he had another backup, and yet another. He had stalked multiple women, switching surveillance from one to another for weeks, taking notes, pondering escape routes. His, not theirs.

He knew that one of the three young women at the house on Hydraulic was named Cheryl. She was a loose woman, in his opinion; he had watched her drink and party at the Blackout, a college bar. He had followed her home, spied on her and her roommates for weeks. Project Blackout, he called her.

Cheryl Gilmour lived with a roommate, Judy Clark. The third "woman" Rader had noticed was Judy's sixteen-year-old sister, Karin, who frequently stayed at the house.

Two doors down, at 1311 South Hydraulic, there was another woman, with three kids. Rader had not targeted her. She just lived in the neighborhood. Her name was Shirley Vian, and she and her kids all had the flu. When the kids got hungry at lunchtime, she called the Dillons grocery store a block away to tell them that she was sending one of her little boys for food.

Steven, age six, bought soup and walked back home, where his mother told him it was the wrong kind.

He walked back to the Dillons and got the soup she wanted. Just before he got back home, a tall man with a briefcase stopped him and asked him a question.

Shirley Vian's son Steven Relford

• • •

The primary target at 1207 South Greenwood had not worked out; no one answered Rader's knock. He stood for a moment, holding his briefcase. He thought about breaking in, as he had done at the Bright house, but decided he did not want to risk mussing his good clothes. He decided to go to Project Blackout's house. He walked to South Hydraulic. When he reached the front of Blackout's house, he saw a little boy walking toward him carrying a soup can.

Time to play detective. He pulled out the photo of his own wife and son.

Have you seen these people? he asked.

The boy looked at the photograph. No, he said.

Are you sure?

Yes.

The boy walked away.

Rader watched him for a moment, and then walked to Blackout's door. He glanced down the street again and saw the boy looking at him.

Rader knocked on Blackout's door. When he got no answer, he walked to the boy's house.

Steven's brother and sister were playing when Steven came home; Bud was eight, Stephanie four. Steven crawled into bed with his mother. Moments later, he heard a knock and sprinted for the door. So did Bud; they liked to race. Steven beat Bud this time and opened the door, but only a crack. He peered out. It was the briefcase man.

Steven's mother put on her housecoat and went to the door. The man towered over the children as he peered through the crack. When he saw their mother, he pushed the door open.

I'm a detective, he said.

He showed Shirley a fake business card. He took a step inside, then another. Then he pushed the door shut and pulled out the gun.

Don't hurt us, Shirley said.

Rader said disarming things to Shirley, similar to what he had said to the Oteros and Brights. But then he embellished his story: he had a sex fantasy problem. He would tie her up, have sex, take some pictures. It would not be a pleasant thing, he said, but everyone would be okay.

He saw that she wore a blue housecoat over a pink nightgown and looked sick. She had lit a cigarette. He looked at her with distaste: she was a mess. The kids are sick, she said; we've been sick for days. She tried to talk him into leaving as he pulled down the shades. He spoke harshly. It's going to happen, he said.

The phone rang.

Someone was calling to check on her, Shirley said, because she was sick, because she had kept the kids home from school.

Should we answer it? Steven asked.

No, Rader said.

They let it ring. It made him nervous; the caller might decide to stop by. He would have to move fast now. He told her he was going to tie up the children.

Don't do that, she said.

I've got to, he said. He opened his briefcase—his hit kit, he called it. He took out rope and started to tie up the older boy, who started to scream.

Frustrated, he told her to help shut the kids in the bathroom, which had two doors. He tied the west door shut from the inside, looping cord around the knob and tying it under the sink. There were toys on the

Rader threw blankets and toys into the bathroom where he'd locked Shirley Vian's children to keep them quiet while he killed their mother.

living room floor: an airplane, a fire truck, a little car. He dumped them into the bathroom for the kids and tossed in blankets and pillows. Comforting them, he said later. You guys stay in here, he told the kids. They looked frightened, but he was talking quietly to keep everyone calm.

He took their mother into her bedroom, shut the east bathroom door, and shoved her bed against it to block it. When he got done with the mother, he might hang the little girl, if there was time, but he was upset about the phone ringing. Someone was always interrupting.

He stripped off the woman's clothes.

Oh, I am so sick, she said.

He wrapped electrical tape around her forearms and calves. There was a sequence to what he did: he taped people first, because that got them under control quickly. Then he could take his time binding them with knotted cord.

Rader tied her wrists with cord and a nylon stocking, then tied her ankles with cord. In the bathroom, the children were screaming, pounding on the door. "Leave my mother alone, leave my mother alone, get out of here!" Steven yelled. "I'm gonna break out of here!"

I don't think you want to, Rader shouted back. I'll blow your head off!

With the shades drawn, it was dark in the bedroom at midday. He made the woman lie facedown on the bed, her head at the foot of it. He tied her feet to the metal head rail, and ran a long cord to her throat.

She threw up on the floor.

Oh, well, he thought. *She said she was sick.* And he had said this would not be pleasant. *Not for her, anyway.*

He walked into the kitchen and fetched her a glass of water, to comfort her, or so he said later. He considered himself a nice guy. When Julie Otero had complained that her hands were going numb from her bindings, he had adjusted them. When Joe had said his chest hurt from lying on the floor with broken ribs, he had fetched Joe a coat to rest on. Now, in the darkened bedroom of the house on Hydraulic, he gave the sick woman a sip of water.

Then he took a plastic bag out of his hit kit and pulled it over her head. He took the cord that was tied to the bed and wrapped the far end of it around her throat four or five times, along with her pink nightie.

And he pulled. He had rigged the cord so that it tightened as she struggled. The kids screamed louder and hammered their hands on the wooden door as their mother died.

He stood up, disappointed.

He wanted to do more—suffocate the boys, hang the girl. But the phone call worried him.

Before he walked out, he stole two pairs of the woman's underpants.

March 1977

A Vigorous Debate

Bud, the eight-year-old, picked up something hard and shattered the bottom pane of the bathroom window. They were all still screaming, and Steven now worried that Bud would get in trouble for breaking the window. But after Bud crawled out, Steven followed, dropping to the ground. They ran to the front door, then into their mother's bedroom.

They found the man gone, their mother tied up, a bag over her head. She was not moving.

At 1:00 PM a police dispatcher radioed a cryptic message to Officer Raymond Fletcher: "Call me back on a telephone." Dispatchers asked for a telephone call when they wanted to have a private conversation not broadcast on police scanners. When Fletcher called, the dispatcher gave him an address and said there was a report of a homicide.

On South Hydraulic, James Burnett waved Fletcher down and said

**Bud Relford broke the bathroom window
and escaped to alert the neighbors.**

that two neighbor children had come screaming to his house. His wife, Sharon, had run to the boys' home. In the living room, she saw a little girl sitting on the floor, sobbing. In the bedroom, Sharon Burnett found their dead mother.

James Burnett led Fletcher to Shirley Vian's house. An ambulance was on the way. Fletcher, a former emergency medical technician, searched for a pulse as soon as he saw her, just as he had when he was one of the first two officers to walk into Kathryn Bright's house. He felt a twitch under his fingertips, not a pulse but something faint. Fletcher yanked off the cord and nightie, but took care to leave the knots intact. He began CPR, pushing on the woman's chest. Firefighters were coming in. He told them to preserve the knots—they were evidence.

It was so dark with the blinds drawn that they could barely see. They carried the woman to the living room and restarted CPR.

It was too late.

Fletcher radioed dispatch. Send detectives, he said. It's a homicide.

In the living room, Fletcher saw the girl sitting on a couch, still crying.

He carefully laid the knots aside and studied the rooms and the body. It did not occur to him that this murder could have been committed by the same guy who had killed Kathryn Bright. Aside from a trickle coming from Shirley's ear, there was no blood. But something about this scene rang bells with him: the knots and multiple bindings, the bag over the

Stephanie Relford was found crying in the living room when the police arrived.

woman's head. He had seen things like this written about in the Otero reports. He remembered that Josie Otero had been sexually defiled. Fletcher searched the house, looking for semen stains. He did not find any, but he called dispatch.

"It looks like the same thing as the Otero case."

A lot of cops who showed up at Shirley Vian's house thought the same thing. Bob Cocking, the sergeant assigned to secure the crime scene, said it out loud to detectives when they arrived. They whirled around and told him he did not know what he was talking about. Cocking, feeling insulted, walked away.

But it wasn't just detectives arguing with officers. They argued with each other. Supervisors told them to stop guessing and work the evidence. If BTK had killed Shirley Vian, it meant he was a serial killer, and the brass didn't want to leap to that conclusion or set off a panic.

Some of the cops were already leaking information that would get into the next day's newspaper. Their supervisors then stepped outside and said the evidence of a link was unclear.

The *Eagle*'s new police reporter, Ken Stephens, didn't buy that and wrote a story that noted similarities in the Otero and Vian crimes.

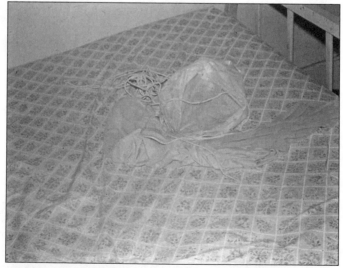

The plastic bag and rope Rader used to kill Shirley Vian on her bed.

• • •

Bill Cornwell, head of the homicide detectives, had visited the Vian scene "just to make sure it wasn't the Otero killer again." He privately noted a number of differences between the cases: there was no semen and no cut phone line at Shirley's house. The Otero children died; Shirley's children survived. But his gut told him it might be the same guy.

Cornwell and LaMunyon also briefly considered whether this case might be linked not only to the Oteros but to the unsolved murder of Kathryn Bright. Most detectives still thought someone else killed Bright. So did Fletcher, a first responder at the Bright and Vian crime scenes.

Shirley's children tried to help the cops.

Steven, the six-year-old, broke down and cried and told them everything he had seen. He had gone for soup, talked to man with a briefcase about a photograph, then let the man in. He blamed himself for that.

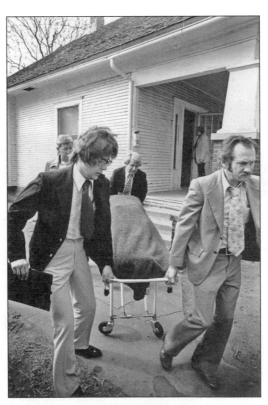

Shirley Vian's body is taken to be autopsied.

He had let in the man who killed his mother. He said the man was dressed real nice. He described a man who was in his thirties or forties and had dark hair and a paunch. But as the boy talked, a uniformed officer walked up.

The boy pointed.

The bad guy looked like that man, the boy said.

The detectives looked at the officer: tall, in his twenties, with a trim, athletic body. No paunch. The detectives glanced at each other and closed their notebooks. The boy's description was useless.

By this time, investigators, including Cornwell, had rejected a theory they had clung to for a long time: that the Oteros died in a drug-related revenge killing.

Bernie Drowatzky, one of Cornwell's better detectives, had been proposing another idea. Some of his bosses didn't think much of it, but Drowatzky was saying that maybe they were dealing with a sex pervert who chose his victims at random. And if the guy who killed the Oteros had now killed Shirley Vian, that meant he was a serial killer.

No, no, other cops said. The FBI said serial killers were incredibly rare.

LaMunyon was not a detective, but instinct told him it was the same

Bernie Drowatzky, one of the primary detectives
during the early years of the BTK investigation.

guy. It seemed obvious. But saying this publicly might cause a panic. If the evidence was there, he would stand before the notepads and TV cameras and say it. It would be embarrassing to admit he could not protect people, but if that was the truth, then he needed to warn people.

In the days that followed Shirley's murder, LaMunyon and the detectives reviewed every similarity and difference. The Otero killer had boldly walked in on them. This killer had walked in on Shirley and her children. The Otero killer had tied hands behind backs; so had this guy. The Otero killer had tied Joe Otero's ankles to the foot of his bed; this killer had tied Shirley's feet to a headrail. At both scenes, a killer had pulled a plastic bag over someone's head.

The cops had not turned up a single useful fingerprint at either house.

Some detectives argued there was not enough evidence to link the murders. What about the differences?

The differences looked small, LaMunyon said.

Detectives pointed out something else: the experts said serial killers couldn't stop once they started. The FBI had only recently begun to study serial killers in depth, but it was saying that no serial killer had taken three years off. It was probably not the same guy.

In the end, based on the advice of some of his detectives and his own desire to be more sure before risking public panic, LaMunyon decided to not make an announcement. He thought publicity might inspire BTK to kill again. He made the decision with one grim thought: the strangler would probably make it necessary to change his mind.

Steven Relford, Shirley Vian's youngest son, would grow up bitter, drinking, drugging, and paying artists to cover his body with skull tattoos. He would remember the screaming.

BTK remembered the screaming too—and that it did not bother him.

10

Autumn 1977

A Turning Point

By 1977, Wichitans no longer felt safe, even from their neighbors. To their regret, they were becoming more accustomed to violent crime. The older generation blamed the sex-drugs-rock-and-roll culture of the '60s. The younger generation countered that Wichita was still so backwater conservative that the '60s would not arrive until after the '70s ended.

A few months after Shirley Vian was killed, Kenny Landwehr saw violent crime firsthand. He was twenty-two, still studying history at WSU. Five years out of high school, he had not yet obtained a college degree. His mother, Irene, later said that Kenny was such a curious kid that he took more college courses than he needed, while putting off taking the science prerequisites that would get him the diploma.

He worked at Beuttel's, a clothing store at Twenty-first and Broadway in north Wichita that sold bib overalls to farmers, cassocks to priests, and hip stuff to their black customers: shoes with stacked heels, long fur coats, and "walking suits" with wide lapels and bell-bottom trousers.

Landwehr liked owner Herman Beuttel, who handed out cigars to employees. Landwehr soon switched to cigarettes because they were easier to smoke on a break.

Going out for lunch one day, Landwehr stepped aside to let two men enter the store. Something about their expressions caught his attention. They looked . . . nervous. Landwehr turned a corner and saw a Cadillac and a third man behind it, leaning against a wall. He looked nervous too.

Getaway car, Landwehr thought. *Shoplifters. We're being set up.* He turned around, walked back into the store, and found himself staring down the barrel of a handgun. The men had pulled nylon stockings over their faces, but they were the same two he had met at the door, and they were not shoplifters. One of them forced him to the cash register.

"Get down on the floor."

Landwehr obeyed. The robbers hog-tied him under the register with electrical cord. They tied up two other clerks. One robber reached under the register and found Beuttel's .45 caliber semiautomatic pistol. He stood over Landwehr and worked the pistol slide, *sha-shink*, jacking a cartridge into the chamber. Landwehr thought he was going to be executed.

But they did not shoot him. They searched for money. As customers came in, the men bound them with neckties. The robbery lasted only minutes, but to Landwehr it seemed to last for ages.

After they left, a badly shaken Landwehr told police that one of the robbers had called the other one "Butch." From that name and Landwehr's description, the detectives concluded that he was Butch Lee Jordan, a small-time thug.

The police went to Jordan's home, but when they did not find him there, they failed to search elsewhere. That was a mistake. Jordan robbed a liquor store a few days later and shot Police Officer Hayden Henderson in the arm.

When Landwehr heard about that, it made him angry and disappointed; angry at Jordan for shooting the cop, disappointed with the cops for failing to pursue Jordan more vigorously.

The disappointment led Landwehr to make one of the crucial decisions of his life.

Landwehr's family had to scrimp and save. His older brother, David, had been a high achiever, the salutatorian of his class at Bishop Carroll Catholic High School. Kenny had been a high achiever too, winning medals in debate, earning good grades, going out for basketball and drama.

His mother said later that even as a kid two things stood out about Kenny: he was one of the smarter people she knew, and he was an incorrigible smart aleck. She hoped his brains would lead to a career that would bring him security.

Landwehr reconsidered the FBI after the Beuttel's robbery. The FBI recruited people who studied accounting and assigned agents to chase white-collar criminals.

Landwehr had been hog-tied and held at gunpoint by thugs who had walked in off the street.

He wanted to bring justice to people like himself.

For young Wichitans in 1977, the Mall in southeast Wichita was the place to be. The Mall was like an old-town marketplace, where people gathered to buy, sell, and gossip. It was air-conditioned in summer, heated in winter.

In December a young woman took a part-time job at Helzberg Jewelers in the Mall. She was a twenty-five-year-old Wichita native who seemed to make friends easily. She had a keen wit and a blunt-spoken manner. Her name was Nancy Fox. She already worked full-time as a secretary for The Law Company, an architectural firm. She had taken the job at Helzberg's to earn extra money to buy Christmas presents for her relatives.

Nancy already had presents for her two-year-old nephew. She doted on Thomas; she had dressed up in a bunny costume to surprise him at Easter. That December she had also put a ring on layaway for her older sister, Beverly Plapp. The sisters were eleven months apart, and after

**Nancy Fox was stalked by Rader,
who considered her his perfect project.**

growing up competing with each other and sharing a bedroom, they were becoming friends. They had three younger brothers.

Nancy had played flute in junior high and sang in the choir of Parkview Baptist Church on the city's south side. She drove a powder blue Opel, and paid attention to her clothing, makeup, nails, and hair— she wore her blond hair frosted, and she liked to wear scarves around her neck. She was a bit of a neat freak. When she got into a spat with her boyfriend, she would vent her irritation by cleaning.

She and her girlfriends socialized at a few Wichita nightclubs. Scene Seventies, at Pawnee and Seneca, was a favorite hangout on Friday and Saturday nights; Nancy dated the door manager there. On Sundays she'd drive her Opel over to her mother's house and walk into a kitchen smelling of fried chicken. It was Nancy's favorite food.

Nancy did not mind living alone. She told her mother nothing would happen to her.

11

December 8, 1977

Nancy Fox

Rader had cruised Nancy Fox's neighborhood and saw that it was lower middle class, with cheap places to live, which attracted single women living alone. Once he figured that out, he trolled the neighborhood frequently. Be prepared, as the Boy Scouts say.

He first saw her one day when she walked into her duplex apartment, which was painted a cheerful pink. He saw that she was small and pretty and that she appeared to spend time on her hair and clothes. He appreciated neatness. He followed her to her job at the architectural company, to her night job at Helzberg's, and to her home. At Helzberg's he bought inexpensive jewelry, looked her over up close, followed her home again, then got her name by looking at the envelopes in her mailbox while she was at work.

She lived in southeast Wichita at 843 South Pershing, not far from the Mall. She had no man that he could see, and no dog. When he checked the north end of the duplex, he learned that it was vacant—there was no one next door to hear a scream.

He spied on her while he spied on other women. Trolling for women had become nearly a full-time job, in addition to his real-world full-time job, which was working for the security company. He often blended the jobs—he trolled for women, and then stalked them, while driving the ADT van.

He was a busy guy. Besides being an ADT crew chief, he was still going to WSU classes at night, and he had a wife and small child at home.

Still, he picked a date: December 8.

Rader had told his wife he would be at the WSU library that night, which was true; he had term papers due, research to complete. He knew exactly when Nancy would leave Helzberg's. So he had gone to the library an hour or two before to work on a term paper. Just before 9:00 PM, he left the library, changed into dark clothing, and drove his wife's red 1966 Chevelle to Nancy's neighborhood. He parked a few blocks from her duplex, took out his bag of tools, walked to her front door, and knocked. If she answered, his lie would be that he had come to the wrong apartment. But there was no answer.

He knocked next door, found that side of the duplex still vacant, and hurried to the back. He had not left the library as soon as he wanted, so he was running late. He cut Nancy's phone line, then broke a window. He waited, crouching. He worried that when cars rolled through the curves on nearby Lincoln Street the headlights would shine on the duplex and expose him. He watched for lights, then crawled through the window.

What a neat, orderly girl Nancy Fox was: everything was tidy and polished. It was a tiny place, smaller than his, only 600 or 700 square feet. He found her Christmas tree lights on. Photographs of smiling people stood neatly arranged on shelves outside the bedroom. He liked everything he saw. *That Vian woman had been so sloppy.*

He pulled a glass out of Nancy's kitchen cupboard, drank some water, wiped down the glass and put it back. He listened to make sure the phone was dead. He still had the phone in his hand when the front door opened.

Get out of my house.

Nancy had just come in with her coat on, carrying her purse. She stepped to grab the telephone.

I'm going to call the police, she warned.

That won't do you any good, he said. I cut the line.

He moved toward her, showed her his gun.

What are you in my house for?

She had spunk; he liked that. She did not even look nervous.

What are you going to do? she demanded. What's going on here?

I'm a bad guy, he told her. I want sex. I have to tie you up to take pictures.

Get out of here.

No.

You need to get out of here right now.

No, he said sternly. This is going to happen.

You're sick, she told him.

Yes, I'm sick, he said. But this is the way it's going to be.

She glared at him. She took off her coat—a white parka—and folded it onto the couch. She was wearing a pink sweater.

I need a cigarette, she said.

She lit one, watching him.

He dumped her purse onto the kitchen table and took some trophies. He found her driver's license. He talked to disarm her, telling the same story, with variations, that he had told the Oteros, the Brights, Shirley Vian: he had a sexual problem, but he wasn't really a bad guy. She would be all right.

And now she faced him squarely, or so he would remember.

Let's get this over with so I can call the police.

He agreed.

I need to go to the bathroom, she said.

He looked in the bathroom, made sure there wasn't a sharp object she could turn into a weapon.

Okay, he said. Make sure you come out with most of your clothes off.

He blocked open the bathroom door with a piece of cloth, then sat on her bed to wait. He looked around in admiration; clothes, closet, jewelry kit—everything neat. When she came out of the bathroom, she was still wearing her pink sweater, her bra, and purple panties. She saw he was holding handcuffs.

What's that about? she demanded.

This is part of my deal, he explained. It is what makes it happen for me.

Why are you wearing gloves?

I'm wanted in other states and don't want to leave prints.

This is ridiculous! she said. This is bullshit!

She kept talking, but he barely listened. He pulled her hands behind her, fastened the cuffs on her wrists, and made her lie facedown on the bed. He got on top of her. He was half-undressed himself by then, hoping this would convey the lie that he intended to rape her. He pulled down her panties.

Has your boyfriend ever had sex with you in the butt?

He said it to deceive; he did not really want anal sex.

She did not answer; she was gagged now.

He took off his leather belt and looped it around her ankles; he found that he had an erection already. He suddenly pulled the belt off her ankles, slipped it around her throat—and yanked it tight, pressing down with one hand where the belt went through the buckle, and pulling the belt with his other hand. Nancy thrashed under him, found his scrotum with her handcuffed hands, and dug her fingers into him. It hurt, but he liked it.

As usual, it took time for his victim to pass out; when Nancy finally did, he loosened the belt to let her have some air.

In years to come, he would say that this was his perfect hit. There was no man or dog or child to interrupt, nobody tried to kill him, little children did not scream and threaten to come out of the bathroom to fight him.

When she regained consciousness, he bent down to her ear.

I'm wanted, he told her. I killed the four people in that family, the Oteros. And I killed Shirley Vian. I'm BTK. And you're next.

She fought frantically underneath him as he yanked the belt tight again. This time he held it until she died.

He picked up a nightgown and masturbated into it.

12

December 9, 1977

"You Will Find a Homicide"

The next morning Rader was still so elated about what he'd done that he wanted to tell someone. On a coffee break, he drove the ADT van to Organ's Market downtown and stepped to a pay phone outside the door. At 8:18 AM, a Sedgwick County emergency dispatcher took the call.

"You will find a homicide at 843 South Pershing. Nancy Fox."

"I'm sorry, sir," the dispatcher answered. "I can't understand you. What is the address?"

Another dispatcher, listening in, spoke up: "I believe 843 South Pershing."

"That is correct," the man said.

Dispatchers tried to ask the man more, but he had dropped the receiver. The dispatchers listened to silence, trying to make sense of what they had just heard. Forty-seven seconds later, someone else picked up the phone. The dispatchers were still on the line.

Who are you? The dispatchers asked.

The man said he was a Wichita firefighter, off duty. He just wanted to use the phone.

Who was using the telephone just before you? the dispatchers asked.

A man who left the phone dangling, he told them.

Officer John Di Pietra reached 843 South Pershing minutes later, at 8:22 AM. No one answered his knock and the door was locked. At the back, he saw a cut phone line waggling in the breeze. The storm window had been removed, the interior window broken. He could not see through the drapes.

"Is anyone home?"

Di Pietra pushed back the drapes and saw a half-clothed woman lying motionless, facedown on a bed, her ankles tied with a piece of yellow cloth. She was wearing a pink sweater.

After they kicked in the front door, Di Pietra and Det. Louis Brown stepped into what Di Pietra later said was the tidiest home he had ever seen. But then he noticed disarray: there was a half-smoked cigarette in an ashtray beside a chair. A purse had been emptied onto the kitchen table. The phone receiver lay on the floor. Jewelry boxes had been dumped out on the bedroom dresser.

The officers saw a blue nightgown lying on the bed, beside the woman's head. There were stains.

It was a dumb move, making that phone call, and Rader knew it. For weeks afterward he thought he'd be arrested. They had his voice on tape now, they knew which pay phone he had used; someone might remember seeing him drop the phone and get into the ADT van.

But he had felt so happy. Of all his murders, he liked this one most—the only one that ever went according to script. After Nancy died he took off the cuffs, tied her wrists with nylon stockings, took his belt off her throat, and tied another stocking in its place. He stole Nancy's driver's license, some lingerie—nice silky stuff. He liked to play with women's clothing.

When he took Nancy's pearl necklace, he thought he might give it to his wife.

Nancy's mother, Georgia Mason, supervised the cafeteria at St. Joseph Hospital, not far from Nancy's apartment. About 10:30 AM on December 9, she was getting ready to open the cafeteria when she got a call from a security officer.

At the security office, she saw two Wichita police detectives, two security officers, her ex-husband—Nancy's father, Dale Fox—and a chaplain. We have some bad news, someone said. Georgia thought something had happened to Kevin, her youngest, who was sixteen. He had been skipping school.

It isn't Kevin, someone said.

It's Nancy.

Georgia, all five feet of her, beat her fists on the chest of a security officer, then collapsed on a couch.

The detectives showed Chief LaMunyon the crime scene photos and the videotape they took inside the duplex. Strangulation, phone line cut, semen on the nightgown—LaMunyon was sure this was BTK. He saw that Nancy's eyeglasses had been placed neatly on the dresser beside her bed.

LaMunyon had to decide again whether to announce BTK publicly. He leaned toward doing it. They were not protecting anyone by keeping BTK a secret.

Some detectives remained unconvinced this was BTK. So what if the phone line was cut? Some burglars do that. So what if the guy left semen? Other killers had done the same.

They listened to the tape of the call to dispatchers.

The caller's diction was staccato and slow. When he said, "You will find a homicide at 843 South Pershing," he pronounced homicide "*home*-eh-side," as though he didn't know how to say it right. Was he a foreigner?

The detectives had talked to the firefighter who picked up the dangling phone receiver. He told them he did not get a good look at the previous caller. He thought the guy was about six feet tall, that he wore a kind of gray industrial suit, that he drove a van with a painted sign on it. He thought the guy had blond hair.

Nancy's mother went to St. Francis to identify her daughter's body. A staff member pulled down a sheet. Nancy's face looked as though the ordeal had aged her. The staff member asked if this was the body of Nancy Jo Fox.

"Yes," Georgia said. Then she ran from the room.

Georgia helped arrange the funeral. Nancy had been baptized at Parkview Baptist and had sung in the choir. Now the church filled with mourners. A line of cars snaked down the road to Harper's town cemetery.

Beverly Plapp took a leave from her nursing job to collect her sister's belongings from the duplex. Georgia couldn't bear to go there.

LaMunyon turned again to the FBI. Should he tell the public about BTK? LaMunyon thought so, but some detectives warned that this might encourage him to kill again. Should they try to communicate with BTK? The commanders were divided. The FBI guys could not decide. Behavioral science was new, they said. They had not collected or interpreted enough data. They took no position. LaMunyon hesitated—it seemed as though people would die whatever he decided. He decided again to wait.

He did not have to wait long.

Nancy's youngest brother seemed to take her death the hardest. Nancy had liked to take Kevin out for hamburgers; she had let him drive her car. He never went back to school. It would be twenty-seven years before he could talk about her death.

Georgia's doctor did not let her go back to work for three months. When she did, hospital coworkers came to her one by one. She had spent her life holding in feelings, but when they hugged her she would start crying. Her doctor had told her to go ahead and cry.

After Nancy died, Georgia would look out the window on Sundays, wishing Nancy would drive up in her Opel. It would be a long time before Georgia could fry chicken again.

At the family Christmas gathering, one of the presents opened was a Tonka truck, for little Thomas. Nancy had hidden it under the bed where she died.

No one came to arrest Rader, to his surprise.

He got cocky again.

Rader wrote out a poem about Shirley Vian on an index card one night, but as he was scribbling, his wife came home, and he quickly stuck the card in the folds of his chair. Then he forgot to retrieve the card and hide it.

His wife found it a few days later.

What's this?

Well, he said. Yeah, I wrote that, but at WSU we're working on some things, writing things about the BTK murders in my criminology class.

Paula bought the lie.

Later, he reworked the poem and printed it on an index card with a child's rubber-stamping set. On January 31, 1978, he dropped it in the mail.

The index card arrived at *The Wichita Eagle* a day later.

SHIRLEY LOCKS! SHIRLEY LOCKS
WILT THOU BE MINE?
THOU SHALT NOT SCREEM
NOR YET FEE THE LINE
BUT LAY ON CUSHION
AND THINK OF ME AND DEATH
AND HOW ITS GOING TO BE.
    B.T.K.

POEM FOR FOX NEXT

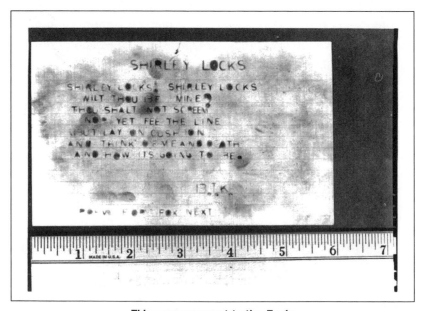

**This poem was sent to the *Eagle*,
but was not immediately recognized as being from BTK.**

No one handling the *Eagle*'s mail that day gave it more than a glance. It looked like a message for a special Valentine's Day section in the classifieds—the holiday was two weeks away. The card never made it to the newsroom. It was forwarded to the *Eagle*'s classified advertising department. There was no money with the card, so the classified people put it in a dead-letter file. Days passed; the *Eagle* published nothing. The poem's author grew irritated.

What do I have to do, draw them a picture?

13

February 10, 1978

Big News

The letter came through KAKE-TV's front door like an angry dog, with its teeth bared. When the receptionist opened the envelope she found a poem titled "OH! DEATH TO NANCY." To the left of the poem the sender had typed "B.T.K." four times, and beside each, he added tiny hangman's nooses. There was a pencil drawing of a woman bound and gagged, and a two-page note with hundreds of words, many of them misspelled.

I find the newspaper not wirting about the poem on Vain unamusing. A little paragraph would have enought. Iknom it not the news media fault. The Police Cheif he keep things quiet, and doesn't let the pubbic know there a psycho running lose strangling mostly women, there 7 in the ground; who will be next?

How many do I have to Kill before I get a name in the paper or some national attention. Do the cop think that all those deaths are not related?

Larry Hatteberg, a KAKE photojournalist, called his news director at home a few minutes later. Ron Loewen was sleeping hard; there was a downtown bar called the Looking Glass, where journalists drank after work, and he'd spent a lot of time there the night before.

You need to come in now, Hatteberg said.

Why?

We have a letter.

Why is it important?

It looks like it could be from BTK.

Loewen hurried to KAKE, his clothes still smelling of stale beer. He had skipped taking a shower.

The woman in the drawing was lying facedown on a double bed, gagged, ankles and thighs bound, hands bound behind her.

Loewen knew who BTK was: the guy who claimed to have murdered the Oteros. But Loewen was relatively new to Wichita, so parts of the letter mystified him. Who is Nancy? he asked. Who is "Vain"? Hatteberg said they were Nancy Fox and Shirley Vian, two murder victims from the previous year.

Had anyone ever connected the Otero killer to the Fox and Vian homicides? Loewen asked. Hatteberg said no.

Loewen realized, as his hands began to tremble, that if the letter was authentic, if BTK had killed Nancy Fox and Shirley Vian, that made BTK a serial killer. That was something the public had not heard before.

He read more:

Josephine,when I hung her really turn me on; her pleading for mercy then the rope took whole, she helpless; staring at me with wide terror fill eyes the rope getting tighter-tighter.

Loewen was only thirty. He had never faced a story this big. He felt sick and alone, as though he'd just been transported to the far side of the moon. What should he do about this letter? He read more, about Shirley Vian's kids:

They were very lucky; phone call save them. I was go-ng to tape the boys and put plastics bag over there head like I did Joseph, and Shirley . And then hang the girl. God-oh God what a beautiful sexual relief tha would been.

In the letter, BTK claimed another victim—#5—whom he did not name.

7 down and many moreto go.

BTK was threatening to kill again. He underscored that point, saying that he would leave a note with the letters "BTK" on his next victim.

We need to call the cops, Loewen said. He picked up the phone.

He wondered whether the cops knew BTK was a serial killer and had covered it up. He wondered whether BTK had been stalking KAKE's female anchors.

• • •

Hatteberg and Loewen drove to city hall as Loewen fretted out loud:

What if it really is BTK, but LaMunyon blows us off and refuses to say? How do we confirm it's really BTK?

Hatteberg did not know what to advise.

What if the letter is real but there is a cover-up? Loewen asked. All they have to do is deny the letter is authentic. Or worse, they could stall . . . tell us that they have to test the letter . . . show it to experts . . . meanwhile there's a killer at large who has pledged to kill again. . . .

Hatteberg said they had to run a story no matter what, to warn people.

Oh, we're going to air the story, Loewen said. No matter what LaMunyon says.

LaMunyon and Deputy Chief Cornwell read the letter slowly, sitting side by side, turning pages. They had said hardly a word since Loewen and Hatteberg arrived.

LaMunyon stood up.

Would you excuse us for a few minutes? he asked. We need to talk about this in private.

Five minutes passed, then ten. Loewen fidgeted.

LaMunyon came back in.

Is it from BTK? Loewen asked.

Yes, it is, LaMunyon said. And I want to talk to you.

This is where they try to tell us not to air the story, Loewen thought.

I'll tell you the whole story, LaMunyon said. I'll tell you everything.

The chief looked relieved, as though he had reached a difficult decision.

We believe we have a serial killer, LaMunyon began. We believe he's killed seven. We have not made it public. We've known about this guy for a while, knew he probably killed the Oteros, and the others, and the only reason we didn't tell the public was that some of our people thought going public might make him want to kill again.

Loewen braced himself: *This is where the arguing begins,* he thought.

We know now it's time to talk, LaMunyon said. For the good of everybody, it's time we tell what we know. We've got to warn people.

Loewen sank back in relief; LaMunyon wanted the secret revealed.

Loewen told him KAKE would broadcast the story on the 6:00 PM newscast. He asked LaMunyon to show up at KAKE to give an exclusive live interview. LaMunyon agreed but said he would also call a news conference afterward and tell the other media.

Loewen told him he intended to go on the air himself to tell the BTK story. He worried that BTK would stalk whoever broadcast the story, and he did not want to ask anyone else to face that. He did not have a family; he had less to risk. Maybe BTK was already stalking KAKE people, Loewen said. LaMunyon agreed that was a possibility. BTK stalked women, and might stalk KAKE's female anchors.

As Loewen and Hatteberg left, Cornwell handed Loewen a police revolver and bullets and told him to keep them in his glove compartment.

Back at KAKE, Loewen tried to write the story himself. But this was a crazy day; he was talking to his station manager about the story, talking with the police, trying to run the rest of the newsroom. He struggled to write it. Finally, Hatteberg did it for him.

KAKE's evening co-anchors were Jack Hicks and Cindy Martin. Loewen called Martin, and told her to come in early—"now."

**Wichita police chief Richard LaMunyon,
announcing the presence of a serial killer in the community.**

When she did, he told her she was off the air that night and why. He and Hicks would deliver the news. Martin was furious; Loewen was firm. BTK's interest in women and in KAKE prompted LaMunyon to order police protection for Martin, weekend anchor Rose, Stanley, and Loewen, even though BTK had made no threats against them. Police followed Martin home that afternoon and checked to see whether BTK had already been there.

Six o'clock came quickly. Loewen sat in one of the two anchor chairs, looked into the camera, and began to report matter-of-factly that a serial killer was stalking people in the city. Loewen looked nervous on the air, and with good reason: LaMunyon was supposed to be sitting beside him, but LaMunyon was late. Loewen had already read several sentences of the script on the air when LaMunyon walked into the studio. The KAKE staffer who was turning the wheel of the TelePrompTer, distracted by LaMunyon's entrance, stopped. Loewen stopped talking in mid-sentence. He had forgotten that he had a second copy of Hatteberg's script in his hands. He sat frozen for several moments, apologized, and told his audience he would start the story from the beginning. And he did.

LaMunyon, sitting beside him now, looked calm and resolved. When Loewen asked about BTK, LaMunyon bluntly told viewers that police did not know who the killer was or how to stop him.

A little later, LaMunyon called a news conference and made his own announcement. Shocked reporters raced back to the newspaper office and to television stations and began to type out stories.

Police followed Loewen home that night, as they would for the next month. Alone in his apartment, Loewen looked at the gun Cornwell had loaned him.

I'm such a fool, Loewen thought. *I'll accidentally shoot myself in the dark.* He unloaded the gun and hid it.

Martin went back to work the next day. For weeks afterward, when she arrived home from anchoring the 10:00 PM news, she saw a patrol car parked behind her apartment building. When she walked from her car, the officer turned the headlights on and off, *flick-flick,* as though saying good night.

14

1978

Fear and Frustration

LaMunyon had decided the moment he saw the KAKE letter that he had to publicly announce BTK. But in those few moments after Loewen handed him the letter, LaMunyon made a couple of quick phone calls to psychologists. He asked them whether going public about BTK might entice him to communicate more, given that he already seemed inclined to talk to the media.

Nothing the psychologists said dissuaded him. So LaMunyon began to plan his news conference, began to plan how to tell a half million people in and around Wichita that a serial killer lived among them.

He would not release the contents of the typo-filled letter, because he didn't want to encourage copycats, but he would say that BTK probably looked not like a monster but like one of us. BTK himself had said he was hiding in plain sight.

I don't lose any sleep over it. After a thing like Fox I ccome home and gp about life like anyone else.

It would be embarrassing to admit the police were helpless, but LaMunyon had to tell people to watch their backs. Some of his commanders still advised against this, but BTK had pointed out the obvious.

Golly -gee, yes the M.O. is different in each, but look a pattern is developing The victims are tie up-most have been women-phone cut- bring some bondage mater sadist tendenices-no stuggle, outside the death spot-no wintness except the Vain's Kids. They were very lucky; phone call save them.

LaMunyon studied the BTK letter for a long time, trying to discern who the police were hunting.

BTK seemed meticulous. The drawing of Nancy Fox on the bed was fairly accurate. LaMunyon wondered if BTK took Polaroids and drew from them. He wondered why BTK decided not to name the fifth of his seven victims. He was probably creating puzzles for the police, playing games. LaMunyon guessed the unknown victim was Kathryn Bright, though there were two or three other contenders.

It was clear from this note and the 1974 letter that BTK craved attention and wanted fame, like serial killers of the past.

You don't understand these things because your not under the influence of factor x). The same thing that made , Son of Sam, Jack The Ripper, Havery Glatman, Boston Strangler, Dr. H.H. Holmes Panty Hose Strangler OF Florida, Hillside Strangler, Ted of The West Coast and many more infamous character kill. Which seem s senseless, but we cannot help it. There is no help, no cure, except death or being caught and put away . . .

How about some name for me, it's time: 7 down and many more to go. I Like the following. How about you?

"THE B.T.K. STRANGLER", WICHITA STRANGLER", "POETIC STRANGLER", "THE BON DAGE STRANGLER". . . .

LaMunyon held a news conference at city hall after he left KAKE. His commanders had worried aloud: "If we tell people, how do we do it? Stand at a podium and say, 'There's this guy out there who says he's going to kill again and we can't stop him'?"

"Yeah," LaMunyon replied. "That's pretty much what we say."

His announcement was the shocker LaMunyon knew it would be. The next day's headline in the *Eagle* read: CITY'S 'BTK STRANGLER' CLAIMS HE'S KILLED 7. If reporter Casey Scott's opening paragraph sounded a little sensational, it was also true:

A killer claiming responsibility for seven Wichita murders—at least six of them strangulations—still is in the area and has threatened to strike again, Police Chief Richard LaMunyon warned in a terse, bombshell announcement Friday.

"I know it is difficult to ask people to remain calm, but we are asking exactly this," LaMunyon said. "When a person of this type is at large in our community it requires special precautions and special awareness by everyone."

It was the most disturbing news people in Wichita had ever heard. Someone was hunting women and children in their city and strangling them. Parents all over Wichita had to decide whether to tell their children.

Nola Tedesco, a twenty-six-year-old rookie prosecutor in the Sedgwick County district attorney's office, one day found herself examining a copy of the drawing BTK had made of Nancy Fox. Tedesco prosecuted sex crimes, so she'd become accustomed to looking at material like this, but the drawing and the idea that someone in town was stalking young women creeped her out. At night, some of her friends in the office—Richard Ballinger, Steve Osborn, and others—would walk her to her car. When she got home, she would check her phone.

Laura Kelly, now a senior known as "L." at East High School, was asked by her best friend to come over and spend the night. They slept in shifts, like two soldiers on patrol in a combat zone. The friend was too terrified to sleep alone. She had figured out that the roofline of her home would make it easy for BTK to enter her second-floor bedroom window. No amount of reasoning would calm her.

Pranksters heightened the fear by calling women and saying: "This is BTK. You're next." Kelly's mother, Barbara, was home alone when she got such a call. *What if it wasn't a hoax?* She immediately dialed the BTK hot line to report it. As a detective began to talk with her, the phone went dead. Everyone in Wichita knew that BTK cut phone lines. In her panic, she ran between the front and back doors, unsure which exit to take. In desperation, she grabbed the phone again—and heard a dial tone. Shaking, she redialed the hot line number. The detective apologized—he had fumbled the phone and cut her off. Still, she demanded that someone come search the house. The officer who arrived helpfully pointed out that closing shower curtains and closet doors would give BTK places to hide. The fear of BTK warped her emotions so badly that for years she made others, including her teenage daughter, search the house before she could work up the courage to go inside herself.

But if many civilians felt unnerved, it was a now a different story with the cops. Clarity had finally come, and there were no more debates about whether BTK was a serial killer. They knew now that he was.

And they knew now that he was going to be much harder to catch than most killers. Most murderers killed people they knew, for motives as old as Cain and Abel: anger, jealousy, revenge, greed. "Smoking gun" murders, the cops called them; not always easy to solve, but they followed an internal logic. Cain killed Abel because he got jealous. Macbeth killed

Duncan to take his throne. Booth shot Lincoln to strike a blow for the South.

But serial killers follow no logic; there are few dots to connect. BTK killed strangers, at random, probably outside his neighborhood. He planned things, cleaned up, wore gloves.

The FBI was only beginning to study serial killers intensely, but its experts were saying that a serial killer was much harder to catch. Most of the time you have to wait for him to kill again and hope he makes a mistake.

BTK had killed five people in 1974—the four Oteros and Kathy Bright. Then he stopped because he got busier at work and school, and then his wife got pregnant with his firstborn.

He had killed again in 1977: Shirley Vian, then Nancy Fox.

Now he had stopped again. For years afterward, the cops wondered why.

His daughter, Kerri, was born in June.

15

1978

Getting Focused

The opening sentence of the letter to KAKE—*"I find the newspaper not wirting about the poem on Vain unamusing"*—prompted the cops to call the *Eagle*. Someone in classified advertising soon located BTK's "Shirley Locks" poem in the newspaper's dead-letter file. They gave it to police without making a copy for the newsroom.

This was the second time the *Eagle* had muffed a chance to study an original BTK communication. BTK had called the newspaper first in 1974, when he left his letter about the Oteros in a book at the library.

One of the police reporters, Ken Stephens, was tired of the *Eagle* getting beat on a story he said the newspaper should have owned. He began to keep permanent files instead of throwing away notes and news releases. He wrote background memos, told other police reporters to do the same, and collected all the autopsy reports on BTK's known victims.

Eagle reporter Ken Stephens became so obsessed with covering the story that some people came to think that *he* was BTK.

Davis "Buzz" Merritt, the *Eagle*'s editor, had suggested some of this file building. Someday soon the cops will catch this guy, Merritt said, and the paper should be ready to tell the story behind the story.

Part of that story—unknown to all but a handful of *Eagle* staffers—was the uncommonly close relationship that quickly developed between the newspaper and the police chief.

Ken Stephens, Casey Scott, or Craig Stock talked to LaMunyon every day, not for publication. He gave them status reports on the investigation and confided that he wasn't sleeping much and that his wife was "extremely worried" about becoming the killer's next victim.

From the beginning, according to an internal memo in Stephens's file, there was *"much debate on how to handle relationship with police, though no disagreement that it is better to cooperate than to look for good quick scoop. Fear of provoking another murder or in blowing cops chances for catching BTK is expressed. Merritt decides that as long as we aren't getting deceived or feel we're being unfairly used, we will go along with police. Police worried about how to play cards, which cards to play and when to play them. They rely heavily on psychiatrists' advice, LaMunyon confides. Chief worries that if BTK kills again, some persons will blame him and news media for publicizing and encouraging BTK. Much feelings of helplessness on part of cops, newspaper people. New situation for cops and us.... Newspaper makes special arrangements for checking incoming mail and taking phone calls. The usual black humor in the office, quite prevalent in most cases, is notably skimpy on this case. Few jokes about the situation, perhaps because in this case newspaper plays a role. Merritt expresses worry about trying to outguess a deranged mind. Not happy about tailoring news judgment to try to appease a murderer, but not willing to challenge the guy to kill again. Even smallest details are questioned, agonized over to try to figure whether they will provoke killer or blow cops strategy.... 'This is one case in which there isn't any value to having the competitive thing.' Merritt on no point in trying to scoop everybody else. Reporters and editors torn. Desire for scoop and letting readers know everything is tugged at by desire to try to avoid provoking another murder. No one sure whether he or she is making right decision ... Brutality and bizarreness of case frightening everyone, even those who have dealt with weird stories."*

One benefit of covering cops, Stephens pointed out to friends, was that he saw life and death in the raw. It taught lessons: life can be short, so savor it. But it also made him feel safer than other people felt. He knew that BTK couldn't kill everybody, and that there was no reason to be afraid all the time. The chances of dying in a car wreck are much higher than of being murdered, yet most drive without fear.

Covering cops also taught him the value of gallows humor. Like most cops and many reporters, Stephens joked about danger, though some of his single women friends felt especially jittery.

One night Stephens went to a movie with Janet Vitt, a copy editor. They went to a theater in the Mall, where Nancy Fox had worked the night she died. After the movie, Stephens and Vitt went to Vitt's apartment to have a beer. She lived in east Wichita, near Wesley Medical Center and not far from where the Oteros and Brights were attacked. When she opened her door, she reached in, picked up her phone, and checked for a dial tone. It was her nightly ritual, she told him. If she heard no dial tone, she would race downstairs to flee BTK. Stephens thought this was funny.

When they went inside, she began to search her rooms.

"Janet, come on," Stephens said. "If he's here, it's already too late. We'd never get out of here alive."

Just then they heard someone open the building's outside door.

They heard footsteps on the stairs: *Clump. Clump. Clump.*

Stephens stepped out to the stairway to face down whoever it was. He saw a big man coming up to Vitt's door. He carried the biggest pipe wrench Stephens had ever seen.

The man looked startled when he saw the burly Stephens. "Plumber!" he called out, lifting the wrench.

Stephens and Vitt laughed afterward, but Stephens decided he would never make fun of BTK fears again. He had been scared on the stairs. Over the next few months he got so obsessed about BTK that people in the newsroom began to joke that maybe *he* was the killer.

He told the other crime reporters that from now on, whenever they covered any homicide, they should ask: Was the phone line cut? Was the victim strangled? Was the victim tied up?

They added notes to the file month by month.

• • •

On March 10, one month after the news conference, police arrested a man they thought might be BTK. He fit their profile, had connections to some victims, and bought clothesline one day as the cops watched in surveillance.

LaMunyon was so confident they had the right man that he told *Eagle* reporters in the city hall pressroom that this was the guy. He handed them background information about him and said that tests were being done to show that his blood type matched that of the semen found at the Otero house.

The reporters typed furiously, assuming they were writing the most sensational story in city history. But LaMunyon stopped by the pressroom that evening.

"It's not him," LaMunyon said.

Everybody stopped typing.

"The blood test rules him out."

Like the two detectives who were willing to sit in the Otero house with a psychic, LaMunyon was now ready to try any idea. Soon after the news conference, with help from the news staff at KAKE, he tried communicating with BTK through subliminal suggestion. Police in Wichita had never tried it before; they would never try it again.

With his letter, BTK had sent his drawing of Nancy Fox; it was so detailed that it showed Fox's glasses lying on a dresser near the bed. Police thought that might be important.

They had noticed that most of BTK's victims wore glasses. In his first letter, he had mentioned where Josie Otero's glasses were left in the house. Perhaps glasses meant something to him.

By this time, police were even thinking that maybe BTK hunted women based in part on their eye color. Or perhaps it was hair color or age, some said.

LaMunyon arranged a personal appearance on a KAKE newscast to talk about BTK. And as he spoke, an image flashed on-screen for only a fraction of a second: a drawing of a pair of glasses, with the words "Now Call the Chief."

BTK did not call.

Other people did; the cops got hundreds of tips. None panned out.

On October 2, 1978, the police department hired a new patrol officer. He was a native of Wichita, from the rough-around-the-edges west side. He had graduated six years earlier from Bishop Carroll Catholic High School, and he was still a few credits shy of graduating from WSU with a history degree.

That robbery in the clothing store nearly a year before still weighed on Kenny Landwehr's mind. He had decided not to apply to the FBI.

At a family funeral, he had pulled his father, Lee, off to the side to talk. He told him that he was going to drop out of college to enter Wichita's police academy. He wanted to fight crime on the street.

Lee Landwehr sighed.

"Okay," his father said. "But let's not tell your mother yet."

When Landwehr broke the news to her a few days later, she did not complain. But she was more scared than she let on.

At the application interview, a police supervisor asked the twenty-three-year-old Landwehr a standard question: What do you want to do with your career?

Rookie cop Kenny Landwehr never wanted to be chief—his dream was to head the homicide unit someday.

The standard answer from enthusiastic recruits was, I want to be chief of police someday.

But this recruit said, "I want to work in homicide."

His interviewer was surprised: You don't want to be chief?

"No," Landwehr said. "I want to command the homicide unit someday."

16

1979

Ambush and Alibis

On April 28, 1979, more than a year after BTK's last letter, a sixty-three-year-old widow named Anna Williams arrived home about 11:00 PM from a night out square dancing. She found the door to a spare bedroom open, a vanity drawer open, and clothes on the floor. Someone had stolen jewelry, clothing, and a sock in which she had hidden $35.

When she found the phone line was dead, she ran.

Weeks later, on June 14, a clerk opening the downtown post office near Central and Main found a man waiting for her at 4:00 AM. He handed her a package.

"Put this in the KAKE box," he said.

The clerk later described the man as clean shaven, white, about five feet nine, and about thirty years old. He was dressed in a jeans jacket, jeans, and gloves. His hair was cropped short above the ears, and he had gaps between his teeth.

The clerk did not know it, but the man had mailed a similar package to Anna Williams.

Williams's envelope was addressed in block letters. Inside was one of her scarves and a piece of her jewelry. There was a sketch of a gagged woman, nude except for stockings, lying on the edge of a bed. Her hands and feet were tied to a pole the way safari hunters carried home big game in the movies; she was trussed so she would pull her bindings tighter as she struggled. There was also a poem laced with typos and sexual menace. The name Louis had been crossed out and replaced with "Anna" and "A":

OH, ANNA WHY DIDN'T YOU APPEAR

T' was perfect plan of deviant pleasure so bold on that Spring nite
My inner felling hot with propension of the new awakening season
Warn, wet with inner fear and rapture, my pleasure of
*   entanglement, like new vines so tight.*
Oh, A—- Why Didn't You Appear
Drop of fear fresh Spring rain would roll down from your nakedness
*   to scent the lofty fever that burns within.*
In that small world of longing, fear, rapture, and desperation, the
*   games we play, fall on devil ears.*
Fantasy spring forth, mounts, to storm fury, then winter clam at
*   the end.*
Oh, A—- Why Didn't You Appear
Alone, now in another time span I lay with sweet enrapture garments
*   across most private thought.*
Bed of Spring moist grass, clean before the sun, enslaved with control,
*   warm wind scenting the air, sun light sparkle tears in eyes so deep*
*   and clear.*
Alone again I trod in pass memory of mirrors, and ponder why you
*   number eight was not.*
Oh, A—- Why Didn't You Appear.

And there was a strange signature: a B turned on its side to resemble eyeglasses, with a T and part of a K conjoined to look like a smile dangling below. The signature was stylized, as though the author was proud of himself. It was the first time he'd marked a message this way.

The cops wondered why BTK had targeted Williams. Most of his victims had been female, but all had been younger than forty. Perhaps BTK was really after Williams's twenty-four-year-old granddaughter, who often stayed with her.

Williams did not wait for police to figure it out. She left Kansas.

LaMunyon asked *Eagle* editor Buzz Merritt to look at the Otero crime scene photos. Knowing that he would never publish such graphic images, Merritt didn't want to see them. So LaMunyon offered a deal: *Eagle* reporters would get a look at some portions of the secret investigative files in return for a promise not to report what they saw until BTK's capture. LaMunyon was insistent and seemed anxious.

This would take the relationship between the police department and the newspaper to a new level. Merritt thought that soon, perhaps before 1979 ended, BTK would be captured. Getting a look at the file would help build that story in advance. He went to see the photos, then arranged to send the reporters too. Twelve days after BTK mailed the Williams poem, LaMunyon showed BTK's letters and a slide show of Otero crime photos to Ken Stephens and Casey Scott. Stephens copied BTK's signature into his notebook; KAKE had given its package to the cops unopened, but now the *Eagle* knew what was inside.

LaMunyon would not tell the journalists why he wanted them to see the files until much later: he and other commanders hoped that new eyes would see new clues.

They did not.

The Williams letter spurred the detectives not only to more effort but new ideas. Over the next two years detectives Arlyn Smith, Bernie Drowatzky, Al Thimmesch, and others tried to track down which copy machine BTK used for the KAKE and Williams letters. They had noticed something interesting. BTK's first message—the 1974 library letter—had been an original document. Since then BTK had sent copies of photocopies to cover his tracks. The rollers of copy machines leave tool-mark "fingerprints" on the edges of each sheet they process. BTK had even taken the trouble to trim off the margins of his messages.

The detectives resolved to trace the copies anyway. They made themselves experts on every copier in Wichita; there were hundreds. Smith's peers considered him to be a brainy guy. Decades later, Smith still could recite from memory the names of copy machine parts and ink components. He learned that pulp manufacturers used a mix of northern hemlock, spruce, and pine in copy paper. He knew what amounts of what trace minerals would show up in different paper brands—the result of each tree grower using different amounts of fertilizer.

One day Smith looked up after a meeting to see two blue-suited and briefcase-carrying representatives from the Xerox Corporation wanting to talk. They said Xerox had a lab in Rochester, New York, containing all copy machine models ever made. Xerox studied competitors' machines. Would these resources be useful? Hell, yes, Smith said.

Thimmesch sent Detective Tom Allen to Rochester with BTK messages: the 1978 letter and the "Oh, Anna" poem and drawing. Thimmesch worried about letting evidence out of the building. He told Allen, "If that plane crashes, you cover the BTK messages with your body to protect them."

Xerox experts and police eventually figured out that BTK had probably copied the Williams letter at the downtown library. And he had definitely copied the KAKE letter on a machine at the life sciences building at Wichita State University.

Did that mean he was a WSU student?

The cops had already compiled several lists: sex offenders, burglars who had turned violent, Coleman workers, and others. They now compared those lists with lists of WSU students—and also with lists of law enforcement people, because of the police jargon BTK used in messages.

Smith and his partner, George Scantlin, also recruited a child psychologist, Tony Ruark, to develop a behavioral profile of BTK. They showed him copies of the killer's writings and photos of crime scenes. Tell us what drives him, Smith told him. What sort of guy should we look for? Ruark studied the spelling and typing errors. Some cops had suggested BTK wrote that way to disguise a keener voice.

Ruark disagreed. He thought the guy might be careful but stupid or have a learning disability. Because BTK was so disturbing and disturbed, Ruark also wondered whether he might have BTK's real name at the Child Guidance Center. Perhaps the center had treated BTK for emotional problems as a child.

Over two years, Ruark studied files of children on his lunch breaks. Smith had given him BTK's age range: twenties to thirties. Ruark picked out former patients who were the right age and had sexual issues. Eventually he gave Smith more than a dozen names. Smith compared them with lists compiled by investigators.

Nothing matched.

By this time the cops had spent hundreds of thousands of tax dollars, had compared thousands of names, and had eliminated hundreds of men with alibis. They even put the postal clerk who saw BTK under hypnosis.

They learned nothing. In the end, there were only two good things about BTK's invasion of Anna Williams's privacy.

One was that Williams survived.

The other was that Ken Stephens got an alibi.

Eagle newsroom gossips had joked so often about Stephens's obsession with BTK that some cops suspected him for real. But Stephens could prove that during the hours that BTK waited in ambush at Williams's house, he was tending bar at the annual Wichita news media parody show, "Gridiron." LaMunyon was the Mystery Guest on stage that night.

"You were my alibi," he told LaMunyon.

"And you were *mine*," LaMunyon said.

On December 17 that year, Officer Kenny Landwehr and his patrol beat partner, Reginald Chaney, tracked a teenage burglary suspect to a house. The suspect slammed the back door twice on Landwehr's arm, shattering the glass. Landwehr drew his gun when he thought he saw the teenager reach for something. But as he aimed, he suddenly froze—he saw a jet of blood spurting out of his right wrist, spattering onto the coat sleeve of his left arm. The glass had slashed him.

Chaney put the teen on the floor and called for an ambulance—"officer injured." Landwehr, bleeding profusely, took off his necktie and tied it on his forearm as a tourniquet.

At the hospital, a nurse said a caller was asking to talk to him.

"Who is it?" Landwehr asked.

"Your mother," the nurse said.

Irene Landwehr had heard the whole thing on her police scanner. Her son, knowing how she worried about him, had given her the scanner when he joined the force, hoping that listening to his work would prove to her that his job was not dangerous.

The Installer

An alarm installer for the security company ADT became good friends with Dennis Rader when they first began working together in the 1970s. They shared many stories and laughs, even babysat each other's children. There were nights when the installer and his wife would come home to find Rader cradling their child in his arms.

To the installer, who didn't want his name used in this book, Rader seemed ordinary, approachable, and polite. After Rader became a supervisor, he did not allow other workers to swear or tell off-color jokes in front of women.

But he had quirks. The installer thought Rader was sometimes stern and a little controlling. For example, Rader would refuse to issue new

The presence of a serial killer in the Wichita area was a boon for the home security companies. Rader took advantage of the opportunity as a supervisor for the alarm company ADT.

rolls of black electrical tape unless the installers showed him the cardboard cylinders from used-up rolls. That seemed weird.

Rader wore gray Hush Puppies, and in winter he wore the kind of cap with flaps that Elmer Fudd wore in the old Bugs Bunny cartoons. He talked a lot about his church and his family. Rader was always sweet to his wife, Paula, and talked proudly about his two children.

Rader was a capable man. On one occasion, a homeowner in the wealthy Vickridge neighborhood who was in and out of his house a lot asked if an alarm could be installed in such a way that he wouldn't have to fiddle with it every time he came home. Rader devised a clever relay mechanism and timer that eliminated the need to constantly reset the alarm.

The installer rode with Rader in the ADT trucks. Rader always had a dark blue gym bag with him. He seemed unusually protective of it; the installer wasn't sure why. On the job, Rader would sometimes disappear for a couple of hours at a time, saying he needed parts or equipment.

ADT installers sometimes worked in Hutchinson, Salina, and Arkansas City, small cities miles from Wichita. ADT let them stay overnight, but Rader always drove back to Wichita, saying he needed to go to his WSU classes.

Rader carried a pager, and sometimes had to work until the wee hours.

Outside work, the installer and Rader liked beer, jokes, fishing, gardening, and hunting. They went together on a quail hunt one time at Marion Reservoir.

Rader asked one day whether the installer knew of a way to tie up tomato plants to make them more productive. The installer recommended panty hose—strong, pliable, easy to tie. Rader said later that panty hose worked well.

Rader had started working for ADT in November 1974, when Jim Wainscott was a branch manager. Rader was twenty-nine then. Wainscott ran an ADT security guard service and handled some installation and sales.

Like the installer, Wainscott would remember Rader's ordinariness.

In his hiring interview, Rader did not suck up or try to oversell himself. He listened intently as Wainscott described the work. Wainscott thought at first that Rader was trying to get inside his head so he could say what Wainscott wanted to hear, but when Rader answered Wainscott's questions, he was matter-of-fact about what he could do.

Wainscott raised the idea of working as a security guard. Rader said no. He wanted to be a police officer someday, "in the worst way," but working as a security guard at night would not work out—he was taking night classes to finish his administration of justice degree at Wichita State.

ADT installers drank at a bar called the Play Pen on South Washington. They had a secret code. They would radio each other: "PP30." It meant "Meet you at Play Pen at 4:30." Rader loved wry little codes.

Sometimes the two friends drank more than was good for them. Rader sometimes drank a lot but never got falling-down drunk.

Sometimes the installer would get a call from Paula Rader late at night, asking if he knew where Dennis might be.

Police Stories

Arlyn Smith became Landwehr's boss in 1980, when LaMunyon promoted Smith from detective to patrol lieutenant. Smith said later that Landwehr was the smartest officer he ever supervised. Landwehr was a character too. Smith had a theory about that: humor channels stress. And because police work is sometimes brutally stressful, cop humor is sometimes cruel or macabre.

Smith often started his third-shift work with Landwehr at a Denny's restaurant on West Kellogg. Landwehr called him Smitty.

One night there was nobody else in Denny's but a couple with a squalling baby. As the cops left and passed the noisy child, Landwehr joked to Smith: "They don't do that after you hold their heads under water for a while." Landwehr walked out, with Smith behind him. Outside, Smith confronted Landwehr.

"What if that family would have heard you? I'm your lieutenant. What was I supposed to say if they got mad?" Landwehr grinned and walked to his car.

Smith concluded after a long career that cops, including kind ones, use humor like that to blow off steam, especially after they see cruelty at crime scenes. Landwehr had seen his share.

Smith thought of cop humor as therapy.

"I want my detectives loose," Smith would say later. "I want them cracking jokes, and I want them going home at night and sleeping soundly, should they ever have to walk through a crime scene. Why? Because when you don't get emotional, when you get a good night's sleep, that's when you do your best work. Kenny Landwehr was that kind of cop."

The problem with that conclusion about Landwehr was that it wasn't true. Other people who knew him said Landwehr used jokes and pranks to hide a brittle sensitivity. Irene Landwehr, for one, was sure that her son's supposedly cool detachment was an act. She had noticed that when he was a child he seemed easily hurt when teenagers at family gatherings left little kids like him out of things. When he became a teen himself, he included smaller kids in everything. His attachment to children, especially victimized or disabled kids, continued after he became a cop. He volunteered to help the Special Olympics, a charity he would serve throughout his career.

One night, when Landwehr was a patrol officer, Irene saw him sit in uncharacteristic silence at the dinner table, unable to eat. It took him awhile to get it out, but he finally told her why.

Earlier in the day, as he sat in his patrol car, he had heard a distant scream.

He drove two blocks and found the cause: an eight-year-old boy walking home with his five-year-old sister had looked away for a moment as they crossed the street hand in hand. A trash truck had backed up, crushing the girl.

Landwehr called for paramedics over his car radio and began to scream the location. Smith, parked several blocks away, hearing Landwehr's anguish, thought for a moment that Landwehr himself had backed over the child.

Landwehr led the boy to his patrol car and did the only thing he could think of to help him: he lied to him.

"They will do all they can for her," he said.

Later, at his mother's house, he sat in shock.

After nights on the job now, he sometimes drank to forget.

19

1984

The Ghostbusters

Ten years after the Oteros were killed, city officials approached Chief LaMunyon one day and began to ask about BTK. The more they talked, the more they surprised LaMunyon.

No one had heard from BTK in five years, but people were still scared. Gene Denton, the city manager, and Al Kirk, a city commissioner, wanted something done. They asked what it would take to catch BTK.

"Money and manpower that I cannot spare," LaMunyon said.

To the chief's amazement, Kirk said they wanted to make it possible.

The city did not give LaMunyon more money but gave him temporary discretion to move around what he had in his budget. Denton told him he could have a computer. Personal computers were a new thing; LaMunyon realized that a computer could save thousands of man-hours by crunching numbers, holding enormous amounts of data, and giving cops the ability to quickly compare lists of suspects.

When a snag developed about the cops getting one, city official Ray Trail loaned them his.

LaMunyon planned the most sophisticated investigation in city history, employing not only the data-crunching but new FBI theories about behavioral science, and the fledgling science of genetics. The cops had BTK's DNA—in the dried semen stored in an envelope since the Oteros died.

LaMunyon handpicked task force members after talking to commanders.

"Tell me who your best people are," he said.

A few days later, Landwehr's supervisor told him to go to LaMunyon's office for a new assignment. Landwehr felt a flicker of insecurity, wondering what he might have done wrong. When he got to the chief's office, Landwehr saw several men he knew: Capt. Gary Fulton, Lt. Al Stewart, and officers Paul Dotson, Ed Naasz, Mark Richardson, and Jerry Harper. There would be one more, he learned: Paul Holmes, an officer who had been wounded along with his partner, Norman Williams, in a shoot-out at the Institute of Logopedics near Twenty-first and Grove in 1980.

Chief LaMunyon said he was forming a secret task force.

"And you guys are it."

They were an odd group. Holmes, who had killed a man, was short, skinny, and soft-spoken. He took thorough notes in tiny block letters; he was good at organizing. The chief had monitored Holmes's recovery after the gunfight and learned that Holmes and Harper had worked the BTK case for eight years on their own time, studying files and interviewing people.

Stewart knew more than most people about computers.

Dotson, witty and thoughtful, quickly became one of Landwehr's best friends. He felt drawn to Landwehr in part because they were both ambitious, self-doubting perfectionists, and they loved macabre humor.

LaMunyon had monitored Landwehr's recovery from his arm injury and knew he'd helped make Special Olympics the department's official charity. He had heard that Landwehr partied hard but also that he was resourceful.

Except for Holmes and Fulton, none of these guys had hunted BTK, but LaMunyon liked that. He thought it was time for fresh eyes.

"Tell no one what you are doing," LaMunyon ordered them. "Not your wives, not even my deputy chiefs."

Access to their room was granted only to LaMunyon and task force members. One day, when a deputy chief tried to walk in, Holmes shut the door in his face. The deputy chief yelled, "Let me in there *now!*"

"No," Holmes said.

By late 1984, the *Eagle*'s crime team had a new member. Hurst Laviana had come to the paper two years before with a degree in mathematics. He was quiet, analytical, and prone to solitude.

He knew nothing about BTK. One night he went out to cover a homicide. It would turn out to be a routine murder. As Laviana left, Stephens called out.

"Make sure you ask the cops if the phone line was cut."

"Why?" Laviana asked.

Some of the BTK evidence was now ten years old. To store it, the city had sent it underground, to vaults in old salt mines dug under Hutchinson, Kansas, fifty miles to the northwest. The city stored old records there. The first day Holmes went there, he thought, "Wow, I get to go into an old salt mine." By the next day he already dreaded going into the cold, dark caves.

The BTK files and evidence boxes had become scattered. Holmes began to pull them together and index everything: case files, toys from the Vian house, thousands of pages of BTK reports held in red or green three-ring binders. There were at least five boxes of detective notes.

"We read and read and read," Stewart would say later. "For the first month, we didn't do anything but read reports."

They talked to FBI profilers. The Wichita cops in the task force were beginning to think they should communicate with BTK if he ever resur-

Eagle reporter Hurst Laviana (left) formed an important friendship with Landwehr, based on their mutually quirky sense of humor.

faced, and the FBI's behavioral science guys, whom they consulted, were reaching that conclusion too.

Years before, older detectives probing BTK had created a huge index-card file containing names of suspects they had eliminated. The new task force studied these cards, wondering whether these men should be reexamined. It would mean hundreds of man-hours. They decided yes.

They set up their own indexed lists. From state, county, and city records, they compiled a list of men who lived in the county and were twenty-one to thirty-five years old in 1974. Tens of thousands of names.

They had a separate list of men from WSU, a list of people who worked at Coleman, another list of personnel from nearby McConnell Air Force Base, another from the local electric company. They compiled lists of animal abusers, window peepers, sex perverts, prison inmates, and others.

They wanted to find men who appeared on more than one list. A good idea, but unreliable. They didn't know it then, but the man they were seeking was there, on the WSU list. But he didn't have a criminal record. He'd never been stationed at McConnell. And though he'd worked at Coleman like countless other blue-collar Wichitans, it was before Julie Otero and the Brights did; investigators were looking for a coworker. Thousands of people appeared on at least two of the lists, which made them good suspects until blood samples cleared them. The cops ran their own names too—and Paul Holmes, a police shoot-out hero, appeared on *four* lists. His blood sample cleared him.

BTK had boasted that there was another victim, so far not identified—the fifth of his seven murders. After weeks of debate, the task force decided that victim was Kathryn Bright. They added all the Bright files and evidence bags to the BTK evidence, including one of the bullets that struck Kevin Bright in the head.

Because BTK had shot Kevin with a Colt semiautomatic .22 pistol thought to be a Targetsman or Woodsman model, the cops compiled a massive list of people who had bought such guns.

They set up computer programs to compare lists.

At one point they narrowed their suspect list from tens of thousands to 30 men in Wichita and another 185 living elsewhere. Holmes told the task force they should get blood and saliva samples from every one of them.

"How the hell are you going to convince these men to give you a blood sample?" LaMunyon asked.

"I'm going to walk right up to them and ask," Holmes said.

To find these men, detectives traveled to nearly every state, driving circuits in two-person teams, to Tulsa, Dallas, Houston, and so on. They pricked fingers to collect blood and touched paper to tongues to collect saliva. In Hutchinson one night, Holmes met with a suspect and his wife. "Your name turned up on a BTK suspect list, and I want to eliminate you from it," Holmes said. "I need your blood and saliva sample."

"Don't give these guys a damned thing," the woman told her husband.

"Then I'll have to interview your employers, and your neighbors, and do a complete background check on you," Holmes said.

"Don't give these people *anything*," the woman said.

"Excuse me for just a moment, Officer," the man suddenly said.

He turned to his wife.

"Shut up, bitch," he said. Then he turned to Holmes. "Take whatever blood you want."

The cops tracked down former wives of suspects.

Sorry to ask this, they would say. But does your ex-husband like bondage during sex? Does he like to penetrate from behind? Does he like anal sex? They asked because BTK had accentuated the buttocks of the women in his drawings.

The cops had thought people would argue or refuse their requests for samples and information. But nearly everyone cooperated. "Most people are law-abiding citizens who want to help police do their jobs," Stewart concluded.

Every one of these suspects was eliminated; the chemistry of their bodily fluids did not match that of BTK. This surprised the task force. They started new lists.

In October 1984, FBI criminal profilers, including Roy Hazelwood, provided the cops their first detailed impressions of BTK. Hazelwood thought BTK practiced bondage in everyday life, that he was a sexual sadist, a control freak, and could interact with others only on a superficial level. "You know him but you really don't know him." The profiler felt that although BTK would do well at work, he wouldn't like anyone telling him what to do. "He would love to drive. . . . People would associate him with driving."

Hazelwood also thought BTK collected bondage materials and read crime books and detective magazines. That caught the cops' interest. They considered detective magazines to be instruction manuals showing how to get away with murder. After Hazelwood told them that, Holmes, when he entered someone's home, looked around for detective magazines.

They were working sometimes seven days a week. "It's terrible," Landwehr said later. "You'd be up for one week, and down for three because you don't have anybody that looks good and you don't know where he went. There's times you don't even want to come to work."

After work, they sought a traditional cop stress remedy.

"We needed to get drunk," Stewart said. "The guys were working twelve, fourteen hours a day on their own."

One day, not long after the task force started, Holmes overheard an officer ask: "What are those guys doing in that closed room?"

"Chasing ghosts," someone said.

Someone taped a poster to their office door. It advertised a Bill Murray movie about ghost-chasing pseudoscientists in New York.

Ghostbusters.

A catchy name.

But the Ghostbusters caught no one.

In 1985 Stephens took a job at the *Dallas Morning News.* He made a copy of the BTK file and took it with him. He had long ago showed the original file to Laviana.

"You need to study this," Stephens told him, "in case he comes back."

If BTK ever sends a message to the *Eagle* again, Laviana should take it to the cops, but only after making a copy, he said.

Right after Stephens left, BTK killed again.

April 26–27, 1985

Marine Hedge

Marine Hedge stood not much more than five feet tall and weighed about a hundred pounds. She was a fifty-three-year-old grandmother with a southern accent that slipped off her tongue the way molasses drips slowly off a spoon.

She liked jewelry, dressing with care, and stocking her closet with shoes to match every outfit. She made small look stylish. She liked cooking from scratch and taught younger in-laws how to fry hush puppies and catfish the way she learned when she grew up as little Marine Wallace in Arkansas.

Her husband, a Beechcraft worker, had died in 1984, leaving her feeling lonely in their house at 6254 Independence in the Wichita suburb of Park City. She dealt with loss by giving to others, to friends, a son, three daughters, and grandchildren. She enjoyed seeing customers she

Marine Hedge lived only six doors down from Dennis Rader.

had served for a dozen years at the coffee shop at Wesley Medical Center, second shift. And there was bingo, and her friends at Park City Baptist Church.

Rader timed Hedge's comings and goings, looked for men, and even visited the coffee shop at Wesley, where he learned she started work at 2:00 PM and got off about midnight.

He realized it might be a dumb move to murder someone who lived six doors down. But he had grown lazy in the years since he had stalked Nancy Fox, and he had studied serial killers and wanted to flout the wisdom of the FBI profilers.

Probably loners, they said. Probably not family men. Serial killers can't stop killing.

None of that had applied to him. Now he would prove them wrong again. He would kill in his own neighborhood, kill on his own block, kill a tiny lady whom he knew well enough to wave to as he and his wife drove past on the way to church.

The profilers were right about one thing: serial killers feel compulsions. In the eleven years since he had killed the Oteros, Rader had stalked hundreds of women, in Wichita and in small towns all over Kansas, while traveling for ADT—and as he would in 1989 for the U.S. Census Bureau as the field operations supervisor for the Wichita area.

By 1985 he'd grown tired of trolling, scouting back alleys, planning escape routes. He selected his neighbor in part because she was convenient.

He had never grown tired of the excitement these projects gave him, though. So he was still willing to invest effort in making the fantasy real. For this murder—Project Cookie—he planned an elaborate alibi. He would use a Cub Scout outing with his son as cover.

At Camp TaWaKoNi, perhaps twenty miles from home, they set up tents. It had rained, and the ground was soggy. His son loved these Cubby things. Years later, his son would tell people that his dad had always been his best friend.

In camp after dark that night, Rader told the other Scout dads he had a headache. I'm going to bed early, he said. Then he slipped away, leaving his son with the other boys and their fathers.

He drove west five miles or so toward home. On a country road near Andover, east of Wichita, he stopped to unpack his bowling bag hit kit. He took off the Scout uniform and pulled on dark clothing. Then he drove to northeast Wichita. Near the shops of Brittany Center, he parked at a bowling alley, went in, and pretended to get drunk. He splashed beer on his face and clothing, then called for a cab. He put his hit kit bag on the seat beside him.

The boys and I have been partying, he told the driver. I need a ride home.

When they reached Park City, he told the driver to let him out on West Parkview, one block east of Independence.

I need to walk, he told the driver. I need to wear this off.

He slurred his speech to fool the driver. If this ride ever turned up in an investigation, the cabbie would remember only that he was a drunken bowler in dark clothes, and not the Scout dad who slept in the tent at TaWaKoNi twenty miles to the east. If asked, the Scout dads would say that he stayed in the tent all night with a headache.

He paid the driver and walked in his own neighborhood; he could

**One of BTK's signature moves was to cut the phone lines of his victims.
This was Marine Hedge's line.**

have found his way here in his sleep. He walked through a park, then through his in-laws' backyard—and then to the house of Marine Hedge.

Seeing her car bothered him—she must be home already. He had wanted to hide inside and surprise her when she arrived. He hoped she would be alone.

He snipped the phone line with wire cutters and took his time breaking in, trying to be quiet. He slowly worked the door open with a long-handled screwdriver. When he crept in, he found she was not there.

But minutes later, he heard a car door slam, then voices—hers and a man's. BTK hid in a closet, fuming at his bad luck. He waited for an hour, as the man and Marine talked. The man left; she went to bed.

She woke when Rader climbed into bed with her.

The Park City police chief, Ace Van Wey, and an animal control officer named Rod Rem found her nine days later. Her little body had been hidden under brush in a wet ditch on Fifty-third Street North, northeast of Wichita. Her body was decomposing, and animals had gotten to her.

Her stolen Monte Carlo had been found at Brittany Center in Wichita. Her purse, missing all identification, was found miles away. She had been strangled. A loop of knotted panty hose was found near her body. When the Wichita cops heard about this, they wondered about BTK,

Marine Hedge's body, missing for several days, was found next to the culvert, in the water and covered with branches.

whose last known murder had been in December 1977. But as far as the cops knew, BTK had never killed anyone outside Wichita, had never attacked anyone older than thirty-eight, had never taken a body outdoors. And he seemed to fixate on addresses with the number three; Marine lived at 6254 Independence in Park City. The cut phone line caught their interest, but this case didn't fit what they knew about BTK.

After Marine's body was discovered, Rader's neighbors in Park City chattered in fear. He wondered what they would have thought had they known the full story—what he had done with Marine after he killed her. He had dragged her nude body out to her car, wrapped in bedcovers. She was such a tiny thing, but he could barely lift her. After he stuffed her into the trunk, he drove to his own church, Christ Lutheran, where he had spent many a Sunday pretending to be a Christian.

He taped black plastic over the windows, to block the light he now turned on. He had stashed the plastic at the church before he left for the Cub Scout camp.

In the church, he played God: controlled her, strapped high heels to her cold feet, posed her bound body in lewd positions, and took photographs he could savor later.

Then he took her to the country and dumped her.

By that time, night was creeping toward dawn, and he had to hurry back to the Cub Scouts. He dropped her Monte Carlo at Brittany Center with regret—it was a hot car—and drove his own vehicle back to the campout. He got up that morning with all the other dads and lads.

When he heard a rumor among his neighbors that maybe Marine Hedge's boyfriend had killed her, he spoke up.

No, he said. It couldn't have been him.

21

September 16, 1986

Vicki Wegerle

Landwehr's work on the Ghostbusters task force led to his promotion to detective in 1986.

On September 16 of that year, he lay asleep until afternoon—he had been working late. Had he awakened and walked out on his balcony, he might have seen the very man he was looking for getting out of a gold 1978 Monte Carlo.

Rader had been attracted to Landwehr's neighborhood three weeks before, when he saw a young woman getting into that car. It reminded him of Marine Hedge's. After he began stalking the young Wichita resident, he saw that she had a husband but spent a lot of time alone at home. Sometimes, as he listened outside, BTK heard a piano.

Rader thought she played beautifully.

During the first years that Landwehr lived in his little bachelor pad in the Indian Hills Apartments, the maintenance man was a guy named Bill Wegerle. Landwehr thought Bill was a nice person, quiet of manner. Other people who knew Bill said he did not show a lot of emotion.

Bill's wife, Vicki, usually stayed home during the day taking care of their two-year-old son, Brandon, at their little house at 2404 West Thirteenth Street. She spent a lot of time with Brandon and with Stephanie, their nine-year-old.

She also babysat the newborn son and the two-year-old daughter of Wendi Jones, a friend. Vicki liked babies. She volunteered as a babysitter at St. Andrews Lutheran, which she attended, and at Asbury United Methodist, which was in her neighborhood. Wendi thought Vicki had a calm, motherly instinct—she never raised her voice, even when babies tested her patience. Sometimes, when Wendi came to Vicki's home to pick up her kids, Wendi would pull up a chair, and they would talk, watching their daughters play.

Rader liked what he saw: a young, blond woman alone during the workday. He liked listening to her music so much that he called her "Project Piano" in his notes.

After Bill left the job maintaining the Indian Hills Apartments, he became a house painter. On September 16, Bill told Vicki that he was working at a place not far away and that he would be home early for lunch—he would need to stop painting to let the first coat dry. He liked to spend time with Vicki and Brandon, who was now toddling all over the house. It was a pleasant house to come home to: wife, children, music. Sometimes she would play piano while Brandon took a nap.

Rader had modified a business card to look like a phone company identification card. He had a yellow hard hat, provided by ADT. He had cut out a segment of the cover of a Southwestern Bell repair manual

Bill, Stephanie, Vicki, and baby Brandon Wegerle.

and pasted it on the hard hat, hoping to pass himself off as a telephone repairman. The briefcase he would carry looked official but contained the hit kit supplies—rope, cord, knife, gun. He'd put in something new this time: leather bootlaces tied into what he called a strangling rig. "Leathering up," he called it. He thought the leather, thin and strong, might make the strangling go quicker. He had tied knots into the laces to give himself a better grip.

He parked the security company van in the Indian Hills Shopping Center parking lot, put on the hard hat, and walked across the street toward the blond woman's house. But first he went to the home of her elderly neighbors. They let him in, and he pretended to check their phone line. He wanted the blond woman, if she saw him, to see what looked like a telephone repairman working the neighborhood. He entered many houses this way.

When he left the older couple's house, he walked to the blond woman's door. He heard the piano. When he knocked, the music stopped.

At the door, she looked warily at him.

I need to check your telephone line, he said. He saw a little boy in the living room.

She asked whether it was necessary to come in. Didn't he need to go to the backyard to check the phone line? The dog was out there, but she could bring it in.

No, no, he said. He needed to check inside the house.

As he recalled later, she did not like this, but she let him in. She showed him to the dining room phone. He opened his briefcase and made small talk, pulling out a gadget that he'd cobbled together to look like a telephone tester. He fiddled with it and chatted. There appeared to be no man about.

Well, he said, it looks like it works. He put the fake tester into the briefcase and pulled out his gun.

Let's go to the bedroom, he said.

She began to cry. What about my kid? she asked.

He shrugged. I don't know about your kid.

My husband is going to be home pretty soon, she said.

I hope he's not going to be home too soon, he told her.

Rader thought she was probably lying, but he'd watched the house enough to know she did have "a husband thing." He would need to hurry now, and that upset him.

He made her lie down on her waterbed as she cried and tried to argue. He tied her wrists and ankles with leather shoelaces. Vicki began to pray out loud. Suddenly she yanked her hands, broke her bonds, and began to fight, and then everything became noise and fear. The dog outside heard them fighting through an open window and began to bark. BTK hit Vicki in the face, again and again, then grabbed at her throat. She fought, nicking him on the neck with a fingernail. They fell off the bed on the side farthest from the door.

He tried to use his strangling rig, but could not get a grip on it after he got it around her throat. He saw a pair of panty hose nearby. That worked, once he looped it around her neck.

He was disappointed, though. He had wanted to spend time with her, but there was no time to masturbate.

He got his Polaroid camera, arranged her to his liking, pulled her top up to partially expose her breasts, and took a photo. Twice more he tugged on her clothing and squeezed the shutter. Then he packed his things, got into her Monte Carlo, and drove away.

She died in the space between the bed and television cabinet. Anyone looking through the doorway would not be able to see her.

Rader used panty hose from Vicki Wegerle's dresser drawer to strangle her.

September 1986

Prime Suspect

Bill Wegerle went home early for lunch as planned. At Thirteenth and West Street a Monte Carlo passed him going the other way. Bill thought it was his wife's car until he saw a tall man at the wheel.

When he got home, the Monte Carlo was gone, and so was Vicki. That upset him—their son was alone. Bill could not imagine why Vicki would drive off and leave a two-year-old; maybe she had made a flying trip to a store. Bill held Brandon and waited, made a sandwich and ate it, walked around.

Time passed; he grew more puzzled. He needed to go back to work. He walked through the house again. Forty-five minutes passed before he found her.

Moments later, a 911 dispatcher heard anguish in his voice. "I think someone has killed my wife," he said. The dispatcher heard him moan. "Vicki, Vicki, Vicki, Vicki, Vicki, oh God, oh no no no no."

Rader had driven the Monte Carlo west, then north about a mile, to Twenty-first Street. In a trash bin outside a Braum's ice cream store, he dropped the briefcase. In a trash can outside a muffler shop, he dropped the hard hat—after peeling off the Southwestern Bell label. Besides the label, he kept the Polaroids. He drove back to the woman's street, parked the Monte Carlo next to a meat market, and walked to his van, which was parked across from her house.

He heard sirens.

Two firefighters, Ronald Evans and Lt. Marc Haynes, found Bill Wegerle punching the wall of his porch. "If I could've been here five minutes earlier, I could've done something," he told them.

They found his wife in the bedroom. There was a pocketknife beside her head. Bill told them later that he had used it to cut the leather shoelaces and the nylon stocking encircling her throat. There was no room to work, so they carried her into the dining room.

An ambulance arrived. A twenty-eight-year-old paramedic, Netta Sauer, saw Bill in the front yard, talking to a cop and holding a little boy. The child looked calm.

In the dining room, Netta found the firefighters starting CPR, even though Vicki looked dead. Her face was mottled, and the cause was obvious from the ligature mark around her throat. Her hands were tied behind her back; the leather had dug deep into her skin. There were also laces around her ankles. Netta, glancing around, saw toys scattered. The killer had done it in front of the boy. *Had he cried? Had the killer hurt him?*

Netta and other paramedics worked on Vicki for ten minutes, then put her in the ambulance. A television crew filmed them.

As Netta drove Vicki away, she saw the husband still standing in the yard holding his son, talking to police.

At Riverside Hospital's emergency room, doctors pronounced Vicki dead. Netta heard someone say that the cops thought the husband might have done it.

Detectives probing the death of a wife at home usually suspect the husband first. It's standard procedure: quickly rule him out as a suspect, or establish guilt. So detectives asked Bill pointed questions: What time did you say you saw the Monte Carlo? How long did you sit in your house before you realized your wife was in the bedroom? Forty-five minutes? Why so long?

Bill did not show a lot of emotion. His friends knew this was because he was reserved; but to these cops, in these circumstances, Bill came off as coldhearted.

The detectives were trying to move fast. The first few hours in a homicide investigation are crucial. Detectives increase the chances of catching the killer if they press hard from the first hour, stay up most of the first night following leads, questioning witnesses. The more hours go by, the more the trail cools.

They took Bill downtown and grilled him: Were you having an affair? Was she having an affair? What did you argue about? They were not satisfied with Bill's account of what streets he had driven to go home and where he had seen his wife's Monte Carlo as it passed him going the other way. And he sat in the house for forty-five minutes before he found her? What gives?

The detectives suggested a lie detector test.

Bill said yes. He was innocent, after all.

The doctor who performed the autopsy saw that the killer had strangled Vicki so hard that there was internal bleeding in her throat. She had been beaten—there were scrapes on her right ear, cheek, and jawline. He found a gouge on her left hand and a knuckle that had swollen just before she died. That told him she had fought.

He found a bit of skin under one fingernail. She had nicked her attacker.

The doctor looked for evidence of sexual assault; there was none. He took a swab from her vagina and preserved it, in case there was male fluid in the sample.

Lie detectors record heart rate, blood pressure, and perspiration. The theory is that a guilty person registers physical signs when lying. But cops use lie detectors only as a supplemental tool. Most courts consider them unreliable.

In years to come, Wichita detectives would conclude that a lie detector test should never be given to a spouse or close family member immediately after a murder. If a husband has just lost his wife, his emotions might falsely register as guilt. But that conclusion was in the future. On the day of Vicki's death, detectives gave Bill two polygraph tests—and he failed both.

The cops really got tough after that. Their voices rose. They were questioning Bill on the sixth floor of city hall, and had let Bill's family sit close by. Bill's relatives overheard some of the questions. And they got mad.

Bill told his interrogators he had to go to the restroom. He stepped out where his family could see him. One of them yelled: Stop answering questions and get a lawyer.

Bill told detectives he was done with them.

Under the law, it was his right.

They let him go.

Police never charged Bill Wegerle with his wife's murder, but there were detectives who said privately for the next two decades that Bill probably killed her. That rumor spread through town. Schoolkids on playgrounds sometimes told the Wegerle kids that their dad had killed their mom.

Bill never publicly complained, but he refused to talk to the cops further.

That crippled the investigation. An innocent husband is the investigator's best source because he holds the key to countless leads: he knows the names of his wife's family and friends, the stores where she shopped, the kid she hired to mow the lawn.

Bill had loved his wife—he and Vicki had made love the night before she died. But Bill's cooperation disappeared after he walked out.

Hours after Vicki died, Ghostbuster investigator Paul Holmes called Landwehr and said a car belonging to a homicide victim had been found within walking distance of his apartment. Landwehr stepped out on his balcony and saw a gold Monte Carlo parked across the street.

Three days after Vicki died, Landwehr and Holmes were sent to the Wegerle house. And that put them in an awkward position.

They studied the scene, the bindings, the reports. Their role was limited to a quick look. But that look convinced them Bill was innocent.

Landwehr and Holmes shared what they had seen with Paul Dotson, another Ghostbuster. He reached the same conclusion: this was probably not Bill. It might even be BTK. That ran counter to what the detectives working the Wegerle case thought. Dotson's brother, John Dotson, was the captain supervising the homicide section. Landwehr and Holmes decided not to press their conclusions on the other detectives. Landwehr did not want to contradict the assigned detectives based on his quick look at incomplete evidence.

But Bill's two-year-old son had told police, "Man hurt Mommy." No child, in Landwehr's opinion, would say "Man hurt Mommy" if he had seen his father do it.

Landwehr also thought it unlikely that Bill would strangle Vicki in front of Brandon. Bill would know that Brandon could speak a few words and might tell what he saw.

The most convincing evidence of Bill's innocence, Landwehr thought, was that the killer had stolen Vicki's driver's license, leaving behind her wallet, money, and credit cards.

That's not a husband killing a wife, Landwehr thought. It's a sex pervert stealing a trophy.

Landwehr felt sorry for Bill, felt bad that his wife was murdered and that some cops thought he had killed her. But Landwehr also thought Bill should have stayed in the interview room, even after the cops badgered him. "If it was my own wife murdered," Landwehr said much later, "those cops would have had to fucking *throw* me out of the room to make me quit talking to them. I would have never shut up, I would have just kept throwing ideas at them until they figured out who did it."

But that is not how it worked out.

23

1987 to 1988

Failures and Friendships

Had the city known that BTK had killed again, the Ghostbusters would have stayed together. But by the time Vicki Wegerle was killed, LaMunyon had begun to scale back.

By the next year, 1987, most of the Ghostbusters had been reassigned; only Landwehr remained.

He packed the files in a cabinet and in thirty-seven boxes; the boxes ended up in the basement of city hall.

LaMunyon let the *Wichita Eagle* interview the Ghostbusters. Bill Hirschman spent hours tape-recording interviews with Landwehr, Capt. Al Stewart, and others. His transcripts revealed frustration. Stewart broke down and cried when he talked about Josie Otero; he thought he had failed her.

"You feel the frustration of the investigators before you just by reading their reports," Landwehr told Hirschman. "It's always gonna be there: Why can't we find him?"

They had tried everything they could think of: Landwehr had been assigned, for example, to test the theory that BTK was dead. To do this, he had taken a list of every white male who had died in Wichita since 1980 and had done background checks on them. It was boring work. The Ghostbusters task force spent thousands of hours and hundreds of thousands of tax dollars, and they imposed terrific strains on themselves and their families.

Paul Dotson never shook his disappointment. "When I think of the Ghostbusters all I can think of is what a failure it was, and what I didn't do and how I could have done more if only I'd been smarter."

Was it worth it? Hirschman had asked.

Probably yes, Landwehr told him. If BTK ever resurfaced, Landwehr would know a lot about him. He knew an important BTK flaw—arrogance. That might prove useful. The Ghostbusters had eliminated hundreds of potential suspects, so if BTK showed up again, the cops would not be starting from scratch.

What keeps you going on this case? Hirschman asked.

"I still believe that he can be caught," Landwehr said. "I still believe that he's out there." He speculated that BTK might be in prison for a minor crime, and if so, "he will probably get out sooner or later, and I believe that if he does get out that he will not stop."

Landwehr was just as resolved in private. Dotson, sharing disappointment over their failure with Landwehr, was surprised by what his friend said in reply.

"Don't worry about it," Landwehr said in a grim tone.

"But why?"

"Because we still might get him." Landwehr pointed out that they now had a plan that they had polished in the days when they got nowhere: if BTK ever resurfaced, they would deliberately use the news media to play to his ego and keep him sending messages until he tripped himself up. Landwehr also reminded Dotson that the study of human DNA was still developing. BTK had left them DNA at three of his murders.

But with all Landwehr's upbeat talk about finding BTK, Dotson could see that the investigation had taken a toll. Self-doubt nagged at Landwehr; Dotson could see strain and fatigue in his friend's face. They tried to joke each other out of these moods. But at bedtime, Landwehr often found himself unable to sleep. He was drinking more.

Just before the end of 1987, the Wichita Police Department, which had promoted him to detective the year before, assigned Landwehr to the homicide unit, a job he had sought for nine years.

The Ghostbusters never truly disbanded. LaMunyon said they would never disband unless they proved that they had run down every lead. So even as Landwehr began to investigate other cases, he thought about BTK every day.

On the last day of 1987, a woman named Mary Fager, who had been out of town visiting relatives, arrived home at 7015 East Fourteenth Street and discovered her husband and daughters were dead.

Sherri, sixteen, had been drowned in the hot tub. Kelli, nine, was strangled hours later and dumped in the tub with her sister. Their father, Phillip, had been shot in the back.

Landwehr was assigned to assist the lead detective, Jim Bishop. The girls' bodies had soaked for more than a day. When Landwehr got home and undressed after working the scene, the odor of boiled flesh was clinging to his clothes. For the rest of his life, the warm-water-and-chlorine smell of a hot tub would remind him of the Fager house.

In Stuart, Florida, a few days later, police tracked down William T. Butterworth, the thirty-three-year-old contractor who had just finished building the sunroom that housed the hot tub.

The cops were sure Bill Butterworth was the killer. He had driven away from the Fager home in the family's car, stopped at the Towne East shopping center to buy new clothes, then headed to Florida. Butterworth told police he was so traumatized when he found the bodies that he fled with a case of amnesia. They did not believe him.

The evidence he helped gather against Butterworth seemed to Landwehr like a slam dunk.

A few days after her husband and daughters were murdered, the widow Mary Fager opened her mail and read the first line of a rambling, taunting poem from an anonymous sender:

A ANOTHER ONE PROWLS THE DEEP ABYSS OF LEWD
   THOUGHTS AND DEEDS

The message came with a drawing of a young girl, hands bound behind her, lying beside a tub, a look of fear on her face. In the lower right corner of the drawing was a symbol. Police noted that it looked similar to the symbol BTK signed to his fantasized drawing of Anna Williams: a letter B turned on its side. This time, however, the legs of the K formed a frown.

The writer did not claim he had killed the Fagers. Instead he wrote in admiration of the murderer:

OH GOD HE PUT KELLI AND SHERRI IN THETUB
SUN AND BODY DREWING WITH SWEAT _WATER,FEMININE
   NAVETTE

THE BUILDER WILL CHRISTEN THE TUB WITH VIRIN
    MAIDS . . .

Landwehr saw that the sketch, unlike BTK's drawing of Nancy Fox, was inaccurate—drawn by someone who had not been at the murder scene.

No one had heard from BTK since the letter to the burglary victim Anna Williams in 1979, more than eight years before. BTK had killed no one, as far as they knew, since Nancy Fox in 1977.

In fact, the cops were not sure BTK had sent this letter. But Butterworth's attorney, Richard Ney, filed motions arguing that the Fager killings looked similar to the seven BTK murders from the 1970s. Perhaps BTK had killed the Fagers, Ney said.

A judge ruled that Ney could not bring up the letter during the trial because he could not prove a link to the older killings. Landwehr was relieved. But the newspaper and TV stations heavily covered the case and the BTK connection before the trial. So even though BTK wasn't mentioned during the trial, he was on everybody's mind—including jurors'.

The jury found Butterworth not guilty, but the police considered the case closed.

In this same year, 1988, Netta Sauer rode her ambulance to a home where someone had been bitten by a dog. There was a cop working the case who made her laugh.

Netta had been a new paramedic on the day she had tried to save Vicki Wegerle two years before. She was more experienced now and had seen several more murder scenes.

At the dog bite house, the young cop began to tease her in a friendly, engaging way. She teased back. His name was Kelly Otis.

They met several times more, both of them working accidents or crime scenes. Over time, this led to a breakfast meeting, then dates, then talk of marriage. Netta thought guys with a keen wit were highly intelligent, and Otis was unusually witty. She saw character under the teasing. He had grown up the son of a hardworking single mother. Like Netta, he was an adrenaline junkie: it was why he'd become a cop.

She did not tell him about that day at Vicki Wegerle's house. The Wegerle murder was a cold case, interesting only to detectives, and Otis had no interest in becoming a detective. He loved street patrol.

Netta met Otis's closest friend, a patrol officer with an impassive face, big shoulders, and a brusque manner. Dana Gouge's father had been in the military. His mother was Japanese and owned a fabric store in the little town of Tonganoxie, Kansas. Gouge had a reserved manner, but Netta saw it was a mask: Gouge was warmhearted, shy—and one of the few people funny enough to put Otis on the floor, shaking with laughter.

The Butterworth verdict had political consequences.

LaMunyon blamed District Attorney Clark Owens for assigning the case to two prosecutors LaMunyon claimed were inexperienced. He wasn't the only person who was unhappy. Weeks later, Nola Tedesco Foulston, the tough young lawyer who long ago had checked her phone and accepted escorts to her car out of fear of BTK, announced she would run against Owens in the November elections. She declared the Butterworth verdict a travesty, vowed to assign herself some homicide cases, and promised that her assistants would go into trials well trained and prepared. Owens was well known in Wichita. Foulston was known hardly at all. But Foulston beat him 82,969 votes to 55,822.

Foulston wanted a new start for the district attorney's office and asked everyone in it to reapply for their jobs if they wanted to stay on. When she made her selections, several people involved with the Butterworth case were not rehired.

Landwehr vented his bitterness over the Butterworth verdict in bars. Sometimes he got drunk at home, as well, and tried to humor himself out of bad moods by knocking golf balls out the balcony door of his third-story apartment. Sometimes he would shift his stance a bit and splash a few balls into the apartment complex swimming pool. Then he'd laugh his ass off.

LaMunyon heard rumors that Landwehr wanted to resign over the verdict. The chief warned commanders: "No paperwork involving the job of Kenny Landwehr had better cross my desk. If such paperwork comes, I'll dispose of it."

Landwehr later denied that he tried to quit. If the chief heard that, it was an "urban myth." The Butterworth verdict didn't bother him that much, he said.

But that was a myth too.

24

1988 to 1990

The Rescuer

By now people like Cindy Hughes had forgotten BTK, or no longer worried. Cindy had other problems: she was a divorcée with a daughter and an extended family with a penchant for trouble. Her brother had just made Sedgwick County's Most Wanted Criminals list.

She had a female friend who one night told her about a Wichita cop who supposedly had quite a wild streak.

"He hangs out at Players," Cindy's friend said. "Let's go see if we can find him."

"Are you dating this guy?" Cindy asked.

"No," her friend said. "But I really want to."

Cindy had a wild streak of her own. She thought watching her friend chase after unrequited love with a cop in a bar would be a fun way to spend an evening.

By the late 1980s, the job Landwehr had worked so hard
to get proved to be a curse as well as a blessing.

At Players, her friend pointed out the cop, who was sitting unsteadily on a bar stool. Cindy saw thick dark hair, a tanned face, a lit cigarette in his hand. He was drunk, and he was yelling at a woman beside him who sat unperturbed, sipping a drink. The cop was hollering about injustice and some guy named Butterworth.

He went on yelling until he finally fell off the bar stool with a thud. The woman beside him acted cool, as though this wasn't the first time. Cindy found this entertaining.

She did not talk to him much that night. But on subsequent nights, when her infatuated friend took her along, Cindy began to study Kenny Landwehr.

He appeared to be the Party Guy From Hell. Landwehr drank at west-side bars: Players at 21st and West, or Barney's at Ninth and West. He walked in every night wearing a $300 black leather bomber jacket given to him by a former girlfriend. He would order a drink, tell a funny story, order another drink, tell another story. He bought drinks for Cindy, for his friends, for her friends. He would listen intently to the stories of others. Once in a while, somebody would push his buttons and mention Butterworth and he would yell about injustice. After Cindy heard the full story, she understood why.

At first she thought Landwehr was merely one of those quick-witted people who like to tell tall tales in bars but had little else going for them. He seemed like such a bad boy, chain-smoking, getting hammered, telling off-color stories. But she soon saw deeper shades to his character. He wasn't like other guys. Landwehr was curious, likable, and empathetic. He had a habit of leaning forward and listening more carefully than other men.

He said outrageous things as a defensive move—he'd been hurt by a few girlfriends, and wanted to keep people at arm's length. But this strategy didn't work with Cindy, who talked as outrageously as Landwehr.

"Why do you have a vanity plate on your car that says 'Skippy'?" Landwehr asked one night, whirling on Cindy with a grin.

"Because I'm proud of what I do for my softball team," Cindy replied. "It means I skip around the bases."

"Bullshit," Landwehr said. "It means you're like Skippy peanut butter—you spread easy."

"You're a witty little shit," she said.

"Where did you go to high school?" he asked.

"South High," she said.

"Really? We used to call South High girls the South High Sluts."

"And we used to call your bunch the Bishop Carroll Fucks," she shot back.

She liked this. She had little use for people who tiptoed in conversation, and though Landwehr could be unusually cagey around strangers, he never tiptoed around friends. And after she became friends with him, she decided that for all his swearing and teasing, he was nevertheless "the most gentlemanly gentleman I ever met." He was curious about her work with special-ed kids for the school district. She helped teach the most damaged of children the most basic of skills; she changed diapers on these children. Her dedication to them touched him.

She learned that he went to dinner at his parents' house every Sunday and had done so all his life. He had friends from boyhood who were intensely loyal to him. Other cops openly admired him. Paul Dotson said he was brilliant, and meant it.

There were former girlfriends still around. She noticed they seemed like herself: nice, but wounded—recovering, like her, from a busted marriage, or abuse, or a bad family. Landwehr seemed drawn to such women. A rescue compulsion, Cindy decided.

Eventually Cindy met his mother, Irene, and from her and Landwehr heard some of the family's favorite Kenny stories: Irene told how Kenny used to be an altar boy, and at Christ the King School liked to drop books on the floor to startle the class. He pulled girls' pigtails, then batted his eyes at nuns to avoid getting whacked with a yardstick. Landwehr himself took pride in telling a story about an elderly nun, Sister Wilfreda Stump, who suffered from narcolepsy—she dropped off to sleep, sometimes in mid-sentence. One day in seventh grade, Sister Wilfreda was talking to Landwehr's best friend, Bobby Higgins. She was talking and pointing at Higgins when she suddenly fell asleep with her finger still pointing. "Quick," Landwehr said to Higgins. "Switch seats with me." Moments later, Sister Wilfreda woke up to find herself pointing at Landwehr. She leaped up, grabbed a yardstick, and chased Landwehr, who ran away cackling.

Years later, after high school, Landwehr was knocked senseless when he collided with a teammate during a softball game. He seemed fine when he got up, but after the game ended he began to repeatedly ask, "What inning is it?" Landwehr regained consciousness the next day in a hospital, surrounded by family and friends. When he saw where he was, his first thought was that he had wrecked his car.

"What day is it?" the nurse asked.

"Monday," Landwehr said.

"No, it's Friday."

"What?" Landwehr said. "Damn. It's Friday, and I'm not out drinkin'?"

Landwehr's friends did not want to see Irene Landwehr's reaction to that. They quickly slunk out the door.

When LaMunyon retired in 1988 he regarded the BTK case as his worst disappointment in his twelve years as chief.

BTK had outlasted entire cop careers. People who had been boys when the Oteros died were now veteran officers. Landwehr had gone from being a kid to a clothing salesman, a rookie patrolman, a Ghostbuster chasing BTK for three years, and now one of the detectives working the city's twenty-five to thirty homicides a year.

Now he took another job. The department promoted him to lieutenant and assistant commander of the crime lab. In the Ghostbusters he had already become well versed in elements of forensic science such as blood chemistry, fiber evidence, and fingernail scrapings. As the lab lieutenant, he worked hard to increase his knowledge. People who saw him in the new job realized he seemed gifted at applying science to criminal cases.

In time Landwehr felt like a weight had lifted off him. He had not realized how much it hurt him emotionally to work homicides until he took up the more detached work of the lab. Becoming a homicide detective was what he had worked for his entire career, and it was unsettling to realize how harmful it was, how much the suffering of victims' families upset him, depressed him, tempted him to drink.

As much as it hurt, though, he missed it.

• • •

About a year after LaMunyon retired, Patrol Officer Kelly Otis answered one of those calls that cops dread—a domestic violence call in the wee hours.

At 3:11 AM on December 9, 1989, Otis and two other officers walked up to 1828 North Porter. Inside was a drunken golf course greenskeeper named Thomas H. Hathaway, age twenty-eight. His girlfriend said he had beaten her. When Otis asked her whether her boyfriend had a gun, she said no, but something about her tone made Otis's Spidey-sense tingle. When Otis approached the front door, he stepped off to the side before he called out.

What answered him was a shotgun blast through the open doorway. The man inside ran out, bare chested in the freezing cold. He whirled on Otis.

Otis dropped to one knee, drew his pistol, and yelled, "Drop the goddamned gun!" Fear warped Otis's senses: Both he and the gunman seemed to move in slow motion. The man raised the shotgun to his shoulder and aimed at Otis's face. The muzzle looked big enough to crawl into. Otis fired and felt a new fear—his gun barely made a sound. Otis, terrified, thought his gun had misfired, but the gunman dropped to the ground like a heavy sack of potatoes.

Otis was puzzled for a moment: on the shooting range, his 9 mm always boom-boomed like a cannon, but this time the only sound was a faint *pop-pop*. But Hathaway was bleeding from bullet wounds in his torso.

Otis was so scared that he had barely heard the sound of his own gun.

In a fire station a few blocks away, the paramedic who had fallen in love with Otis the year before now heard his voice on the police scanner. "We have an officer-involved shooting," he said. Netta Sauer jumped in her ambulance. She knew that the address Otis gave was not in an area covered by her crew, but she raced there anyway, terrified that he had been shot.

Moments later, someone on the radio said that Otis had not been wounded.

She drove back to the fire station.

• • •

Otis tried to unload the remaining bullets in his pistol, but his hands shook so badly that he could not do it. Another officer bent over Hathaway and counted the bullet holes. The five wounds turned out to be from two shots. There were three entry wounds and two exit wounds, one bullet having passed through Hathaway's torso and arm. Otis had fired twice just as he'd been taught on the practice range: Shoot a target twice, then aim to fire again if necessary. It's called "the double tap." Otis felt grateful for his training; when you are scared, training takes over.

Hathaway survived. Otis went back to work a few weeks later. Not long after that, Otis and other officers nearly emptied their gun magazines while shooting at a drug dealer who opened fire on them. Otis got the shakes over that one too.

At a South High School class reunion five years later, Netta Sauer Otis ran into Cindy Hughes, a former classmate. Cindy was with Kenny Landwehr, who looked bored. Landwehr brightened when he realized that Netta's husband was a cop. He stuck out a hand to Kelly Otis.

"Good," Landwehr said, teasing Cindy. "Somebody I can talk to, instead of all these South High losers."

25

January 18, 1991

Dolores Davis

Dolores "Dee" Davis liked to carry wet wipes to scrub the faces of grand-children and other surfaces that harbored germs. She hid matches on top of her refrigerator so that wayward children visiting her home would not find them and be tempted to burn down the house. On hot days, with kids in the car, she rolled the windows down only a fraction of an inch. An open window might cause children to be sucked out by the passing wind.

"Grandma!" the kids would yell. "Can you roll it down some more?"

"No," she'd say. Then she'd hum a tune.

She lived alone at the edge of Park City. Her vistas included open countryside. She was raised a farm girl, near Stella, Nebraska, so she did not dread the night or solitude.

Dee worked more than twenty-five years as a secretary for Lario Oil

Dolores Davis lived by herself in an isolated rural area, not far from Rader.

& Gas Company. She also sold Mary Kay cosmetics; she liked that the company didn't test its products on animals. At home she had dozens of magazines and newsletters from animal rights groups such as the Doris Day Animal League and People for the Ethical Treatment of Animals.

Her family last got together with her at Christmas in 1990. Dee hosted, and she wanted everything perfect. The day everyone arrived—her son Jeff and his family from Florida, daughter Laurel and her family from Colorado—Dee made four trips to Leeker's grocery before she got everything she needed.

She fussed so much about getting dinner right that they did not eat until 9:00 PM. Afterward they watched *All Dogs Go to Heaven*. Some of the family cried. It was a good time.

Jeff and his mother had a tenuous relationship early on. His parents divorced in 1961 after twelve years of marriage. Jeff lived with his father. His sister lived with Dee. Jeff spent most weekends with Dee, but things were strained. Later, they grew closer, phoned every weekend, and talked for hours.

Dee had been retired from the gas company for just a few months on the winter night she heard a rustling outside her window and saw one of her cats batting at the glass. Her other cats appeared to be spooked too.

Dee called Jeff. Someone might have been out there, she said.

Rader had looked through her window blinds for several nights. Her house at 6226 North Hillside lay about a mile from his house, so close that he scouted her by riding his bike from home. He was getting lazier. Killing another neighbor was a risk—but why not? Nine dead so far, and the cops still clueless.

He had used a Scout outing as cover for the murder of Marine Hedge. He would do it this time too. He had lifelong friends in the Scouts. George Martin, a Scout leader, thought the world of him. George could work up tears talking about what Scouting did for boys. It was good cover to have such a friend, and Rader enjoyed helping him.

He knew that Martin and other Scout leaders would have thought less of him if they had seen him masturbating—naked and handcuffed—in the truck on that one Cubby outing, though. When he could not get the cuffs off he became frightened. Having to call for help would have been embarrassing. Much to his relief, he became so sweaty from fear that he was able to slip out of the cuffs.

What would Martin have thought about that?

By the time Dee's cat got spooked by that prowler in early January, Kelly Otis had become one of Wichita's most decorated patrol officers. He had survived two shoot-outs and taken part in drug busts and car chases. One night on patrol, Otis saw a man moving around strangely in a parked car. Otis pulled over—and stopped a rape. The department later named him Officer of the Year for 1991.

Only ten years earlier, Otis's chief interests were beer and billiards. He had dropped out of college. Now friends suggested he take the tests that would qualify him to be a detective.

Otis just snorted. He loved street patrol.

Rader had seen Dee while he drove around. He locked in, as he called it. He liked to use cop jargon. *Lock in* meant to concentrate on something. *Shut down* meant stop. *Put her down* meant kill. He had noticed the dog kennel north of Dee's house on Hillside, so he called her "Project Dogside."

He would kill her during the Boy Scout Trappers' Rendezvous. Every year dads and boys camped out by a lake north of Wichita in January, sometimes freezing half to death as they threw tomahawks and cooked over fires. They camped at Harvey County West Park. This put them in the middle of nowhere, with access only by country roads—but Rader had noticed that the roads east led to the small city of Newton, and Newton was on Interstate 135, which led south to Park City, where both he and Dee lived. The drive would only take half an hour.

That Friday, Rader made sure he was the first dad at the lake and got to work setting up the camp. He left before the other dads showed up with their boys. The camp was halfway ready; his cover story would be that he left to get supplies. He headed south—to his parents' home. It was empty—they had gone south for the winter. He slipped in, dressed in dark clothing, and packed his hit kit.

He drove a few blocks to the Baptist church in Park City. When he killed Marine Hedge he had done the taxicab ruse thing, but that had taken too long, so he was simplifying tonight. He had a key to the church because it was where the Scout troop met. He went in, checked his gear, then went back out—and walked to Dee's home, through wheat fields, through a cemetery. It was close to freezing. His feet hurt by the time he reached her house.

He saw through the blinds that she was alone, reading in bed. He waited, shivering; the low that night would reach thirty-two degrees. Dee turned out the lights.

He tried to figure out how to get in—and simplified some more. A little after 10:30 PM, he picked up a cinder block from outside Dee's shed and threw it through her sliding glass door.

As he remembered it, the glass shattered and Dee came running, wearing nightclothes and a robe.

What happened to my house? she asked. Did your car hit my house? Then she saw him and backed away. He had pulled panty hose over his face.

I'm wanted by the police, he said. I need your car and money.

She argued, like all the others, so he tried to disarm her with the usual lies: I'm going to tie you up and leave you, he told her. I need to get in

**Rader broke Dolores Davis's glass patio door with a cinder block.
She woke up, thinking a car had hit her house.**

and warm up (that was not a lie), then I'm going to take your car and some food.

You can't be in my house! she told him.

Ma'am, he said, you're going to cooperate. I've got a club, I've got a gun, I've got a knife.

She said someone was coming to see her later—a man.

God, he thought. *There's always somebody coming.*

Now he had to hurry, which irritated him. He took her to her bedroom, handcuffed her, tied her feet with her own panty hose—the usual routine. Then he found her car keys, rattled around in the kitchen, opened cereal boxes, made noise to pretend he intended only to rob.

He came back, took the handcuffs off, and began to tie her hands with panty hose.

You say you've got somebody coming? he asked.

Yeah, she said. Somebody is coming.

They'll find you, he said reassuringly. They'll find you and then you call the police. I'm—I'm out of here.

It was another lie to calm her. But then she saw his face and recoiled in fear. He had pulled off the panty hose mask, exposing his face.

Don't kill me, she said.

He picked up another pair of panty hose.

I've got kids, Dee said. Don't hurt me. Don't hurt me.

26

January 19, 1991

Out in the Country

Just after noon on Saturday, a friend of Dee Davis's named Thomas Ray came to work on her car, as he'd promised when he had taken her to dinner the night before. He noticed the porch light on and the curtains drawn. Her 1985 Chevy Cavalier was outside; she always put it in the garage.

Ray got no answer when he knocked. He pulled up the garage door and saw that the door into the house was open. In the house, the phone line to the wall jack had been cut, and a cinder block lay on the living room floor surrounded by glass. Her bedding was missing.

Ray drove off, found a working phone, and called 911.

By that evening, Detective Sam Houston and other Sedgwick County sheriff's officers had mustered search parties to walk along roads all over northern Sedgwick County. Deputies knocked on doors, asking if anyone had seen Dee. In her home, Houston noted that someone had gone through her lingerie drawer. A neighbor had seen Dee's keys on the roof of her garage. Deputy Matt Schroeder found some of Dee's bedding stuffed into a culvert miles from her home. No one found Dee, though.

Her family prayed and braced for bad news. Sheriff's investigators determined that someone had wiped down the doors and trunk of her car.

On February 1, thirteen days after Dee disappeared, a teenager named Nelson Schock took a morning walk. Accompanied by a stray dog, he headed west along 117th Street North, several miles north of Dee's home. The dog trotted under a bridge and would not come out when called. Nelson climbed down and saw a bedspread and a body. Beside the body lay a painted plastic mask.

Nelson was so upset that when he ran for home, he headed the wrong way for a few steps.

Sheriff's investigators photographed Dee's frozen body, diagrammed her location, and studied what they saw: panty hose tied to Dee's throat, wrists, and ankles. Animals had gnawed her.

Houston noticed similarities between this and the Hedge killing, which had occurred six years earlier: both women had been tied up and strangled, their phone lines cut. These facts were similar to those in the BTK cases, the oldest of which had occurred seventeen years earlier.

There were also significant differences: the Park City victims were older women, and they had been taken from their homes. BTK had not done that in Wichita.

Most of the detectives concluded that the Hedge and Davis cases might be related, but they doubted they were related to BTK. Houston wasn't sure he agreed.

Rader had dragged Dee's five-foot-five, 130-pound body out of the house in her own bedding and dumped her in the trunk of her car.

He took her first to a Kansas Department of Transportation lake at Forty-fifth and Hillside, near I-135, the highway that divides the eastern part of Wichita from the west. He hid her in some bushes.

He wanted to tie up Dee in all sorts of poses and shoot pictures in the privacy of an abandoned barn. But it was snowing, and the night was wearing on. He would need to sneak back into the campout soon. He

**Rader used this mask on Dolores Davis
when he took his souvenir photos after he'd killed her.**

decided to take Dee's car back to her home. But first he drove through Park City, to Christ Lutheran, his own church, and stuffed her jewelry box and other belongings underneath a shed out back. Then he drove to her house, wiped her car clean, threw the keys on her roof, and walked the several hundred yards back to the Baptist church where he had left his own car. He drove back out to the lake, picked up Dee's body, and started driving north, toward an abandoned barn that he had a mind to use. He felt the press of time; the Scouts would miss him.

He found a bridge along 117th Street North and dumped her body under it. Then he took the long drive back to the Scout Rendezvous.

**Rader placed Dolores Davis's body under this bridge
before returning to his Boy Scout campout.**

27

1991

Bones

Rader was like a dog with a bone: He would not leave Dee alone. By the evening of January 19, the day after he broke into Dee's house, officers all over Sedgwick and Harvey counties were searching for Dee. Rader had spent the day with the Scouts, but he was curious about the search and wanted to see Dee again.

So in the evening, he made up another lie: I have a headache. He drove to the little town of Sedgwick, supposedly to buy aspirin in a convenience store but actually to see if he could learn about the investigation.

He drove on I-135 to a rest stop north of the Sedgwick County line, went into the restroom, and began to change into dark clothes. A Kansas Highway Patrol trooper walked in, glared at him, and asked what he was doing. Troopers got called to the rest stop when people saw men undressing and doing strange things.

BTK, half dressed, told him a version of truth: I'm with the Boy Scouts. I'm changing into my Scout clothes to go to the Trappers' Rendezvous.

If the trooper asked to search his car, he might be in a lot of trouble. Some of Dee's belongings were in there. To his relief, the trooper walked away.

Rader finished dressing, drove out in the fog, found Dee's body, and took photos of her. Her breasts had deflated. *Not very sexy,* he thought. But he took photos anyway. He had brought something to pretty her up: his mask, made of heavy plastic, on which he had painted red lips, black eyelashes, and eyebrows.

He left the mask with her to impress the police.

After he got home from the Rendezvous with his son, he wrote in his

journal how much he enjoyed killing Dee, how she pleaded. He kept trophies: Dee's driver's license and Social Security card, clippings of stories
published by the *Eagle* after the murder. Some of those stories noted similarities between Dee's killing and the deaths of Marine Hedge, the
Oteros, and other BTK victims.

He missed his mask. He had worn it a number of times, when he put
on women's clothing and photographed himself in bondage, in poses of
distress. He went to his parents' house when they were not at home, put
on Dee's clothing, and took pictures of himself in the basement.

On February 18, 1991, only one month after Dee Davis was murdered, a
jogger trotting through woods south of the small town of Belle Plaine,
Kansas, found a skull sticking out from under some leaves. Belle Plaine is
thirty minutes south of Wichita. Wichita police sent their crime lab team,
including Landwehr. The news media were notified.

At the *Eagle*, Bill Hirschman turned to Hurst Laviana, his teammate
covering cops.

"God, I hope this isn't what I think it is," Hirschman said.

"What do you think it is?" Laviana asked.

"Nancy Shoemaker."

Laviana hoped he was wrong too.

Nancy was nine years old.

Detectives soon determined that the skull belonged to Nancy. She had
disappeared the previous July while going to a Wichita gas station to
buy 7UP to settle her little brother's upset stomach. Her disappearance
touched off prayer meetings, searches, and some of the worst commu-
nity-wide fear in years.

Wichita police formed an investigative squad. Among the detectives
they loaned to the city and county Exploited & Missing Child Unit investigation was Clint Snyder, a lean, intense burglary investigator in his late
twenties who had grown up on a cattle farm near Burden, southeast of
Wichita.

Snyder went to the spot where the jogger found the bones. Among
the people he talked to there was the crime lab lieutenant, Landwehr.
Snyder wanted to get to know him better.

• • •

Paul Dotson, now a lieutenant in charge of the police department's homicide section, was still obsessed with BTK. Two months after Davis's murder, in March 1991, he called a meeting with Sam Houston and other Sedgwick County sheriff's investigators, FBI behavioral scientists, and Landwehr. Dotson's goal was to jointly review not only the Davis homicide but all open homicide cases in the city and county.

The investigators compared files and opinions. The FBI specialists noted that in the Park City murders the bodies had been moved around. They said serial killers usually don't do that. And it wasn't BTK's style.

To Dotson's disappointment, the meeting ended inconclusively. Once again the BTK detectives tried to see links in the killings and concluded, "Maybe, and maybe not."

Landwehr and Dotson had investigated BTK for seven years. No matter how confidently Landwehr talked about catching him someday, Dotson felt only disappointment and doubt.

One day Snyder and the crime lab people processed a car belonging to a man police were investigating as a possible Shoemaker suspect. Snyder got to know Landwehr a little better. He learned a lot.

They talked about what could be done to move the case forward. Landwehr chain-smoked, cracked little jokes, and made useful suggestions, supplementing the street wisdom of detectives with forensic science.

For all his skill, Landwehr was unpretentious, even humble. Not all police commanders were. Landwehr seemed warm, sympathetic, and curious about people. He also seemed to love what he did. That got Snyder's attention because Snyder wanted to continue developing as a detective, and the Shoemaker case had shaken him deeply. He wondered how full-time homicide investigators managed their emotions as they pursued their work.

After work, Snyder would go home and spend time with his daughter, Heidi, only eighteen months old. As they played, he wondered how the Shoemakers learned to cope with the way Nancy had died. Snyder also wondered how cops could learn to cope especially considering the limitations of their own department. Nancy's murder had horrified him;

he could not imagine any job more valuable than finding her killers. But his bosses in burglary pressed him to return to working property crime cases, though Nancy's case was unsolved.

He wondered what kind of beast could torture and kill a child. Like a lot of other detectives, Snyder had to teach himself anger management. Snyder spent a lot of time talking it through with his wife, Tammy, with friends, and with God.

A few months after Nancy's body was found, detectives got a tip from a Wichita man who, by coincidence, had once been landlord to BTK victim Kathryn Bright. The tip led investigators to a man named Doil Lane, who was already under investigation for another murder in Texas. Further investigation led to an acquaintance of Lane's, a mentally challenged man named Donald Wacker. Snyder and another detective got him to confess. Wacker said he watched Lane rape, beat, whip, and strangle Nancy. Wacker told them that she kicked her attackers, demanded to be let go, and fought until the last.

One of the saddest murders in Wichita history was solved. Snyder went back to working burglaries, grateful for what he had learned. Snyder didn't know it yet, but Landwehr had been impressed with him. Landwehr thought Snyder would be a good guy to work with someday.

May 1991

Little Hitler

Four months after Dee Davis was killed, Park City hired a new compliance officer to catch stray dogs and enforce zoning rules. Dennis Rader's résumé appealed to city officials for several reasons. He was a former ADT employee with a good work record. In his four years in the air force, he had been a wire and antenna installer, serving primarily in Mobile, Alabama, and Tokyo, Japan, with temporary duty in Okinawa, Turkey, and Greece. He had been discharged in 1970 as a sergeant. He was a lifelong Park City resident who attended a nearby church and volunteered with his son's Scout troop. He had many friends in town.

People who encountered him after he was hired noticed that he kept his uniform immaculate, that his boots were always polished, that he seemed to relish the power to tell people what to do.

Jack Whitson, who supervised Rader for years, said he tended to tell rather than ask. He'd say "You need to fill this out" rather than "Would you please fill this out?"

Rader wasn't a loner; he would talk if someone engaged him. But he did not kid around—work was work. On breaks he never went a minute over the allotted fifteen. Rather than socialize on downtime, he would sit at his desk and read the *Eagle*. When he chatted about something other than work, it was about either Kansas State University football or his children. Mostly he talked about his kids. When his daughter became a K-State student, Rader attended the school's football games religiously.

He eventually got his own office. When he was there, he always kept the door open, but he locked it when he left for the day. His office had a second door, one that led to the outside and allowed him to come and go without being noticed.

One day, while looking for a piece of paper in Rader's office, Whitson opened a two-drawer filing cabinet. Inside were neatly filed black binders, some with labels. He didn't stop to read them.

Rader had abbreviations and acronyms for everything. Once, Whitson told him, "Dennis, you got to talk English to me. I don't understand your acronyms." Rader had hundreds of them. "IR," for example, stood for "Investigator's Report."

Whitson knew Rader took great care in preparing cases against Park City residents, but he'd also seen Rader help people get back their pets when they had to be taken in. When animals were hurt, Rader insisted they be taken to a vet.

One day a woman brought in a duck with an injured wing. Whitson told Rader that the duck couldn't survive and should be euthanized. Rader said he couldn't bring himself to kill the bird. He took it to a park with a creek to let nature take its course.

Still, his job guaranteed criticism. Dog lovers seldom love dogcatchers, and no one likes to hear a man in uniform threaten to issue a citation.

Many of the Park City residents whom the compliance officer would check up on in his daily rounds were lower-income men who worked two jobs and who took their time about fixing cars in their yards. They would leave oil pans and junk parts and cars with only three wheels lying around. Or they were single moms, juggling kids and school, who had little time for mowing grass.

Not long after Rader got the job, people began to complain.

They said he seemed like some sort of authority nut. He'd step onto their lawns, stick a ruler into their grass, and tell them that it stood a fraction of an inch too tall. When pets got loose, he would take them away and sometimes have them put down.

On occasion he walked unannounced into the homes of single women and asked detailed questions about their workday schedules, their children, their boyfriends. There seemed to be something creepy about this guy.

On Sundays, he took his wife and kids to church.

29

Heading Homicide

On March 12, 1992, Dennis Rader helped Wichita detectives investigate a homicide.

Six days earlier, an avionics worker named Larry A. Bryan, age thirty-six, shot and killed Ronald G. Eldridge, age forty-two. Eldridge was Bryan's supervisor at Collins Avionics near Wichita Mid-Continent Airport, and he had apparently planned to fire Bryan.

Detectives investigating homicides like to "do a neighborhood." They ask questions in the area where a suspect lives, as well as around the site of the homicide. So on March 12, Detectives S. L. Wiswell and Charles Koral drove to Park City to talk to Bryan's neighbors. As a courtesy they visited the town's police chief, Ace Van Wey.

He suggested that Wiswell and Koral interview the city's compliance officer, Dennis Rader, who lived at 6220 Independence, just a couple of doors from Bryan. Wiswell wrote in his report what happened next.

Myself and Det. Koral informed Dennis Rader that we were investigating a homicide in which Larry A. Bryan was the suspect and we were trying to find out any background information on Larry. Dennis Rader states that Larry moved in approx 10 to 12 years ago at the address of 6232 Independence and he described Larry as a quiet person. Dennis states that one thing he remembers about Larry is that Larry never came out during the day time and he kind of got the nickname of vampire around the neighborhood. Dennis also states that he remembers Larry Bryan driving what he described as a hot Chevelle. We asked Dennis Rader to describe Larry Bryan and he stated that he was polite and quiet. We asked him if anyone lived with him and he stated that he did not believe so however he thought that a girl hung around his residence when he first moved in but he had not seen anyone else around the residence. Dennis Rader also states that Bryan has a fascination with young kids in the neighborhood. He recalls an incident approx a month ago where he saw Larry Bryan chasing the kids in the neighborhood around with what he described as a Jason mask. I asked Dennis Rader about the residence of Larry Bryan and he stated that Larry always keeps his shades down and again stating that he has never seen any females over at Larry's house.

By May of that year Paul Dotson had run the homicide section for three years and was "complete toast," as he put it—exhausted. When he was reassigned, his commanders told him he could name his successor.

Dotson wanted Landwehr to replace him but worried about what the job stress—and being on call day and night—might do to his friend.

"I know you want this job more than anything," he told Landwehr. "But you have to promise me that you won't let the pressures break you."

Landwehr gave him a long look. "You know what I'm really about," he replied.

Commanders gave the position to Landwehr. He had spent fourteen years working toward this job, and was hoping, against considerable odds, to stay in it for the rest of his career. He was thirty-seven years old. There would be steady work, he knew: Wichita had twenty-eight homicides in 1991, eighteen the year before that, thirty-three the year before that.

The new job wasn't his only success. He was engaged to Cindy Hughes, the special-education paraprofessional with a wit as sassy as his. When people asked him how Cindy could fall in love with a homicide investigator, Landwehr would shrug. "She spent several years dealing with special-ed kids, so she felt qualified to deal with me."

Cindy was happy too, but Landwehr's promotion prompted her to make an unusual request:

"I want you to run my entire family through your criminal computer."

"Why do you want me to do that?" he asked.

"So that you're not surprised. My brother was on the county's Most Wanted list, and I don't ever want you surprised at work by anything my family has done, or will do later."

"I won't do it."

"What?"

"I won't do it."

"I *want* you to do it."

"No."

"I want you to run them so that you can know what you might be getting into."

He smiled.

"Come on," he said. "I would *never* do that to your family."

"Bullshit, Kenny. I know that you've already done it—you're not stupid. So I'm just telling you to do it so that you know it's all right with me."

"But I haven't done it."

"You're lying."

"No," he said. "And I'm telling you, I would never do that to your family."

"You goddamned *liar*."

He smiled.

Five months after Landwehr took over homicide, officers in a parking lot near Twenty-first and Amidon confronted a man who had tried to kill his wife. When the man jumped toward the open door of his car to get a gun, the officers fired. The medical examiner later determined that he had shot himself just as the officers shot him, so it was part suicide and part officer-involved shooting.

Homicide detectives arrived, along with their new boss.

Landwehr had decided that he should be mostly a hands-off boss—that he should assign detectives to a case, then support them with advice and resources. Unless they fell down on the job, he would stay out of their way. But he had also decided he would walk every scene himself, not only because he might prove helpful, but because he was aware of his own shortcomings. There were supervisors who could look at photographs of a homicide scene and see the whole thing in their minds, but he couldn't do that. "I'm more of a 3-D person," he told people. "I have to see it in the full dimensions myself."

The detectives liked him. He let them do their jobs. He did not have a big head: he didn't say "I'm head of homicide" or even refer to himself as a lieutenant. When he called people, he told them only that he was a police officer.

Landwehr arrived at Twenty-first and Amidon and began to pace inside the yellow police tape that blocked news reporters from getting near the evidence.

Hurst Laviana from the *Eagle* decided this was an opportunity. He had spent eight years covering crime and wanted to develop the new head of homicide as a source, and earn his trust.

Landwehr was dressed, as usual, in a suit with a crisp white shirt. There are habits that the Police Department teaches detectives about clothes and grooming. The male homicide detective must shave close, wear a suit, and must not smile or crack a joke at a homicide scene. If the news cameras catch a detective smiling, TV stations might play the tape repeatedly and make him or her look uncaring.

On this day, after an on-site briefing, the television people packed their gear and left. Landwehr still paced the parking lot. He looked at the brick wall of a nearby building. There had been several bullets fired. Perhaps some bullets had hit the wall.

Landwehr stepped outside the tape barrier and walked to the building. Laviana stepped forward. He stopped a few feet from where Landwehr peered at the wall. Laviana, usually a taciturn man, decided to crack a joke. He pretended to peer around the corner of the building.

"Hey," he said to Landwehr. "Have you checked this dead guy over here?"

Landwehr laughed. An important friendship had begun.

A Year of Changes

Lee Landwehr, a retired Beechcraft tool and die maker, died at age seventy-three on January 24, 1993. Paul Dotson had never seen Kenny Landwehr so undone. Lee had gotten his son interested in reading, had handed him stories about the detective Sherlock Holmes. Together they'd worked on cars in the driveway. Kenny wasn't good at repairs, but he had held wrenches for his father so that he could learn from him and trade stories about news of the day.

After Lee died, Landwehr went over to his mother's house and worked in the garden. Landwehr hated gardening, but it was his mother's garden, and it got weeded regularly.

A few weeks after his father's death, the police department sent Landwehr to a full week of FBI training at Quantico, Virginia. The subject was "vicarious victimology"—how law enforcement officers, including homicide detectives, often hurt themselves by empathizing in an unhealthy way with crime victims. What Landwehr learned gave him much to think about, and it was a lucky break that the training occurred just after his father's death; Landwehr had been drowning his sorrows. What he heard at Quantico stopped him.

Cops often feel so shaken by the suffering of victims and their families that they begin to pursue investigations as though the victim were a member of their own family. That was how Landwehr had felt ever since he joined the police department. He learned that if investigators are already prone to self-destructive behavior—avoidance, drinking, melancholy, depression—working cases gives them every excuse to hurt themselves. The suicide rate among cops is high.

At Quantico, instructors described the dangerous relationship between stress and drinking. Do not assume responsibility for actions you are not responsible for, they said. Not all cases can be solved; not all the guilty get convicted; not all victims receive justice.

In addition to working with a therapist, find people you trust and care about, the instructors said. Talk things through.

After Landwehr got home, he applied what he'd learned. He asked Cindy if he could talk honestly about his work, and she agreed.

He began to talk to her regularly to vent frustrations. She listened, empathized, teased, and consoled him. Marrying her, Landwehr often said later, was the best thing that ever happened to him. "You think you can cope with this stuff alone, but you can't."

Landwehr had spent much of his life partying. That began to taper off now. He wanted to head the homicide section for years to come, and he could see that his drinking was leading to no good. "I just decided to grow up."

Shortly after he moved to Park City in 1993, Jan Elliott bought a young bird dog and trained her to fetch. Jessie was friendly and wouldn't bother anybody. But during storms, Jessie would climb Elliott's ten-foot chain-link fence or slip her leash. Rader, the Park City compliance officer, caught her three times and told Elliott to resolve the problem—or else.

Rader seemed arrogant as he told Elliott he owed the city two hundred fifty dollars.

I don't have that kind of money, Elliott said.

Then I'll have your dog put down, Rader said. And he did.

Elliott got so mad that he moved out of Park City.

But something puzzled him.

He had heard similar stories about Rader from other people, but he'd also heard good things.

Years before, his mother, Thelma Elliott, had lived across the street from someone she described as "a wonderful girl"—Paula Dietz—who had married Rader. Elliott's mother liked Rader. She said he was "the nicest person."

On April 7 that year, Rader's parents, William and Dorothea, marked their fiftieth wedding anniversary. The family planned a dinner and put a notice in the *Eagle*.

William Rader had served in the U.S. Marine Corps during World War II. He had worked for thirty-seven years for the local utility, Kansas Gas & Electric, before he retired in August 1985.

Dorothea Rader had worked for twenty-six years as a bookkeeper at a grocery, Leeker's Family Foods. She had retired in January 1986. She was a gentle person, appreciated by her neighbors and others who knew her.

The elder Raders took their four boys to church and Scout meetings and encouraged them to explore the great outdoors. They tried to do right by Dennis, Paul, Bill, and Jeff, although Jeff, as he admitted later, was a hell-raiser.

Now that they were retired, Bill and Dorothea were pleased that Dennis, their eldest, was so attentive. He worked close to home, and he and Paula lived only a couple of miles away. They stopped by frequently and went to the same church. Dennis and Paula's daughter, Kerri, had shown up on school honor roll lists for years. Their son, Brian, was becoming an Eagle Scout.

Landwehr married Cindy Hughes on April 24, 1993. Paul Dotson served as best man. The Landwehrs honeymooned in Cancun, Mexico.

In the third-floor apartment where Landwehr lived for the thirteen years before his marriage, he had knocked so many golf balls outside his door that his sand wedge had worn a wide hole in the carpet. But Cindy was settling him down now. She used to worry that he felt attracted to her because he thought she needed rescuing.

But she had rescued him.

Late that year, Park City got its first phone directory. Brian Rader put it together as his Eagle Scout project to provide a service for his community. Scout leader George Martin, a longtime friend of Dennis Rader, liked to point out that there was no way to complete such a demanding project unless the boy got a lot of help from his father.

Brian's phone book was so well received that *The Wichita Eagle* did a cheery story about it on October 28:

Park City residents will soon be flipping through their own directory to find local phone numbers, thanks to the PRIDE Committee and an Eagle Scout.

"It will be handy," said Cecile Cox, PRIDE president. "I think it's nice for a small town to have a directory because the Wichita book is so large and you have to hunt up things."

Brian had organized ten other volunteers and compiled the book by hand, picking names and numbers out of public information sources and cross-directories. The new directory spelled out the names, numbers, and addresses of every business and person in town.

"We had to use maps to tell who lives where and stuff like that because two other cities have the 744 exchange," Brian told the newspaper. The books were sold door-to-door, for a dollar apiece, to offset the cost of printing two thousand copies.

Brian's father already knew the names and addresses of many people in town. Some women thought Dennis Rader seemed incredibly nosy—he was unusually interested in their comings and goings.

Landwehr's first year as head of the homicide section was busy. Fifty-seven people were killed, a record.

Because the first hours after a homicide are crucial, Landwehr and the detectives often worked without sleep for forty-eight hours straight.

During 1993 and in years to follow, people in Wichita would become familiar with Landwehr's face and flat television-interview delivery. As the supervisor, it was part of his job to give news briefings. On camera, Landwehr looked a little stiff and talked in a monotone.

Laviana, interviewing him alone, saw a much different personality; Landwehr would brighten with humor and warmth. His laugh betrayed the rasp of a frequent smoker.

One day Laviana misspelled the name of murder victim Kristi Hatfield. In his story, it was "Hartfield." Landwehr showed up at the police department's daily news media briefing and gleefully announced to reporters that Laviana had apparently found a new homicide victim.

"Where's the body?" Landwehr demanded. It was a careless error that would be corrected in the next morning's paper.

The lieutenant felt so comfortable with Laviana that in one important interview, Landwehr began to talk in the relaxed, no-bullshit tone he used with friends. The subject was the record-breaking number of homicides in 1993. Landwehr showed Laviana a chart, paying particular attention to the fourteen cases still unsolved.

"Magallanes, we have a suspect," Landwehr said as he started down the list. "Anderson, we're clueless. Marvin Brown, clueless. Menser, we have an idea.

"Kocachan, clueless," Landwehr continued. "Gonzalez, clueless. Adams, that's another one of those where everybody was shooting at a party. Hatfield, clueless."

His use of "clueless" showed Landwehr's self-confidence: He did not mince words. He said "clueless" because that's how he saw it.

But after Laviana's story appeared, Landwehr took some heat from his detectives and others in city hall. Unlike many public officials in similar situations, however, he didn't get pissy and blame the reporter. He merely told Laviana, with a sheepish grin, "I wish I hadn't said it, but I did."

In 1993 some of the Wichita cops had a strange encounter with the Park City compliance officer. It was a story that Tim Relph and his friends would retell many times.

Relph became interested in joining the police force in part because he got arrested in 1979 as a teenager. He'd been shooting a BB gun he had modified to make a loud bang. Two officers, Darrell Haynes and the future Ghostbuster Paul Holmes, threw him facedown and handcuffed him, in part to frighten him away from a life of crime.

That arrest, and his own reevaluation of his life, led Relph one day to enter the police academy. Like Landwehr and Dana Gouge, Relph was first in his academy class.

Relph, a devout Roman Catholic with a gregarious and meticulous nature, joined the homicide unit in December 1991, a few months before Landwehr took command. By 1991, Relph had many cop friends, including the officers who had once arrested him, and John Speer, a long-haired undercover cop Relph had met when both worked street patrol.

In October 1993, Speer needed to reroof his house in Park City. He asked Relph and twenty other cops to help. It was a hot, nasty job. Toward the end of the day, some cops noticed a man in uniform standing outside Speer's house, taking Polaroid photographs.

"Everybody stop," Speer said. He climbed off the roof.

Relph watched Speer confront the man, who was standing beside a Park City truck. The man spoke to Speer in a cold, official manner about needing a work permit.

Speer argued. Relph watched this with some amusement. "This guy must be pretty brazen," Relph thought. None of the men were in uniform, but with their haircuts and the cop jargon that Speer talked and from the way that they all stared, Relph thought it should be obvious to the compliance officer that this was a flock of cops perched on the rooftop.

But the Park City compliance officer insisted Speer needed a permit; he didn't leave until the the cop agreed to get the proper paperwork.

Speer's friends thought the guy was arrogant. But they teased Speer about getting lectured by a guy wearing a uniform and quoting regulations, chapter and verse. Something about that guy's cold manner stuck out enough that the cops remembered it for a long time.

31

1994 to 1997

BTK as Antiquity

The *Eagle* published Bill Hirschman's twentieth anniversary story about the Otero family murders on January 15, 1994. Hirschman knew that he needed to write it as though many of the newspaper's readers had never heard of BTK.

The trail had grown cold; many readers didn't know about the killings, and others had lost interest as their fear faded. BTK had not killed, as far as anyone knew for certain, since strangling Nancy Fox in December 1977. Some cops thought BTK might be dead or in prison on unrelated crimes. So when Hirschman wrote his anniversary story, most of it was background information.

Like a lot of crime reporters, he did what he did because cruelty upset him. To stop it, you write about it to make people care. The idea that BTK had become old news bothered Hirschman. He wanted the monster caught.

Before Ken Stephens left the *Eagle* in 1985, Hirschman had listened to him talk about BTK at a newsroom party. Stephens had related it as a ghost story, and Hirschman had watched chattering friends grow silent, listening in the dark. He remembered that as he wrote his story:

Failure to convict BTK is always mentioned as the one lasting regret of every retiring police officer who worked the case, ranging from LaMunyon to Sheriff Mike Hill, once head of the police homicide squad.

"*No, it's something you don't ever get rid of,*" LaMunyon said.

Shortly after the story ran, Hirschman left the *Eagle* and joined the newsroom of the *South Florida Sun-Sentinel,* in Fort Lauderdale.

Perhaps Hurst will get to write the big BTK story someday, he thought.

At Hirschman's going-away party, newsroom staffers gave him a mock front page with a banner headline:

HIRSCHMAN LEAVES; BTK CASE SOLVED

Laviana thought that was really funny. Like Stephens before him, Hirschman had been identified in town gossip as a BTK suspect.

BTK was not an old story to Detective Tim Relph.

One night, while working a two-month night-shift rotation, Relph got bored. He looked at the gray four-drawer cabinet sitting in a corner. People seldom opened it. Relph fetched a key, opened a drawer, and began to read the Otero files.

It took Relph back to when he had felt terrified as a child after the murders. He had been in seventh grade then, and he had worried that something like that might happen to his family.

Now, in the investigations room, he read old files for a long time.

The next day, Relph went to lunch with Landwehr and surprised him by saying he wanted to study the BTK files.

Landwehr needled him.

"What are you doin', Relph?"

"What?"

"Are you tryin' to fuckin' take my job?"

"No!"

"No no no, you fucker—you're tryin' to take my job, I know it!"

"No, I'm not. I just want to understand it."

Landwehr stopped teasing and grew thoughtful.

"I've been thinking I need to have someone else study BTK, in case I ever leave," he said. "Are you serious about wanting to learn?"

"Yes."

Landwehr began to coach him, at lunch and in the days that followed. Landwehr talked so fast, and with such enthusiasm, that he sometimes lost his train of thought. Relph listened, enthralled. As Relph described it later, Landwehr gave a master clinic on how to hunt BTK—and how to become a great detective.

• • •

Not all of Landwehr's detectives praised him at first. Some of them thought that the details of management bored Landwehr and that he was a better investigator than administrator. Clint Snyder, who joined the homicide section in 1995 and admired him a lot, joked that Landwehr's brain sometimes worked on a different frequency than his mouth. Detectives had to know the context to understand what Landwehr was talking about, Snyder said. "He'll say something about 'needing to get the deal' or 'do the deal' or something like that. But you know what he means."

When Dana Gouge first joined the unit, he had a little trouble with Landwehr's attitude about supervision. In other units, bosses had told Gouge what to do. It puzzled Gouge at first how little Landwehr talked to him. The work worried Gouge—it was hard, and he wanted to make sure he never accused the wrong person of murder, or accused the right person but saw the killer walk free because of a mistake in the investigation. But Landwehr barely talked to him unless Gouge asked him something. Gouge's initial impression was that Landwehr wasn't much of a teacher.

That impression slowly changed. At crime scenes, Gouge began to study what Landwehr looked at, listened to questions Landwehr asked, and tried to think what Landwehr was thinking. Gouge concluded that when he watched Landwehr he learned a lot.

Landwehr's own assessment of his coaching was cold and simple: "The one thing I cannot teach anyone is IQ points. You either have the brains to work in this unit or you don't."

The detectives all noticed Landwehr's memory. Other people had to study a case; Landwehr could glance at reports and recall the details with precision years later.

One day Relph got into a lively argument with Landwehr over a point of Roman Catholic teaching: is Ash Wednesday a holy day of obligation? Relph, a student of Catholicism, said yes; Landwehr, a backsliding Catholic, said, "No, it ain't."

They investigated; Landwehr was right.

"It doesn't bother me that you know more about forensics than I do," Relph said. "But it pisses me off that you know more about church teachings."

To some extent the detectives' attitudes, even their humor, became a reflection of their boss. They needled each other, and Landwehr, sometimes cruelly. They dropped the f-word in casual conversation—even Relph, who could talk eloquently about his religious beliefs. They had a plastic rat that they put on the desk of the detective due to take the lead on the next homicide. They carried on a Dotson-era practical joke tradition of sometimes calling a sleeping detective to say "We've had a triple homicide" just to jolt him awake. They bonded. The stress of this work would have been unbearable to most people, but whenever a detective would get upset, someone would weigh in with a smart-ass comment and lighten the mood. Over time they realized that Landwehr used humor with calculation. It dawned on Relph that after reading his reports, Landwehr would say funny things that sometimes stung. Landwehr embedded criticism in humor. After that, Relph began to listen closely when Landwehr made him laugh.

Not every funny thing Landwehr said was intentionally funny. One day Gouge, Snyder, and Landwehr worked the murder of a Wichita prostitute. The killer had dumped the body in Harvey County, near Newton. Gouge and Snyder went into the Newton police interview room to talk to the suspect. They could not take their handguns in, so they handed them to Landwehr, who paced outside. Landwehr, who had his own gun in a holster, stuck theirs in his waistband.

Gouge and Snyder interviewed the suspect, then separately interviewed his wife. Their stories did not match. Gouge and Snyder went to Landwehr and excitedly told him this. Landwehr was delighted; they were solving the case.

A Newton detective rounded a corner and saw Landwehr with three guns jutting from his clothing, rubbing his cheeks vigorously, yelling: "God, I *love* this job!" The detective thought Landwehr was a nutcase.

The work wasn't for everyone. Snyder left in 1997, trading the horrors of homicide investigation for the grim task of outwitting narcotics dealers.

Kelly Otis joined the homicide section in 1997, after taking the test to qualify for detective on a whim. One day the strain of building a particularly tough case got to the new investigator, and he walked into Landwehr's office to vent. He worried that it might be picked apart in court. In frustration, he kicked a sofa.

"No no no," Landwehr said coolly. "Just follow your chain of evidence and let your case speak for itself. Don't ever worry about anything else."

Otis's case held up.

"Landwehr, ever since I've known him, has had this steely eyed confidence that we're going to win our cases," Relph said later. "He gets us that way because he knows how to build a case."

They usually won, but not every time. Relph once saw a man he had investigated walk away with an acquittal. It horrified him.

To his relief, Landwehr stood by him all the way.

"Here's where detectives get themselves lost," Landwehr told Relph the day they first talked about BTK. "They get lost in some guy's story. A guy looks good as a suspect; if you have maybe twelve criteria for being the right guy for the crime, and this guy meets ten of the twelve, then he's looking good. And so the detective gets enthralled, chases his story—and goes off on a tangent, a wild-goose chase. Because if the guy's DNA doesn't match the DNA from the crime, it's not him. And then you have to drop him like a rock."

Relph began to apply this advice while reading about BTK and working on other cases.

"How do you not get lost in all these thousands of pages of evidence?" Relph asked.

"Don't try to get into all that peripheral evidence," Landwehr said. "Just read the actual case files. Focus on the essentials."

That advice worked with BTK and with every new homicide Relph handled.

He realized, with some pride, that Landwehr had helped him become a better detective. And if BTK ever resurfaced, Relph would be ready to help Landwehr put him in a cage.

32

1996 to 1999

Covering Crime

In the Landwehr house in Wichita there is a photograph that Cindy sometimes shows to family and friends. It shows the back of a man's head and a baby reaching a tiny hand to the man's face. The face is turned away from the camera, but anyone familiar with the family would recognize the narrow head and thick, dark hair of the chief homicide investigator for the Wichita police.

The boy was born in 1996.

Ken Landwehr had thrown himself into fatherhood with enthusiasm even before he became a father. Cindy had worked with special-needs kids for years and had talked Landwehr into becoming a foster parent with her. In the first three years of their marriage they served as temporary foster parents to ten children. That's how they found the baby they wanted to adopt. They named him James.

Cindy had worried—most men want their own children, but she could not give Landwehr any. He waved off her concern. "That doesn't bother me at all," he said.

He was now responsible for shaping a child's life. He soon saw that the boy was changing his life too. The Party Guy from Hell now stayed home changing diapers.

In that same year Bill Hirschman, working at the *Sun-Sentinel* in Florida, heard that a fellow reporter was leaving for *The Wichita Eagle*. Hirschman met him for coffee. Roy Wenzl, a Kansas native, was anxious to move home. At the *Eagle*, Wenzl would join the newspaper's crime team, Hirschman's old group. Hirschman was delighted. He had spent fifteen years at the *Eagle* and became almost weepy talking about Wichita and Kansas and people he missed.

You will work with Hurst Laviana, he said. He's a resourceful investigative reporter. Wichita is a much safer place to raise children, more neighborly and relaxed, much friendlier than South Florida, Hirschman told Wenzl. There's some crime, he said, and of course there is BTK, the big one that never got solved. Some people think he's dead, Hirschman said. Or in prison. But he and Laviana thought BTK may have just quit killing.

Maybe BTK will never be solved, he said.

Wenzl looked puzzled.

"Bill," he said. "What's a BTK?"

A year later, at the *Eagle*, Laviana told Wenzl the whole story. The newsroom was empty, it was dark outside, and Laviana told it as a ghost tale, how the killer took his time strangling people, performing perversions. There is an old file in a drawer here, Laviana said. It has a copy of the first BTK message.

He waved a hand at the newsroom, which contained more than a hundred desks.

"If he ever docs surface again, you're going to see this entire room full of people head out the door with notebooks in their hands. Because that is what we'll do to cover the story. It will be that big. Like the beginning of World War II."

Paul Dotson, now a captain, took command of the Crimes Against Persons Bureau in 1996, which meant he became Landwehr's supervisor. One of the first things he did was to issue a directive that other lieutenants in the bureau had to serve on a rotation, at staged intervals, to supervise homicide investigations. Landwehr would no longer be on call for all homicides twenty-four hours a day, seven days a week.

Landwehr hated it, but Dotson ignored his opposition. Every detective in the homicide unit had a habit of self-delusion, Dotson thought. They told themselves they could keep going on a case after forty-eight hours without sleep. They all had to have that kind of work ethic to do their jobs, but Dotson remembered how the unrelieved stress of investigating every homicide had nearly ruined his health when he did it. When Landwehr continued to gripe about it, Dotson brushed him off. "Come on, Kenny," he said. "Look at how tired you look." From now on, unless there was a huge case, Landwehr would get to take a break once in a while.

On the night of June 17, 1996, a one-story wooden home in the 1700 block of South Washington burned. Firefighters found a woman dead and her toddler daughter in critical condition.

The *Eagle* sent Laviana to the house the next day. He was surprised to see Landwehr and his detectives there. Was this a homicide?

Not long after the television reporters had finished their noon live shots, a big man in his twenties approached Laviana and said he was looking for the injured girl's father. Laviana told him he was probably at the hospital with his daughter, then offered to drop the man there on his way back to the newsroom.

During the ride, Laviana tried to ask the man about the family. The man's answers seemed odd and evasive. When they got to the hospital, Laviana handed him a business card and asked him to call. "What's your name?" Laviana asked.

"Mike Marsh," the man replied.

The little girl died six days after the fire. Meanwhile, Landwehr's detectives had arrested Marsh. It became Wichita's first death penalty case in decades.

Not long after Marsh's arrest, Landwehr gave reporters a briefing about another homicide. Someone asked what detectives were doing to catch the killer.

"We're going to see who Hurst drives to the hospital and arrest him," Landwehr said.

One day Laviana heard a truck back up into the driveway of his home.

Laviana found Landwehr outside. Laviana was bewildered; the two men never socialized. Now the homicide chief had come to his home with a peculiar look on his face.

"Where do you want it?" Landwehr asked bluntly.

"Where do I want what?"

Landwehr waved a hand at what lay in the bed of the truck—a moldering, eight-foot-tall playhouse. It looked like a big piece of junk.

And now, with the help of Laviana's wife, Landwehr unloaded the playhouse, heaved it over the chain-link fence, and dragged it to the middle of Laviana's backyard. Landwehr avoided looking at him, but he was smiling. Laviana's wife said Cindy Landwehr had told her that she had a playhouse she wanted to give away; Laviana's wife thought that their three daughters would like it. Laviana just rolled his eyes. His daughters never entered the playhouse; they said it had cobwebs.

Capt. Al Stewart had never forgiven himself for failing to catch BTK. When he retired in 1985, he took copies of some of the old files with him to study. He had been through a lot on the job. When he was a young officer, a sniper's bullet had knocked his police cap off his head. When he was a Ghostbuster, he had driven himself to tears and drink with frustration.

He spent his last years dying of emphysema. He warned his son Roger one day that he did not intend to suffer much longer. He was down to ten percent lung capacity; it took him half an hour to walk across the hall from his bedroom to the bathroom.

On March 31, 1998, Stewart, lying in bed, put a .25 caliber pistol to his head. He was only sixty-one.

On the nightstand beside his body, his family found one of his BTK files lying open. He had studied it until the end of his life.

The phone call came to Patrick Walters's law office around 11:00 AM on August 3, 1998. Someone who lived near the lawyer's mother in Park City was on the phone. There was a guy in Barbara Walters's backyard, the neighbor said, shooting at a dog with what looked like a tranquilizer rifle.

When Walters got to his mother's house, he found Park City compliance officer Dennis Rader inside her fenced yard.

Patrick Walters asked him to get off the property. Rader would not leave. The Park City police chief happened to drive up then; he tried to calm both men. Then Walters noticed the dog was gone. A neighbor told him that Rader had opened the gate.

Three days later, Rader delivered a citation to Barbara Walters, saying she had allowed the dog, Shadow, to run loose.

She had received several tickets from Rader. He seemed obsessed, driving by slowly several times a day. She decided to fight the latest ticket. She was sure Rader intended to catch her dog and kill it.

One of Patrick Walters's fellow attorneys, Danny Saville, agreed to represent Barbara Walters in Park City Municipal Court.

By the time of the hearing, Rader had supplied the judge with a half-inch-thick stack of papers supporting his case. He had audiotapes and videotapes of the dog. He had annotated, cross-referenced notes. The judge continued the case twice because Rader kept saying he needed time to prepare. All this over what would be a twenty-five-dollar ticket.

The judge found Barbara Walters guilty. She appealed, then settled before the case reached Sedgwick County District Court.

She got to keep Shadow but paid a fine.

She was glad to save the dog. Shadow had one characteristic Barbara Walters now cherished: he despised Rader.

On February 26, 1999, a man named Patrick Schoenhofer went out to buy Tylenol and was shot to death by a robber lurking near his apartment. Schoenhofer was only twenty-three.

Roy Wenzl from the *Eagle* knocked on his widow's door two days later. Erika Schoenhofer let him in and talked calmly about Patrick for a few minutes. But then a little boy came out of a nearby room. His name

Park City compliance officer Dennis Rader took Polaroid photos of Shadow, a dog he claimed was a nuisance to the neighborhood and should be put down.

was Evan Alexander Schoenhofer, and he was two years old. He crawled up into his mother's lap with a questioning look.

"Daddy?" he said.

Erika Schoenhofer hugged him.

"Daddy's not here," she said. She had turned her face away from her child as she hugged him, hiding tears.

Earlier that day Wenzl had talked to the cop assigned to the case, a detective with a crew cut named Kelly Otis. Otis was helpful and fun to talk with. He was also wary.

"Do not quote me," he said. "I'll talk enough to help you figure it out yourself, but keep me out of your story."

Wenzl agreed. As he left to see the Schoenhofers, Otis looked hard at him.

"Treat those people right when you talk to them," he said. He did not phrase it as a request.

That same week, Wenzl learned that a Wichita lawyer named Robert Beattie had recently spent forty-five minutes interviewing Charles Manson.

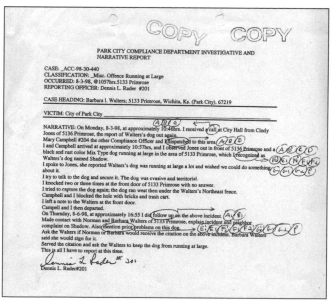

**Rader's annotated report for the Shadow court case,
one of a half-inch-thick pile of documents he'd prepared.**

Manson's hippie clan had murdered a movie star and several other people in California in 1969; for decades afterward, Manson was the most notorious murderer in national history. Beattie gave Wenzl a transcript of the Manson interview. In spite of the killer's fame, Beattie said, any reader of the transcript would see what a dull person Manson was. The media had made Manson the personification of evil, but in conversation he was boring.

Beattie had interviewed Manson to put together a mock trial for his college students. At Newman University in Wichita, Beattie taught sophomores about juries; citizens should know about jury duty before they perform it, he said.

He wanted to do similar interviews involving other cases. The Oklahoma City bombing. Maybe BTK. When he had mentioned BTK to his sophomores, Beattie said, most of them gave him a blank look.

It was ancient history, though they'd grown up in Wichita.

33

2000

The Joy of Work, Part 1

By February 2000, Wichita's murder rate had dropped. Community policing, a crackdown on local gangs, and the booming economy all played a role. Landwehr told his detectives: "Let's see if we can go back and pop some bad boys in the cold cases."

Otis and Gouge, who had been partners for two years, picked a file at random, a thick document in a three-ring binder labeled "Vicki Wegerle." Landwehr didn't tell them much about the case. He didn't want them working with preconceived notions. They knew that detectives at the time had thought Vicki's husband killed her.

Otis and Gouge read the file at work and at home. One night Otis told his wife what he was studying. Netta, surprised, told him that as a paramedic she had tried to save Vicki's life. She told him how sad it was to see Bill Wegerle holding his little boy.

Otis noticed right away that the killer had stolen Vicki's driver's license. From that he reached the same conclusion Landwehr had years before: This was a serial killer taking a trophy.

"What do you think?" Otis asked Gouge.

"I don't think Bill Wegerle killed his wife," Gouge said.

"I don't think he killed her, either," Otis said.

In years to come, Paul Dotson would say that Landwehr made a crucial decision about BTK in the late 1980s. He refused year after year to test the DNA preserved from the semen found at the Otero and Fox crime scenes.

DNA testing was helping solve high-profile cases around the nation. The temptation to test the BTK samples was strong. But a test, Landwehr told Dotson, would use up the samples they had, and would show only what BTK's DNA signature looked like. It would not tell who BTK was.

"I want to be patient," Landwehr told Dotson. "DNA technology is like computer technology. It gets a lot better every year. The longer we hold off, the more we're gonna learn when we test it."

Examining the evidence in the Vicki Wegerle case, Otis and Gouge found the autopsy inventory included bits of skin found under one of her fingernails. Perhaps DNA analysis of it would lead to a suspect. And if the killer wore no gloves, pulling on the leather laces and nylons as he tied and strangled Vicki would have scraped skin cells off his hands. They might find the killer's DNA there as well. They decided to also test the covers from Bill and Vicki's bed. The killer had fought with her and might have sexually abused her there, leaving DNA.

They also sent the lab a blood sample taken from Vicki's body during the autopsy and a bag of trace material vacuumed from the floor of Vicki's bedroom the day she was killed.

They needed to talk to Bill Wegerle to learn everything he knew about Vicki, especially the names of men she knew. They could swab those men for DNA and see if it matched the fingernail sample.

They also needed a sample of Bill's DNA, for comparison.

But Otis realized that Bill might not talk. The transcript of Bill's interrogation showed Otis that the cops had given Bill a hard time. Otis concluded that if it had been him, he would have walked out on the cops too.

Otis approached Bill indirectly, through one of Bill's relatives who had a job at the Sedgwick County Courthouse.

"We're taking another look at Vicki's death," Otis told her. "I can't promise anything, but I've looked at the evidence, and I'm leaning toward the idea that Bill didn't do it. We might be able to prove it." He explained that he was requesting Bill's cooperation and a DNA swab.

Otis waited a month.

Through the relative, Bill said no.

On February 14, only one week after Otis and Gouge had submitted Wegerle evidence for DNA analysis, they got some lab results in writing.

There was no result yet on the full DNA profile. That would take time—with DNA analysis, cold cases took a backseat to new cases.

But the lab had determined, nearly fourteen years after her death, that the skin found under Vicki's fingernail contained human male DNA.

By early December 2000 the homicide team had worked only twenty-three new homicides for the year, less than half the number they worked in the record year of 1993. Landwehr had kept his team working on cold cases, including Wegerle.

But on December 7, all spare time came to an end.

Four bodies were found in a house at 1144 North Erie. The dead were Raeshawnda Wheaton, eighteen; Quincy Williams, seventeen; Odessa Laquita Ford, eighteen; and Jermaine Levy, nineteen. Williams and Ford were cousins. Ford was renting the house. Detectives began to compile the names of people who knew these teenagers.

Within hours, detectives had suspects and began to plan arrests.

For a few days, as they worked without sleep, Landwehr and his detectives thought this would be the biggest case they handled all year, one of the biggest since BTK.

One week following the quadruple homicide, Landwehr and his detectives felt numb from fatigue. One of the people they had quickly arrested was Cornelius Oliver, age eighteen. He told the cops that he had gone to the house because he was mad at Wheaton, his girlfriend. But he gave no clear reason why he killed: "I just did it."

On December 14, Otis and Landwehr worked into the night, Landwehr doing paperwork, Otis investigating what looked like a suspicious death. Landwehr headed home after midnight. Otis determined his case was an overdose, stayed to do paperwork, and drove home about 2:30 AM. It was twenty-five degrees outside, wind-chill fourteen, snow everywhere.

Otis had worked a seventeen-hour day; Landwehr had worked nearly as long and would be in bed by now. Otis pulled into his driveway just as a voice spoke from the police radio he carried.

"Potential homicide," the dispatcher said. "Multiple victims . . . Thirty-seventh and Greenwich Road."

"Jesus," Otis thought.

He pulled into his garage.

This can't be, he thought. *Multiple victims again?* He sat still, his car's engine still running.

"Caller says four of her friends have been shot in a field," the dispatcher said.

Otis didn't believe it. *This has to be some drunk,* he thought. *Somebody's drunk and calling 911 and messing with us.*

Two minutes went by.

The dispatcher came back on with the correct address, the voice urgent:

"Sheriff's deputy at the scene at Twenty-ninth and Greenwich Road reports four bodies in a field. . . ."

Otis backed out and drove east at high speed. *Holy shit,* he thought. *Unbelievable. A second quadruple homicide in eight days.* He called his boss on his cell phone.

"Landwehr," Otis said, "we've got a quadruple."

Silence.

"Oh, *fuck you,* Otis," Landwehr said and hung up. He thought Otis was pulling one of the old jokes.

Otis dialed again.

"What?"

"Landwehr," Otis said, "we've got a quadruple homicide at Twenty-ninth and Greenwich Road."

"That was *last week,* dumbass!"

"No, no, Landwehr, listen to me," Otis said. "We've got a quadruple homicide, *another* one. At Twenty-ninth and Greenwich."

Landwehr hung up again.

But this time he got out of bed.

Five people had been shot execution-style in that snowy field at Twenty-ninth and Greenwich. The two men who did it then drove their stolen truck over the bodies. Incredibly, one of the victims got up, bleeding from the wound in her head, and ran naked through the snow to summon help. When Otis met her at Wesley Medical Center, she gave him information that within nine hours led to the capture of two brothers, Reginald and Jonathan Carr.

34

The Joy of Work, Part 2

Landwehr looked at the naked bodies in the bloody snow.

Jesus Christ, he thought. *What's the world coming to?*

After the arrests, Dana Gouge and Rick Craig interviewed the Carr brothers. One of the first things they did was have a nurse take samples of hair, blood, and saliva to learn whether the suspects' DNA matched DNA found on the victims' bodies.

At the hospital, Jonathan Carr asked Kelly Otis: "What happened to those boys who shot those kids?" He was asking about the other quadruple homicide case the week before.

"They've been charged with capital murder," Otis replied.

"What's capital murder?"

"Anyone convicted of capital murder can get the death penalty," Otis replied.

"How's that done?"

"Lethal injection."

Carr sat silent for a long time before he spoke. "Do you feel anything?"

"We've never been able to ask anyone," Otis said.

Tim Relph went to the hospital to ask the surviving victim more questions. Relph regarded her as a hero. In the next few months, as he helped "H.G." prepare to testify, he came to regard her as a friend.

Relph had seen horrible things as a homicide detective, but what she told him was worse than most things he'd heard about cruelty. The dead were her fiancé, Jason Befort, twenty-six; Brad Heyka, twenty-seven; Aaron Sander, twenty-nine; and his friend Heather Muller, twenty-five. Over the course of three hours, the two intruders had beaten the men, repeatedly raped and sodomized the women, forced them to take money from their ATM accounts, made all five kneel naked in the snow, then shot them.

Relph pondered how cops internalized cruelty in different ways. Gouge appeared to rise above anger as he followed chains of evidence. Otis, in contrast, allowed himself to feel rage, then channeled it. Snyder, helping to solve the murder of a little girl, had sunk into despair, pulling out of it with the help of prayer and talks with his wife. Landwehr's remedy for a day's work in homicide had been widely known, though he didn't often take that remedy anymore.

Relph had felt the anguish too, as he stood at the edge of the bloody soccer field. He thought about his family. Relph had four children, and his wife was pregnant with their fifth. *These killers wiped out four people,* he thought. *Four lives and loves like mine.*

Still, he thought he fared better than most of the other homicide investigators, and told them so. His faith had been a blessing for his work. The first time he saw the photographs of Josie Otero in her basement, he studied them with calm detachment. His faith ensured that he could quickly recover his composure, even standing in that field. Like most people, he had questioned God at times. Some cases brought him to tears. But they all served only to confirm his faith, as he saw it: God did not make these five people kneel in the snow. God did not hang Josie Otero or strangle Nancy Fox. God is never one-sided or cruel or blameworthy. There is a devil in the world; evil people do evil things by their choice.

And when they do, it becomes necessary to hunt them down.

Robert Beattie, the Wichita lawyer who had put the Charles Manson case through a mock trial at Newman University, got back in touch with the *Eagle* in the summer of 2001. Beattie was corresponding with the Oklahoma City bomber, Timothy McVeigh, who was soon to be executed for killing 168 people. Beattie told Roy Wenzl that he was planning mock trials beyond McVeigh. He had corresponded with the science fiction writer Arthur C. Clarke and planned to put him on trial for creating the evil computer HAL, which killed astronauts in *2001: A Space Odyssey.*

Beattie said again that he might do something similar with the old BTK cases.

• • •

In Park City that October, Mayor Emil Bergquist presented city compliance officer Dennis Rader with an award for ten years of service.

Rader was restless. He and Paula were empty nesters now; their son and daughter were grown and gone.

When Rader patrolled streets, he took solace in an unusual collection. He cut advertisements out of the *Eagle*, the slick ads that pictured women and girls modeling outfits and underwear. He had collected hundreds of these pictures. He pasted many of them on index cards and wrote notations on the back about fantasies he entertained.

Earlier that year a woman named Misty King moved out of Park City because the compliance officer had harassed her for nearly three years.

He would park outside her house and sit, watching. He did this at least twenty times in one six-month stretch. Sometimes she would glance up and see him peeking through her kitchen or living room windows. He handed her one citation after another for code violations.

It hadn't always been like that.

She first met Rader in 1998, the night she came home from the hospital after her husband was critically injured in a Toughman amateur boxing match.

Rader asked if he could do anything to help. He checked on their well-being even after her husband returned home.

When her marriage ended, Rader continued to offer to keep an eye on things.

Then a boyfriend moved in.

She began getting citations. Rader claimed the grass next to her fence was higher than the grass in her lawn. He issued a citation because her boyfriend was working on a car in the driveway, even though her former father-in-law had done the same thing in the same spot for years without a citation.

There were at least six citations between 1999 and 2001. She called the police several times to complain about Rader.

They said he was just doing his job.

More than once, Rader told her all her problems would go away if she got rid of her boyfriend.

In the fall of 2001, she came home to find a note from Rader: Her dog, a big Saint Bernard–chow mix, had gotten out of her yard. Rader had taken it to the pound.

When she went to get the dog, she was told she had to meet with Rader first. She went to see him but was told he wasn't available. By the time they met the following Monday, the dog had been put down.

There were streaks of gray in Landwehr's hair by the time the Carr brothers went to trial in the fall of 2002. Maybe it was his age (forty-seven); maybe it was stress. The burdens on his unit had been immense from the day of the soccer field murders, and the workload did not slacken in the year and a half it took to bring the defendants to trial on ninety-three criminal counts in a death penalty case. Landwehr's cell phone rang day and night.

All the evidence held up. The trial was covered live on television, and the work done by the cops prompted praise.

To his friends, Landwehr seemed happier now: calm, resolved, and content.

Cindy Landwehr had done much to steady him, but his bond with his son seemed to deepen his maturity. After work, he would help James build forts out of sofa cushions and bedspreads in their basement. Within fifteen minutes, Landwehr would feel the weight of the world slide off, and he would read storybooks to his son and tuck him into bed and no longer dwell on work. His detectives were so experienced now that he did not have to deal hands-on with homicides. The detectives did most of the work, while Landwehr coordinated, gave advice, and ran administration.

He and Cindy were talking about building a new house; he was thinking about finishing that history degree he'd started working on twenty-nine years before.

Laviana had a little quirk that Wenzl liked to tease him about in the newsroom. Laviana would hear about a big event and say that it wasn't really big enough to be a story. In 1998, for example, after the biggest grain elevator in the world blew up just south of Wichita, Wenzl had assigned Laviana as the lead reporter and teased him. "What do you think, Hurst? Is this a story or just a two-inch brief?"

But Laviana was a reporter of great skill. On May 4, 2003, the *Eagle* published a story by Laviana showing that more than two dozen people had been killed in the previous four years by prison parolees who should have been more closely supervised. Murder charges also were pending against parolees in eight other cases.

Reporting the story had taken years and a legal battle with the state that reached the Kansas Supreme Court. The story later won one of the biggest national awards the *Eagle* had earned in its 131-year history.

Laviana cared little for awards. He went back to writing cop stories.

A few weeks later, lawyer Robert Beattie started sending e-mails to Wenzl, telling him that he was teaching BTK as a class—and working on a BTK book. He suggested Wenzl write a story about this.

Wenzl turned to Laviana. "You're the house expert on BTK," he said. "Do you want this?"

Laviana made a face. "It's a pretty old case," he said.

Otis and Gouge had submitted Vicki Wegerle's fingernail scraping and vaginal swab to the Sedgwick County Regional Forensic Science Center three years earlier, but the lab people had to give priority to new homicides. In August 2003, Otis and Gouge finally got the DNA results they'd been waiting for.

The DNA found under Vicki's fingernail was different from the DNA found in the semen on the vaginal swab. To Otis, this was one more reminder that Bill Wegerle had told the truth in 1986. Otis had read in the interrogation transcript that Bill told detectives that they had no marital problems and that he had made love with Vicki the night before she died. Bill also told the cops he'd had a vasectomy shortly after his son was born.

Men who have a successful vasectomy ejaculate semen but no sperm. Gouge and Otis did not have Bill's DNA to prove beyond doubt that the semen was Bill's, but the lab tests showed it was semen with no sperm.

The finding prompted Otis and Gouge, with Landwehr's blessing, to immediately request that the lab test samples of semen that BTK left at the Otero and Fox crime scenes. Those DNA profiles could then be compared with the DNA found under Vicki's fingernail.

They still needed to get a mouth swab from Bill.

He had refused to cooperate three years earlier.

Now, Otis talked through options with Deputy District Attorney Kevin O'Connor. They decided that they could use a subpoena to compel Bill to give a DNA swab.

Otis wrote out a request for a subpoena. Once it was signed by a judge, it would be good for only seventy-two hours before it became void. Otis showed the subpoena request to O'Connor, who said it was written properly. But then Otis stuck the request in a desk drawer, unsigned by a judge. He would keep it, like a card to play down the road. For now, he could not bring himself to compel Bill Wegerle to do anything. Otis had read the interrogation transcripts from 1986 and knew how rough the cops had been on Bill. He thought the guy had suffered enough at the hands of the cops.

He would use the subpoena if he had to, but he wanted to talk Bill into giving a swab voluntarily.

Beattie sent more messages to Wenzl about his BTK book, and Wenzl kept putting Beattie off. But one day Wenzl went to Laviana: "Are you sure you don't want this?"

Laviana said he wasn't interested.

But Bill Hirschman in Florida was still obsessing about BTK, almost ten years after his departure from the *Eagle*. A few weeks later, Hirschman wrote Laviana a short e-mail.

Just six words.

35

January 12–March 19, 2004

An Anniversary Story

"Do you know what Thursday is?" Hirschman wrote.

Laviana had to think for a moment: *Today was Monday, so . . . Thursday would be January 15.*

Why does Hirschman care about January 15?

He typed an e-mail reply:

"It has to be Otero."

Hirschman replied two days later. "So are you doing a thirtieth anniversary BTK piece?"

"I will now," Laviana wrote.

He didn't want to do it, though.

Hirschman liked anniversary stories. Laviana disliked them—they didn't involve news.

Laviana took the idea to Tim Rogers, the *Eagle*'s assistant managing editor for local news. Laviana had to explain who BTK was; Rogers had worked at the paper less than three years.

"I'm not a big fan of anniversary stories," Rogers said.

"I'm not either," Laviana said.

"Let's see if there's anything new," Rogers said. "If there is, we can do something."

Laviana walked away, past Wenzl's desk. No story, he thought.

Then he stopped.

"Roy," he said. "Who was that guy who's doing something with BTK?"

"Beattie," Wenzl said. "A lawyer."

"Do you have his number?"

• • •

Laviana's story ran on Saturday, January 17:

It was a routine followed by thousands of Wichita women in the late 1970s:

- *Upon arriving home, check the phone immediately.*

- *If the line is dead, get out.*

"I don't think people today realize the kind of tension there was in Wichita at that time," said lawyer Robert Beattie. . . .

Beattie said he wanted his book to document a chapter in Wichita history and prompt someone to come forward with information that would solve the case.

"I'm sure we will be contacted by both crackpots and well-meaning people who have little to contribute," he said. "But I do not think we'll be contacted by BTK."

BTK case unsolved, 30 years later

BY HURST LAVIANA
The Wichita Eagle

It was a routine followed by thousands of Wichita women in the late 1970s:
■ Upon arriving home, check the phone immediately.
■ If the line is dead, get out.
"I don't think people today realize the kind of tension there was in Wichita at that time," said lawyer Robert Beattie, who was a West High School student at the time.
"There was a lot of anxiety and fear," recalled Al Thimmesch, a

retired Wichita police official. "Of course, a serial killer will do that."
It was 30 years ago this month that a killer calling himself the BTK strangler murdered the first four of his seven victims. The four — all members of the Joseph Otero family — were strangled in a small, one-story house at 803 N. Edgemoor.
After three decades, the case remains active and unsolved. And Beattie, who teaches a criminal justice course at Friends University, has cut back his law practice and is researching a book about the man considered by

many police officers as the city's most notorious killer.
What made the case frighteningly different for city residents was the fact that the killer sent several taunting letters about the crimes to local media. He cut the phone lines of his victims before killing them, and he took souvenirs from the crime scenes — a pocket watch from one, a driver's license from another.
Beattie has interviewed dozens of retired police officers and witnesses, and he hopes to have a

Please see **BTK,** Page 4A

Fernando Salazar/The Wichita Eagle
Wichita lawyer Robert Beattie sits at his desk with a scrapbook containing newspaper clippings on some of the BTK murders. Beattie has conducted 60 interviews and is writing a book about the case.

Hurst Laviana's story in the *Eagle* about the thirtieth anniversary of the Otero killings. The article caused BTK to resurface.

• • •

In fact, BTK regarded the *Eagle* story and Beattie's comments as a collective personal insult. He could hardly believe what he read:

Although the killings remain firmly implanted in the minds of those who lived through them, Beattie said many Wichitans probably have never heard of BTK.

He said he used the BTK case during a segment of his class last year and was surprised at the reaction.

"I had zero recognition from the students," he said. "Not one of them had heard of it. . . .

"I'm hoping someone will read the book and come forward with some information—a driver's license, a watch, some car keys," he said.

It had been thirteen years since BTK's last murder. In that time Rader had confounded the experts, resisted the temptation to flaunt himself, and remained silent and safe. He had gotten away with murder ten times over.

But he found this story outrageous, and impossible to ignore.

Did they not remember him? Did they no longer feel the fear?

He would show them.

He went to his trophy stashes. He pulled out the three Polaroids he had snapped of Vicki Wegerle seventeen years before. He pulled out Vicki's driver's license.

Did the lawyer want a driver's license?

Then he would have one.

Lt. Ken Landwehr was forty-nine years old and looked healthy again after the stress of the Carr brothers case had abated.

He had been a cop for twenty-five years; he had supervised the homicide detectives for nearly twelve, far longer than the three years that had nearly ruined the health of his predecessor. One night a week, he taught a class on serial killers at Wichita State University.

He had sad brown eyes, but laughed easily, unless he was pacing a homicide scene. He was going gray, but he hadn't let himself go—a lot of women considered his creased face to be handsome. His face and hands were so brown that some people assumed he had Lebanese or Hispanic ancestors, but the tan was from playing golf. The rest of him was a blinding pale white.

He was still a sharp dresser: silver wire-frame glasses, dark brown or charcoal gray suits, white shirts he ironed himself, and dress shoes. A gold watch with a stretch band, a tiny silver cell phone attached to his left hip, his police badge attached to his right hip.

He was a pack-a-day smoker of Vantage cigarettes, but his son was nagging him to give up the habit.

Because of Cindy and James, he was content and happy.

That was about to change.

The letter arrived in the *Eagle* newsroom in an ordinary white envelope on March 19, 2004, a Friday. It was one of about seven hundred pieces of mail delivered to the paper every day.

It's a wonder this one didn't get tossed in the trash. Newsroom people throw obscurities away, and the sender of this message had made its contents obscure.

The first newsroom person to touch it was Glenda Elliott, the assistant to the editor. She sliced open the envelope and shook out a sheet of paper. She saw a grainy photocopy of three photos of a woman lying on a floor. And a driver's license. Some strange stenciling at the top: *GBSOAP7-TNLTRDEITBSFAV14.*

It looked like routine nut-job stuff.

Then, in the lower right corner, she noticed a faint, graffiti-like symbol, the letter B tipped over and made to look like breasts, the T and the K run together to make arms bound back and legs spread wide.

Elliott felt goose bumps. As a police reporter, she had covered the Otero murders. Four years later, when Chief LaMunyon and Deputy Chief Cornwell sought advice about what to do about BTK, Cornwell had pulled her into an office one day and shown her parts of the BTK file.

The cryptic letters stenciled across the top of the letter that BTK sent to the *Eagle*.

She had seen a symbol with a B made to look like breasts. This one wasn't identical, but it was close.

She laid the letter and the envelope on the desk of Tim Rogers, the editor for local news. She didn't say anything to anyone about who it was from; she was sure they would know.

But they did not. After twenty-six years, Elliott was the only remaining person in the newsroom who remembered what BTK's signature looked like.

"Hurst," Rogers called out when Laviana walked into the newsroom. "Come check this out." Rogers handed him the paper and envelope.

Laviana was mystified. He walked over to Wenzl.

"What do you make of this?"

Wenzl looked, and shrugged. "I don't know."

"It's weird," Laviana said. "It looks like crime scene photos."

"Why would anybody send us this?"

"I can't figure it out."

Laviana was working on two stories, and was in a hurry. The paper puzzled him, but he had not studied it closely; he had not noticed the signature, or the name "Vicki L. Wegerle" in the driver's license.

It was nearly time for the 10:00 AM police briefing. Laviana decided to take the letter with him.

It did not occur to him that the message came from BTK. But he re-

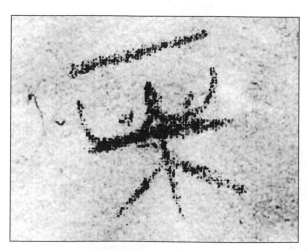

The faint penciled-in symbol at the bottom of the letter was Rader's BTK signature, his attempt to create a "brand" for his killings.

membered Ken Stephens saying nearly twenty years before that the *Eagle* had blown its chances to have its own copies of BTK's first two messages.

So he made a copy.

The daily briefings were run by Janet Johnson, a civilian who served as police spokeswoman. This morning there was much to relate: officers had shot to death a man who waved a knife at them the previous night. His relatives had told the *Eagle*'s Tim Potter that the man was mentally ill and probably didn't understand the officers' commands to drop the knife.

Laviana took notes to pass along to Potter, then waited. After the other reporters left, he went to Johnson and to a police commander who happened to be there, Capt. Darrell Haynes.

Laviana handed them the paper.

Haynes was fond of cop abbreviations. A crackpot, for example, was CCFCCP: "Coo Coo for Cocoa Puffs."

Haynes looked at the paper and thought it was CCFCCP. Johnson agreed. Cops get a lot of tips from kooks.

Probably nothing, they said.

But Haynes took the paper and envelope.

"I'll show them to the homicide section," he said.

Back in the newsroom a short time later, Laviana took a closer look at the copy he had made. What he saw suddenly made him very agitated.

A driver's license.

A blond woman smiling.

"Wegerle, Vicki L."

"Date of Birth 03/25/58"

When he had first seen the sheet of paper, he had almost tossed it away. He realized now that if he had paid more attention, he would have taken it to Landwehr's homicide section himself.

He knew who Vicki Wegerle was: an unsolved homicide. She had lived only a mile from him. Laviana knew one of her relatives, and he had talked with her occasionally about Vicki's murder.

Laviana handed the letter to Potter, who sat next to him.

Potter pointed out something Laviana had not noticed: the envelope's return address.

Bill Thomas Killman

1684 S. Oldmanor

Wichita, KS. 67218

"The initials would be BTK," Potter said.

That hadn't occurred to Laviana. Interesting, he thought. He had written that anniversary BTK story only two months before.

But still . . . he thought it was a hoax. The newspaper got letters from crackpots. BTK had not killed anyone, as far as Laviana knew, since Nancy Fox in 1977. Twenty-six years had passed.

He studied the sheet a few more moments. Potter had noticed the return address. Maybe there was more.

And then Laviana saw it.

He walked to Wenzl.

"Look at the photos," Laviana said curtly.

Wenzl looked.

"What?"

"Those are *not* crime scene photos," Laviana said, jabbing a finger at the photos. "Look at her arms. They've been *moved*. They are *not* in the same position in all the photos. The cops *never* move a body around when they shoot photos at a crime scene."

"This is creepy," Wenzl said.

Eagle reporter Tim Potter spotted the initials BTK in the return address
of the letter from "Bill Thomas Killman."

"Potter just pointed out that Bill Thomas Killman's initials would be BTK," Laviana said.

"What do you think?" Wenzl asked.

"No."

"Why?"

"It's a hoax," Laviana said. "It can't be."

"Did you run the name of the woman?" Wenzl asked.

"I already know the name. Vicki Wegerle was a murder victim, 1986. Unsolved."

"Was Wegerle one of BTK's victims?"

"Not that we know of. But it is an unsolved homicide."

Wenzl looked at Wegerle's face in the driver's license.

"You have to tell the editors about this," Wenzl said.

Laviana did.

Then he went to his computer and searched court records for a Bill Thomas Killman. He found nothing.

Rogers walked over to Wenzl.

"You think there's anything to this?" he asked.

"I don't know," Wenzl said. "But if it is BTK, we'll see whether Hurst thinks it's more than a two-inch brief."

The "Oldmanor" return address turned out to be false. And there was no trace of a Bill Thomas Killman. The name sounded like a tongue-in-cheek clue. So did "Oldmanor." BTK liked to taunt people and talk about himself. He would be an old man now.

That evening, in the newsroom, Wenzl called out to Laviana, "Did the cops ever get back to you?"

"No."

Laviana e-mailed Johnson: "Anything to that letter?"

She e-mailed back that no one in homicide had seen it and that Landwehr had been out of the office all day.

"Have a great weekend," she wrote.

36

March 22–25, 2004

The Monster Returns

On Monday, Laviana covered the daily briefing again, and stepped into Haynes's office afterward. "Whatever happened to that letter?" he asked.

Haynes looked sheepish. "I forgot about it."

He grabbed it and headed upstairs.

Landwehr at that moment was at Riverside Hospital hoping he could avoid work—he was standing beside a gurney on which his wife was resting. Cindy was minutes away from gallbladder surgery. She had timed the surgery for spring break, so that she could recover without missing work at West High School.

Landwehr had left his cell phone turned on.

In the homicide section, Detective Dana Gouge watched with mild amusement as Haynes walked in and looked into Landwehr's empty office. *Supervisors apparently like to talk only to other supervisors,* Gouge thought.

"Can I help you?" Gouge asked.

"I was looking for Landwehr," Haynes said.

"He's not here," Gouge said, stating the obvious.

Haynes shrugged. "I have something I wanted to show him. Hurst brought it to us."

"Can I see it?" Gouge asked.

"Yeah," Haynes said. "Why don't you look at this?"

Gouge looked at the envelope without touching it. Something about it caught his eye. He stepped away, pulled on a pair of latex gloves, then took the envelope and pulled out the paper inside.

One look was all it took.

He turned to Kelly Otis, standing nearby. "Look at *this*!"

Otis looked.

"Shit," he said.

Landwehr's cell phone rang just after a nurse stuck a needle into Cindy's arm and started the saline drip that precedes surgery.

"This is Landwehr," he said.

"You're not going to believe what we just got," Gouge said.

"What?"

"It's a letter from BTK."

Landwehr said nothing for a moment.

"Why?" he asked.

"It's got the BTK signature," Gouge said. "Wegerle's driver's license. Photos of her in her bedroom."

"Where did this come from?"

"Hurst brought it to us."

"Bring it to me."

Landwehr closed his phone and looked down at Cindy.

He waited.

His detectives sometimes teased him. "Kenny's getting excited," Otis would say, mocking him. Landwehr had a cool head. He said nothing now to Cindy. He preferred to see things for himself.

Gouge and Otis drove to Riverside mostly in silence.

They had studied the Wegerle case thoroughly in the past four years. They knew no cop had ever taken a photograph of Vicki lying dead on her bedroom floor. Otis's own paramedic wife, Netta, had told him that. The firefighters had carried Vicki's body out of her bedroom and into the larger dining room the moment they found her; they needed the extra space to start CPR.

So these images had to have come from the killer's stash.

But had the letter come from the killer? Otis was doubtful. Maybe some asshole had found BTK's trophies and was playing with the cops. Maybe it was a son, or a nephew, or somebody who had bought the killer's house.

Whoever he was, he knew secrets that only the cops and Vicki's killer knew. Only the killer could have shot these Polaroids.

The shit is going to hit the fan now, Otis thought. *No cop is going to sleep tonight. We may not sleep again for a long time.*

Cindy did not ask Landwehr about his phone call, and he did not tell her. He was always getting calls. He had worked on more than 400 homicides. Maybe 450—he had lost count.

The doctors were going to start the surgery in minutes. Landwehr looked up when Gouge and Otis walked into the room. Gouge had photocopies in his hand.

Nurses were working around Cindy's bed, asking her how she was, making sure the saline dripped properly. Landwehr led his detectives out of the room and looked at the papers.

"Fuck!" Landwehr said. "It's him. Oh, shit, shit, shit!"

Otis glanced down at Landwehr's feet and began to grin in spite of the moment. Landwehr dressed sharply for work, but in the hospital he was wearing a golf shirt, khaki pants, and the sorriest-looking pair of cheap tennis shoes Otis had ever seen. *Old man shoes,* Otis thought: white with Velcro straps, the sides of the shoes stained green from mowing the lawn.

"Jesus, Landwehr," Otis said. "Why don't you buy decent shoes?"

Landwehr did not laugh. He looked like he was in shock.

"We're in so much fucking trouble," he said. "Fuck!"

Landwehr walked back to check on Cindy. He talked to her for a moment, then came back out.

His first thought, he said later, was *I hope I don't screw this up.* Homicide section leaders are like anybody else: They feel doubts at the beginning of a case. *Will I fuck this up? Have I already fucked this up by missing something important in the last twenty years? What if we don't catch him? What if this asshole decides to kill somebody again?*

He realized he was holding his career in his hands.

Think fast. Laviana and the newspaper would want to publish a story immediately about BTK resurfacing. This time around, the shit storm would hit the police department the moment the story was published.

The national media would show up, 580,000 people in the metro area would feel twitchy about opening their front doors at night, and everything the cops did, everything Landwehr did, would be put under a giant microscope.

He needed to ask Laviana to hold off on the story long enough for his detectives to set up a task force and a tip line with a tap on it. They needed to be ready in case BTK called the tip line himself. Landwehr needed Laviana to be reasonable.

If he could get the newspaper to hold off for two days, he might be able to get the lab people to do a quick turnaround on the DNA found at the Otero, Fox, and Wegerle scenes, then run it through the federal criminal database. Maybe BTK really had been in prison all these years and was now out. CODIS—the FBI's Combined DNA Index System—contained the genetic profiles of more than 1.5 million offenders. If they got a match, it could be over before the newspaper printed a story.

"Call Hurst," Landwehr told Otis. "Tell him we need time."

Otis made a face.

"How much time?"

"Ask him if he can give us a couple of days to get organized."

Landwehr went back into Cindy's room. She studied his face.

"What's up?" she asked.

"Just some work."

She rolled her eyes.

"Come on, Kenny. Two of your guys walk in here, in the surgery room, dressed for work, with papers in their hands."

"Yeah."

"Well, what is it?"

"We just got a letter they needed me to read."

"A letter."

"Yeah."

She studied his face. "It's from BTK, isn't it?" she said.

He sighed. "Yeah. It is."

"Oh, fuck!" she said.

"Yeah."

He opened his cell phone, turned away from Cindy, and called the

Sedgwick County Regional Forensic Science Center. "That cold-case DNA stuff I asked for last year about Otero and Wegerle," he said. "It's not a cold case anymore. I need that stuff *now*."

He paced the room. A nurse spoke to Cindy. "Can I bring you anything?"

"Tequila," Cindy said. The nurse smiled.

Landwehr paced. Cindy felt sorry for him.

"Guys," Cindy said to Otis and Gouge. "Get him out of here. Just get him the hell out of here."

The three men walked out. Landwehr told the detectives to start pulling the BTK files together and to call Laviana. Landwehr would call police commanders and the FBI. He would need manpower. He would stay with Cindy but would start up a task force with his cell phone.

Landwehr turned back to Cindy's room.

Until this ended, there would be little time for his wife and son.

I'll be lucky to see James today, or tomorrow, or for weeks to come. I'm going to have to live in my office until we catch this asshole. And we might never catch him.

The nurses took Cindy to surgery moments later.

Landwehr took out his cell phone again.

While we hunt BTK, will BTK hunt us?

He's seen my picture on television. What if he follows me home? What if he sees James? And Cindy?

What if he kills somebody just to show us he can do it?

Landwehr called his commanders and gave them the news.

When he hung up, he quickly made another call, to his former partner on the Ghostbusters, Paul Dotson, now retired from the WPD and working as police chief at Wichita State University.

"Come over here right now," Landwehr said.

To Dotson, Landwehr looked as unstrung in the hospital corridor as he had on the day his father had died eleven years before. Landwehr hurried Dotson to a stairwell, put a piece of paper in his hands, and watched him. Dotson took one look at the BTK signature and the image of Wegerle's stolen driver's license and felt the hair stand up on his neck.

"So what do we do?" Landwehr asked.

Someone walked into the stairwell. Dotson and Landwehr looked at each other, separated quickly, and by instinct made sure their hands were visible. They suddenly felt embarrassed—they didn't want anyone thinking that two men were doing or smoking strange things in a hospital stairwell. They almost laughed.

Landwehr asked again: "What do we do?"

Dotson felt compassion for Landwehr—and gratitude. At the pivotal moment of Landwehr's career, he had reached out to him.

Dotson began to talk fast. "Your world as you know it is over," he said. He began to tick off a list of what Landwehr would need: Money. Cars for detectives. An off-site headquarters for a new task force, to eliminate leaks to the media. Police departments have office politics, jealousies, and gossip like any other organization. Landwehr needed to get his task force out of city hall.

It was time to implement the strategy the Ghostbusters had devised twenty years before: communicate with BTK through the news media, play to his ego, get him to make mistakes that would reveal his identity. Put one face on television to communicate with BTK.

"But whatever you do, do not become that face," Dotson warned. "You can't run the investigation and also be the face that talks to BTK. The workload will tear you to pieces."

He looked at Landwehr as he said this. What he saw brought him up short. Landwehr no longer looked shocked—he looked resolved. It was clear that Landwehr intended to do both jobs.

"Look," Dotson said coldly. "It's not my job to tell you what you want to hear. It's my job to talk straight. You can't do both jobs."

Landwehr just looked at him.

Dotson prepared to leave.

He was so worried about Landwehr that he felt almost sick. He knew how smart Landwehr was, but also what a self-doubter his friend was, how Landwehr disguised a deep need to be liked, how much Landwehr ached when he felt that he had failed at something. Now the whole world would watch Landwehr as he faced a hidden monster, with his ass on the line and lives and careers at stake.

One thing they had agreed upon, after they got control of their nerves: this letter might be opportunity knocking.

As Dotson left, Landwehr began to punch in phone numbers.

Maybe this asshole had given them the key to catching him.

After prodding Capt. Haynes about the strange letter, Laviana had gone back to the newsroom to work on other stories.

His phone rang. "This is Hurst," he said.

"This is Kelly Otis."

"What's up?"

"I need two days." Otis let the words hang.

It took Laviana half a moment to register what he had heard. "What?"

"We're asking if you can give us two days before you put anything in the paper."

What was this? It had to be about that letter. Maybe it was a big deal. Or maybe the cops were just being careful. Whatever it was, this was weird.

"I can't promise anything," Laviana said.

Otis sounded polite but cryptic. "Give us as much time as you can so we can get ready."

Ready for what? Laviana thought. *Ready to do what?*

"I'll do what I can," Laviana said.

"Good." Otis hung up.

Laviana stood up slowly and looked around the room. He would need to clue in the editors. This could be big.

Maybe whoever had killed Vicki Wegerle was hoaxing the paper and police. Maybe the real killer was posing as BTK.

Maybe it was BTK.

But no.

He didn't believe it.

Landwehr called the FBI's Behavioral Science Unit in Quantico, Virginia; he asked to speak to a profiler. He found himself talking to Bob Morton, a behavioral analyst he had never met. Landwehr did not know it at that moment, but Morton would become a key player in the task force he was hurriedly forming. Morton—thin, muscular and balding, a former state trooper standing more than six feet tall—had studied serial killers for years. His work involved predicting not only their criminal behavior but also how to lure them into making mistakes. Morton suggested the same strategy for trapping BTK that Landwehr and the Ghostbusters had decided to adopt years before. He now helped to fine-tune the tactics:

- **BTK likes publicity.** Call news conferences to say things about him. Make them look like real news conferences, but make communication with BTK the real purpose. Read scripted statements and answer no questions from reporters.

- **Pick one person to conduct all the news conferences.** Give BTK a face to fixate on. That could be dangerous for the person doing it, but the risk was necessary.

- **Imply that you are making progress on the case.** BTK does not want to get caught, Morton said. If he thinks you are breathing down his neck, he might be reluctant to kill.

Over the course of the first frantic day, Landwehr and police spokeswoman Janet Johnson talked frequently with Morton to prepare a presentation for Chief Williams and his staff.

Landwehr wondered whom they would choose to be the face talking

FBI profiler Bob Morton (far left) confers with Landwehr on the BTK case.

to BTK. Probably himself. He knew Cindy would dislike that. How could he tell her that she and James should feel safe or that BTK might not stalk him? But Landwehr thought it was the right move. He had pursued BTK for twenty years; he had run hundreds of news briefings and knew how to do them right.

There was one other reason to do it himself. Landwehr didn't want anyone else to take the risk.

Landwehr called another retired Ghostbuster. Paul Holmes—sharp nosed, sandy haired, and small, at 148 pounds and five feet eight—had spent his four years of retirement laying bricks with his brother Larry. But he still jogged six miles a day, three times a week, a compulsion resulting from a vow never to let other street cops down by showing up for a fight out of shape. He still had that bullet wound from 1980, and still carried a .40 caliber Glock strapped to his hip on most days. And he still worked privately on BTK, reading files, trying to find something they had all missed.

"He's back," Landwehr said.

Holmes drew a breath.

He did not ask who "he" was.

He asked only one question.

"Is there anything I can do to help?"

Like Holmes, Kansas Bureau of Investigation Director Larry Welch was Landwehr's friend. Welch faced many of his own problems: the KBI, which fought crime statewide and assisted sheriff's offices and police departments with specialists and experts, had been fighting an expensive campaign for years against the worst drug scourge since crack cocaine. Hundreds of methamphetamine cooks had appeared throughout rural Kansas, setting up illegal labs in homes, abandoned barns, and sheds. They stole propane, anhydrous ammonia, and other hazardous ingredients and used them to cook common cold medicine into a cheap street drug.

Welch had some of the best detectives in Kansas working for him, and they were stretched to the limit. But he knew how bad BTK was. Welch had been an FBI agent; he had run the KBI for ten years. For years he had lived in Goddard, just west of Wichita. He and Landwehr had been friends since Landwehr was a patrol officer. Landwehr explained the situation. Welch then made a generous offer.

You can have some of my agents, he said, and whatever other help I can provide.

He soon sent Larry Thomas and Ray Lundin to work with Landwehr for however long it took.

"We'll give you those two days," Laviana told Otis later that afternoon. "But after two days, we want the story, and we want it exclusive."

Otis did not like that. But he conceded that when the letter first arrived, Laviana could have burned the investigation with a huge story in the *Eagle*. Laviana had not done so. The *Eagle* was not in the business of panicking people with hoaxes, and at this point, the editors had no proof that this was anything but a letter from a twisted prankster. The paper's best shot at getting a comprehensive and accurate story was to wait and let Landwehr check it out—then have Laviana sit down and talk with him about it.

Otis told him he would get back to him about the exclusive.

The next morning's newspaper contained nothing about BTK.

In the stairwell, Dotson had counseled his friend not to set up a tip line unless his commanders gave him enough investigators to check out every tip, every alibi, every background of every suspect. Dotson thought Landwehr would need a battalion of investigators. But Landwehr limited that problem with one decision: the task force would check out tips, but detectives would not wear themselves out running down each man's story. They would merely swab him for DNA and compare it to BTK's DNA. Either the DNA matched or it didn't.

Of all the clever things Landwehr did, Dotson said later, this was one of the cleverest. The strategy might not catch BTK, but it would eliminate thousands of suspects quickly and save hundreds of thousands of man-hours.

For two days, as they set up the plan, the cops worked around the clock. As Otis had predicted, none of the detectives slept.

On the first day, the homicide team set up a tip line and the means to record calls. The chief provided twenty-four-hour-a-day staffing.

They picked a task force: Gouge, Otis, and Relph from Homicide; Thomas and Lundin from the KBI. Landwehr also wanted Clint Snyder from narcotics. Snyder had volunteered, and the commanders approved. Another detective from narcotics, Cheryl James, joined the task force to compile and shape the task force's computer databases and to work with ViCap, the giant database the FBI had established to collect and sift information on violent criminals. James also went out and swabbed people.

Some homicide detectives—Robert Chisholm, Heather Bachman, Rick Craig, and Tom Fatkin—were kept off the task force to work Wichita's other murders. Still, Bachman and Chisholm did that while also reading every BTK tip turned in, and Craig and Fatkin helped run down leads.

Landwehr's task force also enlisted the help of fifty detectives and other officers in the first month, from the undercover, gang, and sex crimes units and from the KBI, FBI, and the Sedgwick County Sheriff's Office.

The task force quietly set up a command post at the city-county Law Enforcement Training Center on the edge of town, miles from city hall.

Otis told Landwehr what Laviana had said about wanting an exclusive when the police confirmed it was from BTK

That could be tricky, Landwehr thought. *The more we reveal publicly, the less effective we will be, and the more likely that some other dumbass out there might send copycat materials to throw us off.*

He did not want to reveal details of the letter. He did not want Laviana to reveal what BTK's signature looked like or that there were stenciled letters and numbers on the sheet. Keeping that information out of the newspaper was vital, but he couldn't tell Laviana what to do. And he knew Laviana's editors must be on tenterhooks, waiting to hear if they had received a big scoop—or just a sick joke—in the mail. The *Eagle* had not plastered the letter like wallpaper all over the front page. Maybe that meant he could get Laviana to agree to hold back some information—the more the better. Landwehr thought that if he tried to shut out the newspaper, the *Eagle* might reveal everything.

He had to give Laviana something.

• • •

As the police spokeswoman, Johnson often worked with Landwehr on the media briefings whenever there was a homicide. She considered him a friend; he had the habit of sensing when she was having a tough day and saying a kind word. She knew he did the same for others.

Now Landwehr wanted her help; they would need to write a series of news releases designed to get BTK communicating. In addition, she'd handle all media inquiries.

She had three big worries, she told Landwehr.

One was that once word got out about BTK, the national media circus would come to town: all the tabloid newspapers and cheesy cable shows, all the networks.

The second problem was bigger.

If the police department refused to answer questions about the biggest murder mystery in Wichita history, it would upset reporters, and they would make her life hell. And Landwehr and the FBI now wanted her to refuse to answer questions.

The third problem might stop the whole thing: Chief Williams might not like the plan.

Wichita had one major newspaper, three major television stations (not counting PBS and smaller affiliates), and several radio outlets. The cops tolerated local reporters. They did not like some of them, but they kept their opinions to themselves. Sometimes, as with the Carr brothers case, the national media would show up, and the cops liked them even less than they liked the locals. Still, Williams prided himself on being open. If reporters asked a question, Williams said he wanted it answered unless the answer would interfere with an investigation. Landwehr and Morton were proposing that the department stage media events at which Landwehr would say tantalizing things and then refuse to take questions. That ran counter to the chief's ideas about openness.

At first, Johnson was right. The chief was skeptical, and so were members of his staff. The deputy chiefs pointed out that keeping people in the dark might feed the public anxiety that was sure to follow the story the *Eagle* was about to publish.

The discussion went on for a long time; at times it looked as if the deputy chiefs would veto the idea.

Johnson finally begged the commanders to do what Landwehr wanted. "Look, guys. If we don't do this, we're screwed. We called the FBI. If we then ignore their advice, they might get pissed off too. And what are we supposed to do if we *don't* do this? What other idea is there? What am I supposed to say to the media about what we're doing?"

In the end, the chief approved the plan; the benefits outweighed the problems, he decided.

He needed to make one more decision now.

Who would do the news conferences? What face would they show to BTK?

It was a dangerous assignment. Williams knew what it was like to be in danger—as a patrol officer, he'd been shot three times. He had risked his life many times. Now he would ask someone else to take that risk.

Williams said he wanted Landwehr to do it.

The job needed to be done right, he said. Landwehr's twelve years of experience with homicide briefings had schooled him in what to say—and what *not* to say. Moreover, people in Wichita were accustomed to seeing Landwehr talk about homicides. It would reassure them to hear Landwehr deliver these messages.

But was this the wise decision?

Dotson had warned Landwehr not to do this while running the task force. Dotson had helped develop a manual for the National Institute of Justice on how to run high-profile police task forces. He'd spent time consulting with some of the most experienced hunters of serial killers in the nation, including the cops who had pursued the Green River killer in Washington. They had warned Dotson about how they had worn themselves out trying to do too much at once.

But Chief Williams and his command staff now took care to make sure that didn't happen. Landwehr would run the task force and be the face communicating with BTK. But Johnson would write all the scripted news releases, and other police commanders would relieve Landwehr of many administrative duties. Landwehr's friend Lt. John Speer would run the regular homicide investigations.

The plan looked manageable.

But when Landwehr told Cindy he'd be talking to BTK, she became upset, as Landwehr had known she would.

"Why you?" she asked. "Are they just going to make you stand out there alone?"

"No," he said.

Laviana had given the cops their two days and had heard nothing from them. Now he wanted the story. He called Landwehr on Wednesday morning.

"Come on over," Landwehr said.

Laviana reached the fourth floor of city hall minutes later. He found Landwehr and Johnson sitting in the conference room adjoining the chief's office. Landwehr, as usual, was wearing a white shirt and a dark suit. Laviana looked at Landwehr's face, long and tanned, with deep creases running vertically down the cheeks. What Laviana saw now gave him a moment's pause.

They had known each other for twelve years, had encountered each other on the job hundreds of times, and had needled each other good-naturedly every time. Landwehr had always been articulate, helpful, and funny—sometimes hilariously profane. But Landwehr's face showed there would be no joking today.

Was it really BTK?

There was a lot hanging in the balance with what the two men would say to each other now. If it was BTK, Landwehr might demand that Laviana keep a lid on the story.

If so, Laviana would refuse. People had a right to know if a serial killer had resurfaced in their midst.

Maybe Landwehr would ask him to suppress only *part* of the message. If so, Laviana was prepared to deal. The newspaper had a responsibility to readers, but it would not hinder a homicide investigation.

Laviana was glad that he had photocopied that message, just as Ken Stephens had told him to do twenty years before. He could see another copy of the message now, lying on the table between Landwehr's hands.

He started to ask a question, but Landwehr interrupted.

"Before we start, can I ask *you* a question?" Landwehr said.

"Sure."

"Did you make a copy?"

"Yes."

"Can I have it?"

"No."

That settles it, Laviana thought. *Wow. It's BTK!*

Landwehr leaned forward and slid the copy across the table so that Laviana could see the three photographs of Vicki Wegerle, her driver's license, the strange stenciling, and the signature symbol in the corner.

"I want this," Landwehr said, pointing to the symbol.

"I want this," he said, pointing to the stenciling.

"And I want this," he said, pointing to the driver's license.

In cop shorthand, he was asking that Laviana not write anything about those details. Laviana and his editors had anticipated this.

"I can give you this," Laviana said, pointing to the signature.

"I can give you this." He pointed to the stenciling.

"But I can't give you this." He pointed to the license.

Landwehr did not look offended. Laviana had just told him that he would agree to two of his requests and not publish anything about the signature and the stenciling.

But he would reveal that BTK had resurfaced. He would reveal that BTK now claimed to be the killer of Vicki Wegerle. And he would reveal that BTK had sent the newspaper a message with photocopies of Vicki's driver's license and pictures of her bound body.

Landwehr sat back, waiting.

Laviana realized with a thrill that Landwehr had decided to answer questions on the record.

"Is the letter from BTK?" Laviana asked.

"I'm one hundred percent sure it's BTK," Landwehr said.

"Is the woman in the picture Vicki Wegerle?"

"There's no doubt that that's Vicki Wegerle's picture."

"Is there a Bill Thomas Killman?"

"There has never been a Bill Thomas Killman."

"Why would he resurface now?"

Landwehr shrugged. He did not know.

"How do you know it's BTK?"

"No comment."

• • •

The *Eagle* first broke the news March 24 on its website, Kansas.com, just hours after Landwehr talked to Laviana. The editors also shared the story with KWCH-TV, one of the local TV stations, to promote the next morning's paper. Rival KAKE-TV also broadcast a short story that night based on an anonymous police source.

Eagle editors topped the printed story with one of the most unsettling headlines Wichitans had ever· seen. The headline stack ran four inches deep.

Laviana's lead paragraph was straightforward and blunt:

A serial killer who terrorized Wichita during the 1970s by committing a series of seven murders has claimed responsibility for an eighth slaying and is probably now living in Wichita, police said Wednesday.

The story did what Landwehr had expected. It frightened people. The tip line phones rang and rang.

Landwehr tried to calm fears, appearing on live television that morning to talk in the dry tone he always used in public: "We're encouraging citizens to practice normal safety steps—keep their doors locked, keep their lights on."

BTK's return is front-page news.

He began to talk directly to BTK, though he didn't tell any reporter what he was really doing. Landwehr, Johnson, and Morton had worked out how to do it. Morton had e-mailed suggestions ranging from keeping the overall tone positive to telling BTK how to reach Landwehr by e-mail, telephone, and post office box.

Landwehr talked reassuringly in a room packed with reporters and photographers. The 340-word statement confirmed that Vicki Wegerle was a BTK victim and subtly encouraged BTK to keep talking: "This is the most challenging case I have ever worked on, and the individual would be very interesting to talk with."

Then came the next part of the strategy: make BTK too cautious to kill. Landwehr encouraged people to contact the department with tips. He said that the case was the department's top priority, and that the sheriff's office, KBI, and FBI were helping.

"I wouldn't ever want to comment on any other cases around the nation, but it is without a doubt the most unusual case we've ever had in Wichita."

All over Wichita, gun stores did brisk business. People who had feared BTK when they were kids now feared him again, and they walked into their houses as though walking into an ambush.

Reporters from across the country began to pack their bags and look up Wichita, Kansas, on a map.

37

March–April 2004

The Swab-a-thon

In the first twenty-four hours after the *Eagle*'s story appeared, police received more than three hundred tips. In the next twenty-four hours, they collected seven hundred more. Landwehr had fifty cops, most of them detectives, assigned to him in the first days. Besides working tips, police located tens of thousands of pages of documents from the previous thirty years and coordinated investigators with a big chart.

The KBI's cold case unit immediately began to scan tens of thousands of pages of old notes, photographs, and documents from the BTK file cabinet and the thirty-seven boxes of investigative files accumulated since 1974. The KBI and the FBI turned everything into a huge searchable database. The work would take eight months.

"The KBI cold case people were awesome about what they did," Landwehr would say later. "And they didn't ask us for a damned thing in return."

Nola Foulston, the Sedgwick County district attorney, sent help. The cops would need to coordinate many of their moves with her prosecutors, in case there was an arrest. She assigned Kevin O'Connor to shadow Landwehr's task force, day and night if necessary, and to advise them both as needed. "From now on, you're Kenny's bitch," she told O'Connor.

O'Connor researched whether BTK could be sentenced to death if the cops caught him. To his disappointment, he learned Kansas did not have a death penalty law during the years BTK had murdered people.

Three days after Landwehr got BTK's letter, he drove to the home of the retired Ghostbuster Paul Holmes.

"Wow!" Holmes said when he saw the letter. Then he asked again: "What can I do to help?"

Landwehr didn't want to ask for anything. Holmes was running a bricklaying company with his brother. But Holmes had helped build the massive Ghostbuster files that the new task force was going to reexamine now; he was the most organized note taker Landwehr knew. He knew how to keep his mouth shut.

"You know," Holmes said, "I did a lot of work on those files. I could help you a lot with that."

"I know you could," Landwehr said. "But you know there's no money to pay you for something like that."

"I don't give a damn about that," Holmes said.

Relph, Gouge, Otis, Snyder, and Landwehr all knew how bad some retired cops felt about not catching BTK. The older men had often asked, "Did we miss anything? Did we fail to do something we should have done?"

Landwehr did not think so. But on the day that Laviana's story ran in the *Eagle*, Laviana found Bernie Drowatzky working as chief of police in tiny Kaw City, Oklahoma. Drowatzky touched on the guilt: "I think there's something somewhere we missed that's going to take them to him."

Otis didn't drink much but thought he'd become a drunk if this lasted long. He barely slept the first two weeks. He would wake up in the dark and his brain would engage. He would make a pot of coffee, get dressed, and drive in to work.

Gouge slept more and did not fret as much, but he was grateful that Landwehr was running things. Landwehr did not babysit or second-guess detectives, and though there was great external pressure to find BTK, he kept it away from the detectives. Gouge thought the investigation would quickly become a disaster if anyone but Landwehr were in charge.

Gouge, Otis, Relph, Snyder, and other cops would head out every morning, approaching men all over Wichita who had been named by tipsters. The cops asked for DNA samples. When they reached the end of a list, they went back for another. The "swab-a-thon," they called it.

Anybody named in a tip had to be swabbed. A few tipsters suspected Landwehr.

The detectives took it seriously. Police had theorized for years that BTK was a cop. So Landwehr swabbed himself. "I didn't trust Otis or anybody else to stick a swab in my mouth, so I did it," he joked later. But he did it with witnesses. Gouge handed him two sterile Q-tips, then made fun of him while he rubbed them against the inside of his cheek—and watched closely to make sure he didn't cheat.

On the same day that Otis and Gouge saw the new BTK letter, they had gone out to find Bill Wegerle. There was no side-door approach through relatives this time.

Otis told Bill that someone claiming to be BTK had sent a letter, naming Vicki as a victim.

In his coat pocket, Otis had the subpoena that would force Bill to give his DNA if he refused. Otis had asked a judge to sign it, but he was hoping to leave it in his pocket, unused.

Bill listened as Otis explained: "I'm not here to tell you that the cops screwed up in 1986," Otis said. "But I can tell you we'd do things differently today. I am sorry about how things turned out for you. I believe you did not kill your wife, and now I can prove it. But I need your help."

He said that he needed a DNA sample—now.

Bill said okay.

It took just a couple of minutes. Otis and Gouge thanked him and drove away, the warrant still in Otis's pocket.

Two days later, they went to see Bill at his house. Bill, still wary, had a relative sitting beside him—a witness to the conversation.

A test had just confirmed that the DNA profile of the material found under Vicki's fingernail matched that of the man who had killed the Oteros thirty years before. And now the detectives knew: it was not Bill's DNA.

It had taken almost eighteen years, but he had been eliminated as a suspect.

When Otis and Gouge told him this, Bill did not smile or complain about the years he'd lived with the suspicion that he had killed Vicki. He did not complain about how other children had mocked his children at school, telling them that their father had murdered their mother.

"I'm glad you cleared me," he said. "All I ever wanted was for you to find who killed Vicki."

Otis and Gouge wanted the names of people she knew, places she shopped, details of her life. In spite of the passage of nearly two decades, Bill gave detailed answers.

Otis admired him. *He could have told me to go pound sand. He could have told us to stay out of his house. He could have stayed mad at us for the last eighteen years, but he's too good a man to do that.*

In the first week, Johnson turned down requests from thirty-two national media outlets wanting to interview Landwehr or Chief Williams.

Some reporters got rude.

The FBI's Bob Morton encouraged Johnson to ignore them and stick to the plan:

"The media is not going to solve this case," Morton told her. "BTK is a very clever predator; if you put too much out there you are jeopardizing the investigation. . . . Just because you have spoiled the press doesn't mean that you can't change the way you do business on this case. . . . It is very dangerous for you to overtalk. If you brief every day you run out of things to put out there and you say too much and run the risk of causing another homicide. Then, the very press that you were catering to will turn on you and blame you for the homicide."

Some local politicians worried about the flow of information too—but for other reasons. They thought the BTK publicity might scare off tourists and conventioneers, including some of the forty-two thousand people who were expected in Wichita for the 85th Women's International Bowling Congress Tournament.

Johnson e-mailed Morton that the cops were getting a lot of pressure from politicians "to go on TV and say everything is fine."

"Do not do that," Morton said. If BTK killed someone after police sounded the all clear, the city could be liable in lawsuits.

With the investigators off-limits, the television crews descended on anyone they thought had a remote connection to the case: former BTK investigators like Drowatzky; Beattie, who was rushing completion of his book; and Laviana, who had broken the story.

With three daughters at home, Laviana worried about going on TV and talking about the killer. But he knew more about BTK than anyone else at the paper—so he gave interviews the day his first story ran. The media lined up to talk to him after that. (Laviana didn't have cable TV, so he had no idea who Greta Van Susteren was or that she had a national prime-time show on the Fox News Channel.) That weekend he got more than a dozen calls at home from national shows wanting more. "Come to the paper if you want to talk to me," he told them. Within days, he also got calls from Japanese and German television crews, and magazines he'd never heard of.

The *Eagle* published a story about the swab-a-thon on April 2, after three men contacted the newspaper to say their DNA had been collected: "A police spokeswoman would neither confirm nor deny that DNA testing was under way," the *Eagle* reported.

That same day, Landwehr held his third news conference to keep the tip lines ringing. Some callers suspected ex-husbands. Some turned in sons or fathers. Some suspected neighbors or coworkers.

Men were named as suspects for many reasons: because they were loners, eccentrics, or "just mean." Some were known kooks. Others were upstanding citizens.

Some tipsters viewed themselves as amateur sleuths. One theory had BTK and California's Zodiac killer being the same person. Others were sure BTK had strangled JonBenét Ramsey in Boulder, Colorado.

By this time, Landwehr's instructions had been passed along to every street cop: if they responded to a homicide call, burglary or even attempted burglary and noticed a cut phone line, "that's it, clear the house." He had the same instruction for any scene involving a missing person or a female in bondage.

While some detectives read e-mail tips or phone call transcripts, others did computer background checks. They could quickly eliminate people as potential suspects if they were black (because of the DNA profile), if they weren't the right age (at least forty-six), or if they had a provable alibi (such as being incarcerated at the time of one of the murders).

Sgt. Mike Hennessy prioritized which of the others would be asked for DNA.

Tip after tip led to dead ends, and Otis feared that something they overlooked would come back to haunt them.

• • •

Because the BTK news conferences were so brief, television reporters often filled out their stories by getting reactions from people downtown. Young women would say that BTK did not frighten them. They'd point out he was an old man.

Landwehr cringed when he heard that. "He'll take that as a challenge," Landwehr told Johnson. "He'll try to kill somebody to show he still can."

To help the detectives anticipate the killer's next moves, Landwehr brought in Bob Morton, the profiler from the FBI's Behavioral Science Unit.

Landwehr was comfortable working with the FBI. His uncle Ernie had been an FBI guy. So had his close friend, KBI Director Welch.

But many other cops regard FBI agents as arrogant, removed from the street. Morton began his overview of the case by stating the obvious: BTK probably has sexual fixations. He might live in the Wichita area; on the other hand, he might not.

I've got better things to do than listen to this, Otis thought.

He and Gouge walked out.

38

May–June 2004

"The BTK Story"

Landwehr wondered whether BTK might follow him home some night and learn that he had a family.

Probably not. But Landwehr asked supervisors to cruise officers past his house—and his mother's—every hour. He suspected officers were already doing it on their own.

His mother, Irene, did not tell him she was scared, but she conceded it to Cindy. Cindy told her that BTK must be old by now, feeling cautious. But Cindy got in touch with Morton.

She understood why Landwehr had to talk to BTK on television, she told Morton. But he had made himself a target, and now they were telling James, their eight-year-old son, that he could not play in their front yard and must never answer the door to strangers. The boy was scared.

Morton told her that serial killers almost never hunt cops—they prefer defenseless victims. "Take precautions," he said. "But don't dwell on this."

Landwehr worried for weeks about whether the talk-to-BTK strategy would work. His worries went away on May 4, forty-six days after the Wegerle message surfaced.

A receptionist at KAKE-TV found an envelope in the mail with a return address of Thomas B. King—the initials an anagram reference to BTK.

The news director, Glen Horn, opened the package and found several items: a word search puzzle, photocopies of two identification cards, a photocopy of a badge with the words "Special Officer" on it, and thirteen chapter headings for something titled "The BTK Story." It made

CHAPTER 8

```
M   O   A   S   D   D   O
C   R   U   I   S   E   X
P   J   K   W   P   T   H
R   L   E   O   O   A   G
O   Z   F   L   T   I   J
W   N   A   L   P   L   M
L   F   N   O   V   S   N
X   C   T   F   I   V   B
Q   I   A   M   C   L   D
W   O   S   R   T   T   B
T   P   I   N   I   P   U
Y   H   E   L   M   Q   E
X   N   S   T   E   A   M

I   D       T       6   2       2
    2   S   E           0   P   A Y
    5   U   L   I       3   R    1
    9   Q   E   A           D   F
Q   W   E   P   N   R   S   X   C B
A   E   N   H   D   S   H   S   B O
G   N   R   O   E   Z   L   H   O A
S   R   T   N   R   T   2   L   H
F   T   Y   E   S   C       G   C B
H   Y   U   C   O   P       H   U
L   U   I   O   N   F       N   A D
K           A   D   I   8       H L
X           2   T   M   M       S O X
                6                 B K
R   U       S   E   T       Y   U
E   I       E   O   P       F   A
A   N       R   E   M       O   D
L   S       V   F   G       R   H
T   U       I   S   K       S   L
O   R       C   S   T       A   S O X
R   A       E   E   E       L   B
S   N       M   R   Z       E   K
Q   C       A   D   C       V   O
W   E       N   D   I       E   N
X   R       A   A   G       N
    N           M   Y       D
```

Rader's word-search puzzle was sent to KAKE,
filled with clues about how he stalked his victims.

reference to fetishes, "PJs," a "final curtain call," and asked: WILL THERE MORE?

KAKE called the cops. Otis went to fetch the package. KAKE shot video of him picking it up, much to his irritation. He walked out without saying anything, much to Horn's irritation.

The puzzle included a section called "Ruse," that included the words *serviceman, insurance,* and *realtor.* BTK was hinting that he gained access to homes by pretending to be someone on business.

James Landwehr called his father at work one day. "Dad, you need to come home! Why haven't you come home?"

Landwehr and Cindy had not told James what was going on.

It seemed to James that his father had disappeared. Sometimes his dad worked twenty-four-hour days. Or he would come home for a few minutes to put James to bed, then drive back to work. James was an affectionate little soul; once he got to know someone he greeted them with a bear hug. His bond with his father had grown deep, and Landwehr liked nothing better than to help with homework or play alongside him. James was now seeing his father on television, and the boy sensed something sinister.

"You need to come home," he told him.

"James," Landwehr said. "You know how sometimes I need to work late to catch a bad guy. That's what I'm doing now."

The Landwehrs debated about whether to tell him a longer version of the truth. But how do you tell a little boy about BTK? And that his dad is hunting him?

Otis still wondered whether the person sending the messages was BTK or someone who had found BTK's trophies. The items sent to the *Eagle* and KAKE were perfectly clean. The only fingerprints on the papers were from the people who handled them after the envelopes had been opened. There were no stray hairs, no dried beads of sweat.

If it's him, how come the son of a bitch won't just lick the damned envelope, so we can get his DNA and prove it?

Landwehr thought Otis had a point. Perhaps he could prompt BTK to do that.

He called a news conference and replied to BTK on May 10, six days after the KAKE message arrived. In consultation with the FBI's Morton, Johnson had written a paragraph that subtly prodded BTK to prove it was him writing the messages: "We are proceeding on the possibility that this letter is from BTK," Landwehr was to say. "We have turned it over to the Federal Bureau of Investigation. They will do a thorough analysis utilizing the latest technology and forensic science in order to determine the *authenticity* of the letter."

Landwehr practiced reading the script out loud. The moment he said "authenticity," he stumbled over it . . . and broke into laughter. *Apparently I can't pronounce a five-syllable word,* he thought. He tried to read the word again, and stumbled again.

In front of the television cameras, talking to BTK on live television, he fumbled the pronunciation again and had to suppress his own laughter. Embarrassed, he teased Johnson later. "Don't *ever* give me that word again." He should have deleted the word, he thought. He had ignored his training in debate and drama: when you muff a word in rehearsal, you muff it in performance.

On June 9, Michael Hellman saw a clear plastic bag taped to the back of a stop sign at the southeast corner of First and Kansas streets as he walked to his job at Spangles, a local burger chain. From the bag, Hellman pulled out an envelope that had "BTK Field Gram" typed on it.

When Landwehr saw the three pieces of paper inside, he realized it was BTK's longest communication yet. Its misspelled title was "Death on a Cold January Moring." It was a detailed account of what happened inside the Otero house—including how Josie pleaded for her life.

Landwehr waited to pick up James from the school bus one day. The bus was late.

Landwehr had been skipping meals, not sleeping much.

He looked at his watch.

If he did not catch this guy, he might get transferred out of homicide, removed as commander of the task force. The chief had been supportive, but Landwehr knew Williams must be under tremendous pressure to make something happen. Privately, Landwehr had concluded that if he failed to catch BTK in a year, he'd be transferred.

James's safety worried him more.

The bus arrived—a few minutes late. James trotted to his father.

Back at work, Landwehr suppressed a desire to order the swabbing of every school bus driver in Wichita.

BTK's Otero story was written as a narrative, complete with a scene-setting opener—and the usual misspellings.

If a person happen to be out one of these cold morning in a certain part of Wichita, that is the northeast part on a particwalar morining in January he might have notice a man park his car in a store parking lot pause beifly then walk across the street and disappear among the house and commercial building. If they had follow him they would have notice his head bend low to the ground and wearing a heavy parker. If they would have looked closer they would notice his eye dart back and fourth across the street checking the house windows and door. As he near a house on the corner he quickly glance around and jumped the wooded fence surrounding the house.

What followed was a step-by-step description of what BTK said had happened more than thirty years before. It had such detail that Landwehr wondered whether BTK wrote it soon after it happened.

He knew the family left the house approximetly 8:45, and they would walk out the car and leave for school and in aoproximatly seven mintwe the lany, Judie, would return home.

He had earily in the week, saw them leave for school one day He thought to himself, say this may be it, A perfect set up; a house on the corner, a garage set off from the house, a fenced yard, a large space from near by neighbor house. especially the back dor. It was a few days lter that he stop across the street and follow the family car tooss see wher they when that moring. She took the kids to school each day, an return, a perfect setup.

It was close to his fantasy of a victim all too himself, a person he could tie up, tortue, and maybe kill.

Cindy told Landwehr one night that they had to tell James something about what was going on. The boy was getting increasingly anxious about his father's absences—and he was hearing things about his father.

The Landwehrs sat down at the home computer with James. Cindy showed the boy how to call up his father's name on a search. What came up was one news story after another about Lt. Ken Landwehr—and BTK.

James tried to understand.

"James," Landwehr said, "you know how my job is to catch bad guys?"

"Yes."

"I'm trying to catch a really bad guy this time. He calls himself BTK. He has hurt a lot of people. And we are going to catch him.

"That's why I'm going on TV," he said. "That's why I have to be at work a lot."

"What if he tries to hurt you?" James asked. "What if he comes to the house?"

"BTK has got to be an old man now," Landwehr replied. "He hurt people starting thirty years ago, so he's got to be in his sixties now, and slow, and old. We don't think he can hurt anybody."

What James said next surprised his father.

"But what if BTK has a son, and it's the son who's doing this now?"

It was what Otis and Gouge had suggested: that someone else was pretending to be BTK.

"You're way ahead of me," Landwehr said. "That's a good idea. But we don't think so. And we don't think he'll come here."

Finally, about twenty minutes before nine the door unlocked, and the boy step outside, in just a flash he order him back inside, confronting the family armed with pistol and knife he told them that this was a stick up and not to be alarmed.

The family was preparing to leave. the kids were packing their lunchs and had gather their coats by the table. The mother, Judie asked what was going on, and said they had no money of any thing of value. The boy was by his folks side looking scared and the girl, Josephine was beginnging to cry, all of them gather in the hall way he told them his orders. He was wanted, and needed the car, money and food. . . . Joe noitced, his gun hand shake and told the family to settled down and all would be okay.

The dog's barking finally got to him, BTK wrote.

Rex wanted the pest out and told them he would shoot it or them if they try any funny tricks. expressing that the gun he held wax an automatic and held hollww points bullet that would kill. Joe, reassure him that if the dog was out of the way, things sould better. So, agreeing the man let oe put the dog out, bot being very c reful of Joe.

He said he bound the parents hand and foot. He said Julie (he called her "Judie") complained that her hands were going numb, so he retied them.

He began to tie up the girl.

Her hair was to long and kept getting the way when he tries to gag her in the frist place, tears rolled down her face and Rex said he was sorry about piching her hair.

He gagged them, then slipped a plastic bag over Joe's head. The others immediately began to scream. He could see tears on their faces.

He try to cover their mouth with his gloved hand but htey pleaded for him to release the boy ant Joe . . . Joe had moved to the other bed post and rumb a hole in his bag but he was not feeling good and had threw-up and breathing heavy. The boys eye where open now. . . . Josephine was crying and Judie still pledding for him to leave the house, they would not tell.

. . . he produce a ciol of rope and walk over to Judie and in her crying pleading voice " what are you doing . . . he slip he rope around her neck and strangle her slowly. Josephine cry out, "momy—I love you".

It was all horror, and maybe it was all bullshit fiction . . . but the writer obviously enjoyed writing it.

Josephine kept asking him to be carefull bu Rex told her her Mother her Dad would be asleep also after he quit tighting the rope.

He then slip the garrote around the girl neck, she grasp her eye, bulge, then she passout. Judie was by now awake. Her eye opens, slowly moving her head. This time Rex makes a clove hicth and placed it over Judie neck, she cry, "God have mecry on you," before he tighten the noose, her eyes really bluged because of the extreme pressure the tight clove-hicth makes. She grasp and struggle but, soon passout s blood appear eye and mouth and nose.

James Landwehr, one year younger than Joey Otero had been in 1974, tried to be calm after his father's reassurances. But one day he spoke up.

"Dad," he said, "other kids have been talking."

James told him that some kids' parents were wondering whether

BTK might want to kill Landwehr, miss Landwehr's house, and go to the neighbors by mistake.

BTK had saved the killing of the girl for last.

Returning to the basement he found Josephine awake and looking at the ceiling, he then tie her feet together and then around her knees and lower abouiamal. Secure tightly, he pulled up her sweater and cut her bra into. her small oreal expose so probably the first man to lay eye on them except her father. With that done he again checked the area for mistakes, nothing out of place. he return to the girl, she ask him if he was going to do the same things as he had done to the rest, "no," he told her, the rest where asleep. He pick her up and took her tied body to the sewer pipe. There laying on her back, he ask if her Dad had a camera, she asked, no. then gag her . . . , "Please," she said. "Don't worry baby," he said, "you be in heaven tonite with the rest".

James Landwehr could not sleep in his bed anymore. He would crawl into his parents' bed and snuggle beside Cindy, with the lights on.

One day James saw his father on television delivering another message to BTK.

Cindy watched James cover his ears with his hands.

39

July 2004

Sidetracked

On the morning of Saturday, July 17, an employee at the downtown Wichita library named James Stenholm found a plastic bag in the book drop. The bag contained papers with the letters "BTK." Librarians called police.

Landwehr was not happy about what officers did when they arrived. They shut the library down.

"Come on, guys," Landwehr said. "What were you thinking?" Closing the main library drew attention. That meant reporters and other nuisances; the cops might as well have turned on the tornado sirens.

Landwehr saw about fifty homeless men, blinking like a flock of owls. They hung out in the air-conditioned library, and now, standing in the sun, they looked as irritated as Landwehr.

"Jesus, guys, it was just a bag," Landwehr told the uniforms. "I could have walked in here like all I was doing was picking up a book."

Landwehr took the package and studied it with his team.

They were surprised by what BTK had to say at the bottom of the two-page letter:

I have spotted a female that I think lives alone and/or is a spotted latch key kid. Just got to work out the details. I'm much older (not feeble) now and have to conditions myself carefully. Also my thinking process is not as sharp as it uses to be. Details-Details-Details!!! I think fall or winter would be just about right for the HIT. Got to do it this year or next! Number X, as time is running out for me.

But it's what he had written at the top that sent detectives immediately to the telephones. BTK had titled the letter "Jakey," and implied that he had already killed again.

I had to stop work on Chapter 2 of, "THE BTK STORY." due to the death of Jake Allen.

I was so excited about this incident that I had to tell the story.

Twelve days earlier, the Argonia High School homecoming king and class valedictorian had been run over by a freight train about four miles from his family's farm and about thirty-five miles from Wichita. Allen had been a star athlete. His body had been wrapped in baling wire and tied to the tracks, though Sumner County sheriff's investigators tried to keep that fact a secret.

BTK wrote that they had met when Allen had knee surgery, and had gotten better acquainted through computer chats. He said he lured Allen to the tracks by posing as a private detective investigating BTK.

Jakey would be the bait. We would capture him and turn him over to the police.

BTK made taunting references to bondage, sadomasochism, and baling wire. He described the sexual thrills he got not only from being with Allen at the tracks but "while I peck this out." His library package included grainy copies of photos showing someone in bondage out in the woods, a hood on his face, and white tube socks on his feet. He claimed he and "Jakey" had been out playing "games."

Landwehr called Chief Williams to tell him about BTK's threat to kill and his hints that he had killed Allen.

Williams began to look for ways to reinforce the task force.

Otis called the Sumner County Sheriff's Office. Its lead investigator, Jeff Hawkins, and others drove to Wichita that day and studied the letter.

Hawkins was dubious. Forensic tests weren't complete, but the Sumner County team strongly suspected Allen's death was a suicide.

Lundin and Thomas, the two KBI agents, went to Sumner County. The FBI's Morton also looked into Allen's death. The more they looked, the more they agreed BTK was blowing smoke.

Forensics determined that the wire found with Allen's body came from his farm. An examination of Allen's computer turned up no evidence that he had conversations with the serial killer.

Investigators concluded that Allen had wrapped the wire around his body and positioned himself on the tracks.

The Jakey letter touched off an intense debate in District Attorney Nola Foulston's office the day it surfaced. Her first instinct was that the authorities should go public, with a warning that BTK was threatening to kill a child. As the county's chief elected law enforcement authority, she had the power to do that, or make the cops do it.

Kevin O'Connor and Kim Parker, her two top prosecutors, tried to talk her out of it. O'Connor was a loyal Foulston friend, but she always encouraged him to speak his mind, and he did so now. A lot of hot words flew. O'Connor, who had spent four months shadowing the BTK task force, argued that the cops were right to keep as much of a lid on the investigation as possible. They didn't want to give BTK information, or publicity, or a feeling that he was manipulating the chase.

Chief Williams wrestled with the decision too. If they revealed BTK's threat, should they mention the specifics BTK had written about a "latch- key kid"? There were thousands of latchkey children and many after-school programs in Wichita. Revealing the threat would worry thousands of parents, many of whom had to work and leave kids at home. It was clear BTK liked to push the cops' buttons. Williams didn't want to boost his ego.

In the end, they decided they should warn the public but not be specific about the threat. The decision weighed heavily on Williams. If BTK killed someone now, Williams would wonder whether he had blown the call.

The task force cops took the threat personally. Landwehr continued to worry about James, Cindy, and himself: *Every time this guy puts out a package for us to find, is he just trying to draw me away from my house so he can attack it?*

Otis had a twelve-year-old daughter who was alone at home for twenty minutes after school every day until Netta came home from work. After the Jakey letter arrived, Otis arranged for his sister to stay with his daughter for those minutes after school.

Gouge did not worry. Early on, he told his family to be careful when answering the door, but he didn't want to say more and make them worry.

He thought that BTK did not have the guts to visit a cop.

When the Jakey letter was found, Landwehr's BTK task force was down to twenty-three people. Four days later, Williams nearly doubled the size of the task force, to forty. He told Landwehr he intended to keep that number working on the case for a long time. Investigators were brought in to follow up on tips so the detectives most heavily involved could focus more on digging through case files.

There were nights when Williams's home phone rang in the wee hours, and one of his commanders would tell him about some overnight shooting or something else that needed his immediate attention. Now, when his phone rang, Williams's first thought upon waking was a silent prayer: *Don't let it be a BTK killing.*

Five days after police got the Jakey letter, Landwehr appeared at a news conference. In words carefully crafted by Johnson, he said: "Based on the information provided to us by the FBI, and the fake IDs and fake badge that were sent to KAKE by BTK, we think it is important for citizens to continue to practice personal and home crime prevention techniques.

"We want parents to teach these skills to their children also."

He didn't reveal the contents of the library letter, but many people correctly interpreted his words and tone to mean that BTK had made a threat.

Laviana covered the news conference for the *Eagle*.

Otis approached him in a hallway afterward.

"Hurst, need to talk to you," Otis said. "Have you got a minute?"

40

July–August 2004

Landwehr Takes the Offensive

The national media kept pestering Johnson with interview requests. Unfulfilled, they continued to turn to people with less-immediate connections to the investigation. Some news shows backstabbed competitors, insisting that interview subjects not talk to other shows. Laviana refused to cut such deals.

These shows irritated the cops. Serial killer "experts" who knew nothing about BTK appeared on air talking glibly, "blowing smoke," as Otis described it.

A few days after the July 22 news conference, Wenzl saw Landwehr come out of city hall to light up a smoke.

Wenzl knew Landwehr would not talk about BTK, but he also knew from Laviana that Landwehr had a sense of humor. Wenzl pretended to interview him.

"Kenny Landwehr," he said, shaking his hand. "Have you caught BTK yet?"

"No," Landwehr said.

"I have a suspect, if you don't mind me intruding," Wenzl said.

Landwehr listened politely.

"It's Hurst Laviana."

Landwehr's face crinkled into a grin. "No," he said.

"Really? You got to admit, Hurst is a weird dude."

"No," Landwehr said.

"Okay. But we've talked about this in the newsroom for weeks now, and we've concluded that one day Hurst is either going to reveal BTK on the front page, or come to you and confess."

Landwehr took a long pull on his cigarette. "I know for certain that it's not him," Landwehr said.

"But how?"

"Because we have eliminated him as a suspect."

"How?"

Landwehr grinned. "No comment," he said.

A few minutes later, back in the newsroom, Wenzl found Laviana writing a story.

"I've cleared your name," Wenzl said. "I ran into Landwehr outside city hall. We compared notes and concluded you're not BTK."

"Thank you," Laviana said.

"I didn't say you are innocent," Wenzl said. "I said you're not BTK."

Laviana nodded.

"Landwehr said something weird," Wenzl said. "He said they eliminated you as a suspect. He said it like it meant something."

"It does," Laviana said. "The cops swabbed me to get my DNA."

"*WHAT?*"

It was true, Laviana said. After the July 22 news conference, Otis had pulled him aside.

"I hate to do this, but I need to ask for your DNA," Otis said. "You've been named in some of our tips as a suspect."

Laviana shrugged. "I'm surprised it took you this long," he said. He had thought the cops would swab him from the moment he began giving TV interviews. He figured someone would see him on television and call him in as a suspect for knowing so much about the case.

Laviana followed Otis to Johnson's office. Otis shut the door.

The cops had refused to talk about the rumors swirling around town that they had swabbed thousands of men.

Laviana decided he'd try to get Otis to talk.

Otis pulled on latex gloves.

"Some of the television people say you've already swabbed two thousand people so far," Laviana said. "Is that true?"

Otis had picked up a cotton swab. "No, that's not right," Otis said. "It's only about five hundred."

"What makes you decide you need to swab somebody?"

"All it takes is one tip," Otis said.

Otis rubbed the inside of Laviana's cheek, first with one cotton swab, then with a second.

"How long does it take to get the results back?"

"If I don't come looking for you again in two weeks, you'll know you've been eliminated," Otis said. He dropped each swab into a container. They were done.

Laviana went back to work, told his editors that he'd been swabbed, and tried to sort out how he felt about being a suspect. *Weird,* he thought. And you can't keep it secret. *In some ways it's a relief,* Laviana thought. He knew other men who had been swabbed, and it had been awkward asking them about it. But it was also like being in an exclusive club. Once you were in, you could talk openly. He was in now.

He considered whether he should volunteer to write a first-person story about what it was like to be a BTK suspect.

No, he decided. Laviana had three daughters at North High School; he didn't want them teased or taunted.

Before the "Jakey" letter arrived, the task force and Johnson had called news conferences only in reaction to BTK's messages.

Landwehr and Johnson were wondering whether they should go more on the offensive—find excuses to communicate, even when BTK had not written them.

They fretted a lot over the messages. Every word and all the timing was planned. They always sprang the news conferences on reporters with little notice. They did not want to provoke shallow conjecture that would scare people—or cause BTK to delay communicating until after a scheduled news conference. After "Jakey," reporters sometimes got no notice at all that a BTK briefing was coming. Sometimes reporters would arrive at the daily 10:00 AM briefing and be surprised to see Landwehr stride in, script in hand.

In all these gatherings, Landwehr read his prepared statement, then walked out. Sometimes Otis or one of the other detectives would sit in the back, looking for anyone suspicious. They thought BTK might show up. Otis and the others obtained several DNA swabs from strange men they saw at the briefings.

After each announcement, the newspaper quickly posted the news on its website. TV broke into programming with live reports. KAKE sometimes used the clip of Otis picking up the May letter as a background visual. A confused elderly viewer sent Otis sixty dollars to buy new clothes because every time he appeared on TV he was wearing the same suit. Otis sent the money back.

A few small news leaks got out, which put the cops on edge. Were reporters following them when they went out to swab suspects? Were reporters eavesdropping in hallways? Did they have a source on the task force?

Their worries got worse as they lost sleep. Detectives who before March had sometimes chatted amiably with reporters stopped talking even about the weather.

Nobody at the *Eagle* was focused exclusively on BTK, not even Laviana, who was part of the Crime and Safety reporting team. He and Potter kept hearing rumors about BTK connections to the death of the teenager in Argonia; Potter dogged that story while covering day cops. At the end of July, the newspaper's editor, Sherry Chisenhall, pulled in a new team leader to organize the coverage. L. Kelly had grown up in Wichita and had listened as her father, a former detective, talked about the Otero crimes with disgust. She had helped her best friend and mother cope with their fears after Chief LaMunyon announced that a serial killer was in Wichita. She had been with the *Eagle* more than twenty years and had been close to Ken Stephens and Bill Hirschman back in the day.

Chisenhall wanted a sharper effort on BTK coverage. She knew none of the cops were talking—the task force had proven unusually leakproof. But there were plenty of other people to talk to, other ways to move the story forward. She wanted the *Eagle* to own the story. Kelly was eager to get started, but she first had to make an unrelated trip to Toronto.

By the time she got back, Landwehr had made his own plans for moving forward.

• • •

The cops felt their anxiety growing. BTK hadn't communicated since the July 17 library message. Gouge worried that BTK was busy planning a murder; his last letter had been a clear threat.

Morton told the cops to keep communicating and use their scripts to hint that BTK should worry. BTK has to feel confident to kill, so undermine his confidence. Keep him off balance, remind him that police are hunting him. Do not challenge or threaten him but drop hints that you're closer.

This was easy to say and not easy to do. Johnson, a former crime and government reporter at newspapers around Kansas and Missouri, wrote drafts of each message, faxed a copy to Morton, and showed the copy to Landwehr and Williams's command staff.

On August 17, one month after BTK's last communication, Johnson noted after a meeting with Morton: "We are now changing the rules. Instead of us reacting when he sends a letter, we are going to go proactive, and then he will have to respond in order to gain control of the game."

BTK had pushed their buttons. Now they would push his.

Keep Landwehr talking to him, Morton said. From the beginning, Morton wanted BTK to feel a connection with Landwehr so that the killer would confess willingly to Landwehr someday, if the cops caught him.

Morton told Landwehr to get plenty of rest the night before each briefing. His hair was to be combed, his clothing neat. He was to look and sound refreshed, alert, upbeat. The public needed to see him and feel confident. The killer could not see him tired. Landwehr began to study his own face, looking for bags under his eyes.

With every day that BTK did not communicate, Landwehr lost sleep.

41

August–November 2004

P. J. Wyatt

Three days after Johnson told the FBI that police were taking the initiative, the task force made up a flimsy reason to talk to BTK and sucked the news media into playing it big.

On August 20, Landwehr went before reporters and began talking about BTK's 1978 letter. He noted it included a poem, *"OH! DEATH TO NANCY,"* that was an adaptation of the folk song "O Death." It read, in part:

> *I'll stuff your jaws till you can't talk*
> *I'll blind your leg's till you can't walk*
> *I'll tie your hands till you can't make a stand.*
> *And finally I'll close your eyes so you*
> *can't see*
> *I'll bring sexual death unto you for me.*
> *B.T.K.*

Landwehr referred to BTK's message in May 2004, which included "PJ'S" as one of the chapter titles, and noted that English professor P. J. Wyatt had used "O Death" in a class at Wichita State University in the 1970s.

"We are looking for the public's help on identifying anyone who had used this obscure folk song and had contact with Dr. P. J. Wyatt," who died in 1991, Landwehr said. "The FBI profilers have confirmed our belief that there is a definite connection in the reference to PJ in the letter we received last May and the folklore song 'O Death.' "

This was a deliberate stretch. Investigators had consulted Wyatt in 1978 as an expert. After she recognized BTK's poem as a rewrite of the song, they got copies of her class lists. But BTK had not claimed he had taken Wyatt's class or that he knew Wyatt.

It was a fat piece of bait for a wild-goose chase, and reporters chased it enthusiastically. At the *Eagle*, crime reporter Stan Finger, courts reporter Ron Sylvester, and others from across the newsroom worked overtime to learn all they could about the very private professor. They talked to friends of Wyatt in Michigan, former employees of her parents' defunct radio supply business, and countless university sources. The result was two day's worth of stories dominating the front page, with photos, information boxes, even a sidebar story on the history of the song, which was not "obscure." It had been recorded since at least the 1920s and had been featured in the George Clooney movie *O Brother, Where Art Thou?*

The task force's true intentions were noted in Johnson's internal memo: "By doing this release we are inviting a response from him either (1) because he never thought we'd make the connection or (2) to tell us how stupid and wrong we are. In terms of media this will take the heat off the Argonia thing by giving them something else to pursue. It also shows the public that we have other leads and things we are doing besides just the swabbing."

Johnson underestimated the depth of the *Eagle*'s reporting bench and its willingness to pull people from across the newroom to help with BTK coverage. Tim Potter kept writing about the Argonia story, while religion writer Abe Levy and higher education reporter Katherine Leal Unmuth both had major roles in the Wyatt stories.

The investigators also hoped the Wyatt story would make BTK anxious, Johnson noted: "He is so careful and deliberate that he will not commit a homicide while he is feeling anxiety. This will set him back on his heels."

The *Eagle* worked to broaden its coverage beyond Landwehr's news conferences. (Ultimately, the paper would publish nearly eight hundred pieces about the case.) Laviana talked to men whom the task force had swabbed. Potter interviewed former FBI profilers Robert Ressler and Gregg McCrary to paint a picture of how serial killers thought and operated. And Potter flew to New Mexico. There, at the Western New Mexico Correctional Facility, Potter found Charlie Otero, with a goatee and a

shaved head, serving a three-year sentence for aggravated battery in a domestic violence case. Charlie had been a straight-A student and on his
way to becoming an Eagle Scout when BTK wiped out most of his family.
Since then he'd drifted emotionally, taken drugs.

He still hated BTK.

"I want him to go down."

The BTK discussion board became one of the most popular spots on the
Eagle's website. Back in April, the cops had obtained a subpoena, looking
for the identity of some of the people who posted comments on the
board. None of the "Suspicious Six" were BTK. Months later, Johnson
still monitored the site, hoping BTK might join in. It upset her when the
messages criticized the cops. She told Landwehr that some of the self-
styled BTK experts were idiots. Many discussed their far-flung theories
obsessively.

Landwehr avoided looking at the discussion board unless Johnson
brought a comment to his attention. The first time that happened, he
read other comments out of curiosity.

"Some of these people make a case that I'm a dumb son of a bitch,"
he told friends wryly. "After reading what some of them said, I concluded
that they are right: I really am a dumb son of a bitch."

BTK did not respond to the news coverage about Wyatt and the poem, so
the cops invented another excuse to communicate and keep him off-
kilter. On August 26, six days after the "O Death" news conference,
Landwehr stepped before the cameras to talk about the 1979 burglary at
Anna Williams's house and "Oh, Anna Why Didn't You Appear."

"We want to talk to anyone who may have seen the original poem, or
has any other knowledge of the poem," Landwehr said.

BTK did not reply.

By September, Chief Williams had noticed that Landwehr had lost
weight, perhaps as much as twenty pounds. And he seemed to be moving
more slowly. Cindy saw also that when he slept, it was only for a couple of
hours.

But he had now somehow completed the bachelor's degree in history that he had walked away from in 1978. He had been ten college credits short.

He was also overseeing the building of a new house in west Wichita. The house would include a room for his mother. Cindy had suggested it. Irene was eighty-five years old, still living on her own. But someday she would need help. "Why send her to a nursing home?" Cindy said. "I love your mother. Let's take her in." Landwehr had been touched. Cindy had the room designed with a wide door in case Irene ever needed a wheelchair.

One day at the construction site, Cindy saw her husband looking at the workers with an odd expression. She suddenly realized he was wondering whether one of them might be BTK, setting them up for an attack.

Otis rode with him to the site one day.

"Hey, Landwehr," Otis teased. "BTK is probably laying your floor in there right now."

Landwehr did not laugh.

September progressed with no sign that BTK intended to communicate again. Gouge and the rest of them worried that he was about to kill or go further underground. They wondered whether they might end up like the older cops from the 1970s—haunted by failure.

Every time Chief Williams's phone rang, he expected to hear that his officers had found bodies in a house with a cut phone line. The television coverage wore on him. Most of it was speculation, and some stations coupled BTK images with creepy music. That just fed BTK's ego, he thought.

Netta Otis saw her exhausted husband fall asleep in chairs. They fretted over how little time he spent with their children.

On the morning of September 14, the *Eagle*'s fashion writer and social columnist, Bonnie Bing, was standing in the middle of busy Rock Road in northeast Wichita, breathing car exhaust and hawking newspapers as part of a promotion to raise money for United Way.

Bing was a celebrity in Wichita, as well known for her charitable work as her newspaper work. She served on advisory boards, roasted and toasted prominent friends, and emceed dozens of fund-raisers every year.

On this morning, she was bellowing enthusiastically at motorists as they rolled past on their way to work. "Come on, buy a paper!"

A strange man walked up and spoke to her.

He looked intense. He wanted her to tell a former *Eagle* opinion page editor, Randy Brown, to meet him under the railroad trestle on Douglas Avenue just half a block west of the *Eagle* building. He had a story to pass along.

"Randy doesn't work at the *Eagle* anymore," Bing said. "He hasn't worked there for years."

"You can call him," the man replied. "You can do anything you want." He walked away.

A few days later he called Bing and renewed his request. Then he said, "Bonnie, leaks have caused consequences. I'll get back to you."

Bing called Brown, who now taught at Wichita State. He laughed it off. Journalists get cloak-and-dagger requests from kooks like that one once in a while.

A few days later, Bing got a call from a friend, a real estate agent named Cindy Carnahan, who sounded nervous. Carnahan insisted that Bing drop whatever she was doing and come to her house immediately.

A few minutes later Bing found five big men in Carnahan's home. One face looked familiar, and Bing caught her breath. It was Ken Landwehr, the homicide lieutenant who was investigating BTK.

He introduced the others: Dana Gouge, Kelly Otis, Clint Snyder, and Tim Relph. Bing listened in shock as the men talked. A letter had arrived at Carnahan's house. "It has both our names in it," Carnahan told Bing.

The letter said, "I will contact the sociable Bonnie Bing."

And it warned that "leaks have consequences."

"That's what the guy said to me that day," Bing said.

"What guy?" Landwehr asked.

She realized, as her stomach began to turn, that these men thought she and Carnahan were the recipients of a BTK communiqué.

As Landwehr asked questions, Bing saw that he seemed stressed and tired but masked it with little jokes. He had a warm and engaging manner, as did the other men. They spoke compassionately, trying to calm her.

Landwehr gave her his work number, his cell number, and his home number. "Call anytime if you need to," he said.

Bing had walked out of Carnahan's house feeling unsteady. She went all over town every week reporting stories, speaking to groups, doing TV and radio interviews, volunteering for dozens of charities. She couldn't stop doing that.

And Landwehr had asked her to keep her mouth shut about her involvement in the newspaper's biggest story. "I need you to not tell anyone at the *Eagle* about this," he said. This was a homicide investigation. They could not afford to jeopardize it with a leak. Bonnie had agreed but said she had to tell her husband. If she was at risk, he needed to know. Dick Honeyman, a civil defense attorney, asked Landwehr to talk with him. He was worried about his wife. But when Landwehr said the cops would keep close track of her, Honeyman snorted.

"Good luck with that," he said.

Landwehr smiled, but he was almost certain that BTK had picked out a new target.

Within two weeks Bing was told to go to the FBI's Wichita headquarters in the Epic Center. Landwehr wanted Bing to help produce a drawing of the man who had approached her on Rock Road. Landwehr had called the FBI in Quantico, Virginia. "Send me the best sketch artist you've got," he said.

Bing kept her secret. She was sure that she was betraying her profession and her boss, *Eagle* editor Sherry Chisenhall. Twice she walked into Chisenhall's office to tell her what was going on, then stood mute as Chisenhall waited for her to speak. Each time Bing made up an excuse about why she was there and walked out, weighed down with guilt.

Laviana was getting overwhelmed by requests to sit for interviews but was happy to meet with British clairvoyant Dennis McKenzie and the documentary crew that brought him to Wichita; it was a story. Laviana shadowed them as they visited BTK crime sites, including Anna Williams's former home and the Otero house. McKenzie said he thought BTK was a maintenance man. Or a plumber.

"When is your next big event where the public will know you'll be there?" Landwehr had asked Bing at Carnahan's house.

An auction, Bing said. She would be the emcee for the Boo & Brew Bash, a Halloween costume ball to benefit Dress for Success Wichita.

"You mean, where everybody wears masks?" Landwehr asked.

Landwehr smiled and dropped his head in disgust. "Great!" he said. He glanced at Relph, who smiled tightly. "This is just great."

A day or so before the ball, Landwehr called Bing and asked her to meet him outside Century II Convention Hall to plan how the cops would protect her and search for BTK in the crowd. When Bing arrived, she was startled at how tired Landwehr looked. He looked like he could go facedown on the pavement. Landwehr did not tell her this, but he was exhausted. All of them were at their wit's end, almost blind from lack of sleep, wondering if BTK was planning a murder instead of planning another letter.

When the day of the ball arrived, Landwehr sent two detectives . . . dressed as detectives. "If Bonnie waves to you in the crowd at the auction," he had teased them, "don't wave back and accidentally buy something."

The detectives showed up at the ball, acting as though they did not know Bing. This was standard undercover procedure, which Landwehr and all his detectives followed scrupulously, even on their days off. If Landwehr was in a grocery store, and an undercover cop happened to walk by, Landwehr would never acknowledge him even if he was a friend. *Never tip off the bad guys that you know each other.*

At the ball, men wearing masks shook Bing's hand, and Bing wondered with each handshake: *Is this him?*

But how would anyone know?

A month after Bing first met Landwehr, her home security alarm began blaring at 4:00 AM. It indicated that the phone line had been cut.

"This is not good," Honeyman said. He grabbed a seven-iron and marched downstairs to face the intruder. "Stay here," he told Bing. "No," she said. She had already dialed 911 on a cell phone but had not hit the send button yet. As she followed him, someone began pounding on their front door.

"This is the police," a voice called out. The pounding continued.

Honeyman looked outside and saw a young Wichita police officer at the door. He said he had come to investigate the alarm. Bing told him that she believed she had been the subject of a BTK letter. The officer looked startled and said, "Excuse me, I need to call Lieutenant Landwehr."

Minutes later, more officers arrived. They searched the three-story home thoroughly. The phone line to the house was intact, and there was no evidence of an intruder. It turned out that an underground phone line had gone faulty, setting off the alarm. Bing watched through a window as telephone repairmen ripped up her street to fix the line. If you ever want really fast phone service, she decided, just call Ken Landwehr.

The cops finally heard from BTK on October 22, though they wouldn't admit that to the reporters who picked up on rumors posted on the BTK discussion board. A United Parcel Service driver had found a strange package in a drop box near I-135 in the center of the city. Witnesses saw task force detectives at the scene, so it was maddening to reporters that the cops wouldn't confirm "the latest drop."

It contained a four-page document labeled "C2." scrawled to the left of the title: "Dawn." It appeared to be a chronological account of BTK's childhood and early adulthood. There was also a two-page list titled "THREE: 1-2-3: UNO-DOS-TRES: THEORY The BTK Worhl, Works in Threes and is base on the Eternal Triangle." It had long been thought that BTK had a fascination with the numeral three; all of his Wichita murder victims had a three in their home address. The documents had been copied, recopied, and reduced several times, making the words difficult to read, even when the cops enlarged the type. It made for dreary reading. Though the content was meant to be titillating, BTK was a dull writer.

Mother Slept beside me at times, the smells, the feel of underclothes and she let me rub her hair. Railroad sounds and smell of coal, Mother worked somewhere near the RR's. Mother gone all day and days at time. Grandparents took care of me. I missed mother a lot. Warm baths in a washtub. they bathe us. kissing cousin and I on the porch in the summer and by a stove in the winter.

There was also this:

*Masturbation Reflections 10-11 Years Old: If you **Masturbate**, God will come and kill you. Mom words after she found seminal yellow stain in her underwear one day. She tried to beat me. I fought back. she held my hands behind my back and used the Man's belt to whip me. Funny it hurt but Sparky liked it. Mother finally quit and said, "Oh My God What Have I Done."*

He wrote that he used prostitutes; that he was born in 1939; that he had spent time in Texas, Louisiana, or Oklahoma, or down South. As a boy, he secretly looked at "Girly Books" about sadomasochism and bondage. He went window-peeping at age eighteen and stole panties. He had hanged a cat, then a dog. He traveled overseas in the air force in the 1960s, and broke into people's houses while in the service.

He mentioned fantasies, drawings, pictures. "Always had to destroy them when I moved from base to base. Would start over again when the feeling starting coming back."

By his early thirties, he had tried out bondage on prostitutes. Some refused to see him again "because I was too scary."

At age thirty-two to thirty-four, "I was getting the feeling again and it was bad this time."

He listed other serial killers, including Jack the Ripper, the Boston Strangler, Ted Bundy, and Richard Speck. He wrote about them as though he had studied their crimes.

"They all got caught except the Ripper," BTK wrote. "Could I become a Killer and not get caught?"

The rambling, two-page "Eternal Triangle" list included the following:

Universe (God)-Cosmos (Holy Spirit)-Elements (Son)
Women-Man-Sex
Psycho-Serial Killer-BTK
BTK-Victim-Police

Detective-Others-Landwehr
Details-Time-Hit
Hit-Thrill-Kill

It also made reference to "PJ Board Water" and "PJ Little Key."

The last item in the package was a chilling collage: photos of children, cut from *Eagle* advertisements, with gags and bindings drawn on with a Sharpie. The words "Wichita and vicinity"—taken from the cover of the 2003 Southwestern Bell phone book—served as a headline. None of this was released to the public.

On October 26, Johnson e-mailed a short "media advisory" to local newsrooms. From the journalists' standpoint, it was unneccessarily vague: "Recently, the Wichita Police Department obtained another letter that could be connected to the BTK investigation. That letter was submitted to the Federal Bureau of Investigation on Monday, October 25, for authentication." L. Kelly's call to Johnson to confirm she was talking about the package found in the drop box was met with a curt response: "The advisory stands."

One night James Landwehr woke up after a nightmare. It took Cindy a long time to calm him. She asked him to draw and talk about what he had seen.

He was watching television, James said. There was a knock. No one else was home.

"We will never leave you alone in the house," Cindy said, interrupting him.

"But that's what was in the dream," he said.

The knocking persisted, growing louder. James opened the door. Kneeling on the Landwehrs' front stoop was a big man with a black cape and no head. He rushed in and grabbed James, who screamed.

It was a textbook case of a dream describing reality, Cindy thought. The headless man was BTK, whose face was unknown.

Rader had picked out an eleventh victim, scouting her for weeks. She was in her fifties and lived alone. Thinking of what he would do to her made him feel energized.

He'd seen the online message board chatter. He knew that some people dismissed him as old and feeble, no longer dangerous.

Old? He was fifty-nine.

Feeble? He was not feeble, and he wanted to prove it.

In the lady's living room, or perhaps in a barn, he would drill holes in a support beam, install eyebolts, and hang his next victim. He had bought cables and a come-along—the ratcheting tool used to tighten wire fence. He would create his scene like a stage director: a crucifixion, with the victim stretched by cables tied to her arms and legs. He would wrap her in plastic. When all was done, he'd set fire to the scene, leaving Landwehr to ponder what he had done.

In late October, Rader set out to scout the woman one last time. There was road construction near her house. The work slowed traffic on Second Street and constricted escape routes. This worried him; he postponed the crucifixion.

In November, Chief Williams traveled to FBI headquarters in Washington, DC, and to its specialized offices in Quantico, Virginia. He asked for additional personnel and equipment, provided background about the case, and noted that the killer's July letter included a clear threat. Soon the FBI was committing more people and computers. The task force was about to provoke a lot more tips.

On November 30, Landwehr called another news conference acknowledging that BTK "has provided certain background information about himself, which he claims is accurate."

Landwehr read more than twenty items, including the following: BTK claimed he was born in 1939, making his current age sixty-four or sixty-five. He had a cousin named Susan, who moved to Missouri. His grandfather played the fiddle and died of a lung disease. His father died in World War II. His mother dated a railroad detective. He had an Hispanic acquaintance named Petra, who had a younger sister named Tina. He had repaired copiers. He was in the military in the 1960s. He had a lifelong fascination with trains and had always lived near a railroad.

Landwehr asked for help in identifying anyone with a similar background. The amateur sleuths on the online discussion board loved it. Other people did not. A lot of people in town were sick of the BTK coverage. A caller to the *Eagle* complained: "The only reason BTK should be in the news is if he is captured. Period. The media should stop feeding into his ego with all the coverage. The scary music that TV stations add to their BTK stories is humorous, though."

BTK's "clues" led detectives down frustrating paths.

Detectives called the federal Centers for Disease Control and Prevention for help compiling a list of mining locations where people might contract lung disease. They cross-checked their suspect lists with railroad workers and hobbyists.

And how many sets of sisters named Petra and Tina, in the right age range, could there be? Police compiled a list of twenty-seven from across the nation. A dozen pairs were from the Southwest, where BTK hinted he was from. One set was from Wichita, which the online sleuths quickly discovered.

To ward off harassment, the sisters issued a written statement denying any connection to the killer—and pointing out they were of Bulgarian descent, not Hispanic.

42

December 1, 2004

Valadez

At 9:30 AM on December 1, reporter Tim Potter found several phone messages awaiting him at the *Eagle* from a good source who was frantically trying to give him a tip. About twenty cops were about to kick in a door in south Wichita and arrest someone, the caller said. It sounded like the cops thought they'd found BTK.

The address was near railroad tracks.

Potter, reporter Stan Finger, and photographers Randy Tobias and Bo Rader headed toward the location. They fanned out, in separate cars, trying not to alert the suspect. They didn't see any sign of an impending arrest: no marked cars, no signs of surveillance. Perplexed, Potter parked a couple of blocks down and watched the little white house.

At the *Eagle*, other reporters started looking up public records on the man who owned the house. Apparently he was sixty-five. He lived across the street from train tracks. He was Hispanic, as some eyewitness reports and linguists had suggested BTK might be. He had lived in Wichita his whole life.

That afternoon, as Potter drove down a side street in the working-class neighborhood, he noticed a small blue sedan following. He recognized it as one of the unmarked cars used by detectives. Potter pulled over; the sedan stopped. Out stepped Otis, looking irritated.

"What are you doing?" Otis asked.

"Working," Potter said.

Otis gave him a tight smile.

"Stay out of the way, stay out of sight, and stay off private property," Otis said.

• • •

Otis was furious. He walked back to his car, called Landwehr, and told him Potter was staking out the stakeout. Landwehr blew his stack. He told Otis to come back to the office; he called back the other detectives as well.

The *Eagle* was onto an investigation that had started early that morning with another tip. A source the police never named had tipped them that a man named Roger Valadez might be BTK.

When Gouge, Relph, and Otis went to his house to ask for a DNA sample, they saw movement through a window, but no one answered their knock. Potter had pulled within viewing distance as the cops waited to hear whether outstanding warrants—not related to BTK—would give them legal authority to enter Valadez's house.

"What do we do now?" the detectives asked Landwehr, back at their office. They were cursing reporters, dropping f-bombs. Part of it was anger; were *Eagle* reporters hunting them while they hunted BTK? Part of it was sleep deprivation; they were strung out, dead on their feet. Part of it was they really thought that this might be their guy.

Otis wondered whether reporters were following detectives when they left the city parking garage. If so, they were flirting with obstruction of justice charges.

"Fucking assholes," Landwehr called the reporters.

Potter called L. Kelly to say, "I've been made. Otis pulled me over." This sealed it. If Otis was there, it was about BTK. But this also complicated things. The reporter and detective knew the law, and they were both just doing their jobs. The journalists had a right to observe from their cars, as long as they didn't impede the cops' work. Kelly told Potter that if a cop said he was obstructing an investigation and ordered him to leave, he should back off and call her immediately; the editors would sort it out from there. But it didn't come to that. As the day wore on, reporters and photographers waited in shifts for something to happen. It looked as though the cops weren't coming back. But they might.

Dana Strongin, the *Eagle*'s night cops reporter, took her turn as the stakeout stretched into the afternoon. After several hours, Laviana drove out to let her take a dinner break. When Strongin tried to start her car, she found the battery was dead; she'd been running the heater to stay warm. Laviana said he'd jump-start her car, but it took the two of them ten minutes to get their car hoods open. Then they fumbled with cables in the dark.

Finally, about 7:30 PM, Laviana noticed a flurry of activity at the house. Minutes later, *Eagle* photographer Travis Heying's flash captured an image of Valadez being led from his home in cuffs by two uniformed cops and Detective Tim Relph.

Police hauled a few bags and boxes out of the house. They booked the man into the Sedgwick County jail on outstanding warrants alleging criminal trespass and housing code violations from years earlier—minor charges.

After things had been quiet for a while, Strongin walked up to the house. When she knocked, someone peeked out, but no one answered.

Then she saw a man with a flashlight.

"What's your name?" he asked. "Who are you with?"

She told him.

The man said he was with the KBI. Strongin recognized him as Larry Thomas, one of the agency's best homicide investigators. They were going to occupy the house for the night, he said. "You need to get off this property."

At the *Eagle*, reporters checking public records realized that the arrested man had a couple of grown children, and an ex-wife who lived in west Wichita.

Potter went to the ex-wife's address. He told the young man who answered the door that his father had been arrested and that preliminary information indicated police might consider his father to be a BTK suspect. Potter chose his words carefully.

The young man sat stunned. Children scampered around. He said they had just celebrated his father's birthday. He was retired. He'd worked at Coleman most of his life.

At the newspaper, Editor Sherry Chisenhall, Tim Rogers, L. Kelly, and others passionately debated what to report. This was a major scoop, and Potter's interview with the man's son was an *Eagle* exclusive. But what if police had the wrong man? Was it worth possibly ruining an innocent man's life—or risking a lawsuit? Reporters and editors called confidential sources close to the BTK investigation to gauge the situation.

In the end, the *Eagle* reported that something unusual had happened in south Wichita—an arrest involving a large number of police, including homicide detectives and the KBI. But Chisenhall played the story inside the paper, keeping the man's name and address, and the term "BTK," out of the story. She also temporarily held off running Potter's separate story, his interview with the man's son.

Chisenhall's instincts were right. But after the story broke at about 1:15 AM, December 2, on the *Eagle*'s website, local television stations scrambled to catch up and play the story big. They connected the dots by checking the jail's booking log. By 5:00 AM, they'd all gone live with reports from outside the man's home. One television station broadcast the man's name and called him a BTK suspect. So many gawkers gathered by 7:30 AM that radio traffic reports advised commuters to avoid the area. His neighbors were quoted on camera as saying they couldn't believe that BTK lived nearby. Reporters commented on how creepy it was seeing children's toys in his yard. The scene was broadcast on national television.

That afternoon, Chief Williams denounced the news coverage: "It is a travesty when you look at the impact, and you look at what has happened to a neighborhood because of the fact that people assume that the Wichita Police Department was making an arrest in regards to BTK." Officers had no choice but to arrest Valadez because of the old warrants, he said.

Valadez was released from jail about an hour after the chief's announcement, but he was afraid to go home. Crowds watched as cops returned a vanload of items to the house.

After getting so little out of the task force for the past nine months, Potter felt it was a coup when he got Landwehr to say on the record a few days later that Valadez had been swabbed and eliminated as a BTK suspect.

About a month after that, Valadez told Potter his version of the arrest. He had felt feverish and stayed in bed that day. Around 7:30 PM, he heard pounding on his door. Police forced it open. Valadez saw "a bunch of guys with guns." They didn't mention BTK, but they said they had a search warrant for his DNA. We're going to take it from you one way or the other, one officer said. Two officers held him by his shoulders. A third took a mouth swab. For the next several hours, investigators hauled items out of the house: papers, typewriters, photographs.

"They thought they had their man," Valadez said.

He said police trampled his family photographs and knocked holes in his walls. Later, he heard a woman on TV call him a murderer. He sued some of the news outlets over their coverage.

He knew that some facts about him matched some of the BTK background released the day before his arrest: he was the right age, he had served in the military, he lived near railroad tracks. Still, there was more to his life than that. He was a hard worker—he spent twenty-nine years at Coleman, much of that time as a manager. And he was a loving father of three, with three grandchildren. He was baffled about why the police suspected him.

Valadez later won a $1.1 million judgment against Emmis Communications, which vowed to appeal. He died a month later.

The Valadez episode left the cops feeling prickly about reporters. Landwehr reminded detectives to keep their mouths shut.

Otis worried that there was a leak on the task force. He repeatedly asked Potter to tell how he knew to go to Valadez's neighborhood. Otis even offered to trade information—"Give it to me, and I'll give you something you want." Potter declined. Otis appealed to Potter to be a "pal." Potter said he couldn't reveal his source.

As the anxiety about leaks approached paranoia, Otis himself came under suspicion. One day he saw KAKE reporter Jeanene Kiesling outside city hall. Otis thought she looked "particularly fetching" in her skirt that day, so he said hello in a moment of innocent fun. They made small talk for thirty seconds, then Otis joined a group of BTK detectives. They glared at him.

"What were you telling her?"

43

December 2004–January 2005

The First Breaks

Wichita mayor Carlos Mayans told Chief Williams one day that he had received many e-mails about the BTK case, some saying Landwehr should be replaced.

"What do you think about those e-mails?" Mayans asked.

The question upset the chief. "I'm not going to replace Lieutenant Landwehr," he said. "Kenny's the best. Who better knows the ins and outs of this case than Landwehr?"

Replacing him would send a bad message in the midst of the investigation, Williams said. He could not control public opinion, but he could control who ran the task force, and it was going to be Landwehr.

The mayor did not bring it up again. But reporters at the *Eagle* heard rumors that Landwehr was going to retire or be replaced. They asked their sources about it.

"I just want to kill some of these people who complain," Johnson told Landwehr one day.

"You don't want to kill anybody," Landwehr said. Then he smiled, unable to resist a joke. "But if you do kill someone, don't worry about it," he said. "I know how to make *anything* look like a suicide."

On December 8, Rader made another call from a pay phone to alert the media. He had not done such a thing since the day after he strangled Nancy Fox twenty-seven years earlier, but he was enjoying the publicity now. He would tell KAKE-TV where to find the latest BTK package.

"Hello, KAKE-TV," a voice said.

"This is BTK," he replied.

"Yeah, right!" the KAKE worker said. *Click*.

Irritated, Rader looked up another number and dialed.

"Helzberg Jewelers."

"This is BTK," he said. "There is—"

Click.

He tried other numbers, but people kept hanging up on him. Back in the 1970s, pranksters had terrorized women by placing such phone calls; people were determined not to fall for that kind of sick joke now.

He got mad. He called a convenience store at 3216 East Harry.

"QuikTrip," the worker said.

"Do not hang up; there is a bomb in your store. This is BTK."

That got attention. Brandon Saner, the assistant manager, came to the phone. Rader told him to write down instructions.

"I'm calling to tell you of a BTK package at Ninth and Minnesota on the northeast corner," Rader said, then hung up.

Saner called the cops.

Rader walked away from the pay phone steaming about the hang-ups. Some of the people who had hung up on him had sounded young.

This younger generation, he thought. *They don't understand what's important.*

The location Rader had given was near Murdock Park, next to Interstate 135. When Landwehr got there, he noticed an empty *Wichita Eagle* newspaper rack—a likely place to leave the package, he thought. He dug in his pocket for fifty cents. In the bottom of the rack Landwehr found paper and a piece of rope—trash. He began to walk Murdock Park with patrol officers. They looked into trash cans, peered behind bushes. It was getting dark; neighbors could see flashlights dancing like fireflies in winter.

They couldn't find the package.

Three days later, *America's Most Wanted* (*AMW*), a television show that combines crime reporting with theatrics, broadcast a BTK segment that had been filmed in Wichita. The show's producers tried to cozy up to the task force. Producers would call the police spokeswoman and say, "We're not media; we're law enforcement." Johnson would say, "No, you're media!" Undeterred, *AMW* host John Walsh announced on the show that "I'm here to catch BTK." The producers pushed the cops for inside information and gave viewers the false impression that they got it. When Walsh said on the air that he'd been asked to help with the BTK case, Chief Williams was furious; it wasn't true. Walsh's confrontational *We're-coming-after-you!* style irritated the chief because it ran counter to Landwehr's strategy of trying to establish a dialogue with BTK.

AMW aired incorrect information in its broadcast and its live online chat room, where members of the so-called America's Most Wanted BTK Task Force collected viewers' questions and tips. During the online discussion, an *AMW* employee identified as "BTK_Task_Force3" wrote that BTK wore camouflage and hid his face during the 1974 attack on Kathryn and Kevin Bright. Not true.

Not all reviews from the cops were unflattering. "I have nothing but good things to say about Walsh," Relph said later. "He's a sincere man." Relph, Gouge, Otis, and Snyder befriended him and hoped that the show's nationwide reach would turn up something useful. Relph and Otis flew to Washington, DC, to help when the show asked viewers for tips on the case. Otis could not help liking Walsh, whose career pursuing criminals had started when his young son had been kidnapped and murdered. "Something like that never leaves you, no matter what happens after," Otis said later.

Rader first began to give up some of his trophies when he left a package in Murdock Park containing, among other items, Nancy Fox's driver's license and a doll bound up like one of his victims.

In the case of BTK, the show generated lots of attention but no good leads.

Late on December 13, a man named William Ronald Ervin saw a package near a tree as he walked through Murdock Park. He took it to his mother's house. The small white trash bag contained a clear plastic zip bag. Inside was a doll with its hands tied behind its back, several sheets of paper held against the doll with rubber bands, and the driver's license of Nancy Fox, who had been dead for twenty-seven years. Ervin's mother recognized the name. She glanced at the television and saw a news tip phone number for KAKE-TV on the screen.

After a cameraman arrived at the house and shot video of the package lying on the carpet, KAKE called the cops. On Landwehr's orders, an officer walked in, picked up the package, and walked out. KAKE didn't get the shot.

Landwehr was intrigued by how pristine Nancy's driver's license looked; BTK had taken care of it. He had punched a small hole at one edge so that he could tie it with white string to the doll's ankles.

Landwehr and Chief Williams were even more intrigued that BTK had sent them the license. Serial killers never give up trophies, but BTK had. Was he getting rid of incriminating souvenirs? Was he dying and using his trophies to have some fun at the last? Maybe he thought the cops were getting close, Williams suggested—maybe he was unloading evidence.

BTK had drawn pubic hair on the half-naked doll and wrapped panty hose around its neck.

A two-page letter, titled "CHAPTER 9, HITS: PJ FOX TAIL-12-8-1977" showed that BTK was proud of what he had done—and that he wanted to give the cops a lot of information.

I spotted Nancy one day while cruising the area. . . . Found out her name by checking her mail box and tracked her to work. . . . Up close I visited the store where she worked, asking for some jewelry on display and bought some cheap jewelry (By the way the jewelry I stole from Nancy I gave to another girl friend). Natural I didn't tell my girl friend where it came from.

BTK was beginning to write in a confiding, conversational tone.

On that date I parked a few blocks away and walked to her apartment. Cut the phone line and broke in, waiting. She came home, enters and was confronted in the kitchen, she was startled and started to get the phone. I told her I had knife and display the magnum in my shoulder hoister. We talked about sex and the harm if she didn't cooperate. She lit a smoke while we chatted and finally she said lets get this over with, so I can call the police.

He let her go to the bathroom, made her disrobe, then hand-cuffed her.

I pulled down her panties, quickly slip my belt over her head and on to the neck and pulled tight but not the final strangle hold. Her hands found my scrotum and she try to dig into my balls but I pulled tighter this increase my sexual thrill. I release the strangle hold and let her come back after she passed out, I spoke softly into her left ear. I was wanted for the Oteros and others murders and she was next. She begun to really struggle then and I did the final hold, this my torture mental and re-strangle (SBT).

KAKE news director Glen Horn, a thirty-eight-year-old veteran of intense local media competition in South Florida, had reminded his staff to always cooperate with police. But he also thought KAKE and all Wichita news media had been too accommodating to the cops. Horn said he never would have agreed to sit on the "BTK resurfaces" story for two days, as the *Eagle* had done in March. He was tired of how the cops refused to answer questions, even when the BTK messages came to KAKE. He did not think that was fair to viewers, who were also taxpayers and potential BTK victims. He didn't think it was too much to expect to get a few questions answered and video of the cops doing something, such as opening a BTK package.

We should never interfere with the investigation, he thought. *But we should never be naive, either.*

Several of BTK's drop locations were close to I-135 and he was working his way north. Landwehr wondered whether police should put up pole cameras on the interstate so investigators could check every license plate that had passed on days when BTK made his drops. They talked about it, but it just wasn't practical. Thousands of drivers used I-135 every day.

They would get no clear images; some cars would be obscured by other vehicles as they passed at sixty miles per hour.

They decided instead to try to coax BTK into taking more risks.

On January 4, Wichita endured one of the most destructive ice storms in its history. Rain fell heavily and froze quickly on tree limbs, which began to break off and pull down power lines. The breaking limbs sounded like cannon fire for hours. The next day, as tens of thousands of powerless Wichitans filled up local motels, and the *Eagle*'s newsroom had mobilized to cover the storm, Landwehr made another public statement.

"The investigation has revealed that a necklace belonging to Nancy Fox could not be accounted for after her murder. The necklace in question is described as a gold chain with two pearls that were set vertically. Police believe that . . . BTK may have given the necklace to a woman he was dating at the time." He asked that "anyone who believes they have seen this necklace, or received a similar necklace as a gift in December of 1977 or the early months of 1978 please call the BTK tip line. . . ."

Police released a photo of Nancy wearing the necklace. They hoped that someone would recognize it. They also hoped Landwehr's talk would manipulate BTK into communicating again.

It did.

Four days after the ice storm, a man driving a black Jeep Cherokee drove into the parking lot of the Home Depot on North Woodlawn in northeast Wichita. The lot was packed. Thousands of tree limbs had fallen; Home Depot was selling a lot of chain saws. Automated security cameras recorded a blurry image of a vehicle circling the lot a few times, then parking. The driver walked to a nearby pickup truck and stood beside it. He appeared to put something into the bed of the truck.

Then he drove away.

Edgar Bishop worked at Home Depot. His friend Kelly Paul noticed a Special K cereal box in the truck bed. Written on the box in block letters were the words "BOMB" and "BTK PRE—"

Bishop thought it was a joke. When he and Paul opened the box, they found a beaded necklace and several pages of computer-typed notes.

There was a page labeled "BOOM" with a note saying that anyone entering "BTK's LAIR" would touch off an explosion. On another page there was a long list of "PJ'S," including a paragraph about P. J. Wyatt.

It looked silly. Bishop thought someone was pulling his leg. He threw it all in the trash.

The Reverend Terry Fox had grown his Immanuel Baptist Church by hundreds of members in recent years by preaching a conservative religious message and by reaching out to families, including the poor. He'd become prominent statewide a few months before by leading an effort to put an anti-gay-marriage amendment on a statewide referendum. Fox now decided to focus on the city's most prominent worry. He called for a community prayer meeting on January 11 to persuade BTK to confess his sins.

Some local pastors accused him of seeking publicity, but Fox persisted. He had hoped hundreds of people would show, but with people still living in shelters or motels and cleaning up after the storm, the church ended up welcoming only about a hundred people into its gymnasium. Two were cops: Deputy Chief Robert Lee and BTK Task Force Detective Kelly Otis.

Rader left this Kellogg's Special K box featuring actress Courtney Thorne-Smith in the bed of a pickup truck in the parking lot of a Home Depot. This was the beginning of the end for Rader, as his Jeep Cherokee was caught on video by the security cameras.

Fox called the killer to action: "You have obviously made very poor choices, even tragic choices, up to this point. As a pastor, I am calling on you today to make the right choice in surrendering so that you can never hurt anyone again."

No one came forward. At the back of the gym, Otis studied faces in the crowd.

The detectives had donated a lot of off-duty time, but the department was racking up overtime numbers that strained the budget, and there were other bills to pay. So it was with gratitude that the chief took several calls from a Kansas congressman. Republican representative Todd Tiahrt in January arranged that $1 million in federal money be sent to help the cops. To get it, Tiahrt had buttonholed House Speaker Dennis Hastert and Republican Majority Leader Tom DeLay, sometimes in their offices, sometimes on the House floor.

Williams and Landwehr were delighted. They used the money for overtime, rental cars, computers, DNA testing, and a long list of other needs.

Though grateful, they asked Tiahrt to keep his work on their behalf secret. Johnson told him they didn't want BTK to know. Tiahrt agreed.

"But if you catch him, I want to be there," he said.

On January 25, KAKE received a postcard from BTK. The return address was "S Killett" at "803 N. Edgemoor," a reference to the Otero home. This missive was labeled "Communication #: 8."

> *Date: Week of 1-17-2005*
> *Where: Between 69th N and 77th N on Seneca St.*
> *Contents : Post Tosties Box,C-9. PJ-Little Mex. & Doll,*
> *Haunt of KS, Acronym List and Jewelry.*

There was more, but news director Glen Horn told a KAKE reporter, Chris Frank, to drive immediately to the isolated rural road BTK mentioned and see if there was a package.

Horn then tried to decide what to tell the cops. He had tried, as the BTK story had unfolded, to do the right thing, sometimes consulting with journalism ethics experts at the Poynter Institute. He badly wanted KAKE to have exclusive access to whatever happened next.

He called the cops to say KAKE had a postcard.

Landwehr told Otis to go get it.

Otis hurried into the KAKE lobby minutes later and asked Horn for the postcard. To his amazement, Horn started trying to negotiate a deal. Horn told him he wanted video of the cops opening the package if one was found at the location named in the postcard. He also wanted Chief Williams to come to KAKE so they could get video of him.

"This is a homicide investigation," Otis told Horn. "I need that message now." But Horn kept talking, in a brusque tone.

Otis pulled out his cell phone, called Landwehr, and explained in a few curt words what Horn wanted. Otis then handed his cell phone to Horn. "He wants to talk to you," Otis said grimly.

Horn took the phone.

"I am not gonna sit here and play *Let's Make a Deal* with you," Landwehr said. "Detective Otis needs that information now. You will either give that information to Detective Otis immediately, or he's going to start arresting you and your people one at a time until your building is emptied out. He'll arrest you for interfering with a homicide investigation."

"All right," Horn said.

Horn handed the phone back, then handed Otis the postcard.

Otis read it and walked out.

Horn would say later that it would not have bothered him to go to jail. "Throw me a harmonica and I would have sat in jail and played a song," was how he put it. He wondered whether he had been too insistent with Otis. "On the other hand, being nice hadn't gotten us anywhere, and I was tired of it."

The BTK postcard had contained one more cryptic and tantalizing clue:

Let me know some how if you or Wichita PD received this. Also let me know if you or PD received # 7 at Home Depot. Drop Site 1-8-05. Thanks.

Before he called the cops, Horn had sent news anchor Larry Hatteberg to the two area Home Depots: "Start asking around if they've seen anything unusual."

• • •

As he left KAKE, Otis called Gouge and Relph and told them to head to North Seneca.

When Otis got there, he found Gouge, Relph, and several people from KAKE-TV, including reporters Chris Frank and Jeanene Kiesling. Everyone was looking at a Post Toasties cereal box festooned with a red crepe streamer, weighed down with a brick, leaning against the base of a road-curve sign.

Gouge was unhappy. This stretch of Seneca was dirt; the reporters had driven right up the road and swerved close to the sign, obliterating any tire tracks that might have been there. Then they had walked to within a foot of the box, leaving footprints in the soft sand; any hope of finding BTK footprints was gone.

Gouge pointed to cigarette butts lying within a few feet of the box. Cops love to find cigarette butts at crime scenes—they can test them for DNA. Gouge told Otis he was going to collect them until Kiesling told him they were hers. The more Otis heard, the more he got pissed off. They would have to swab Kiesling now. Maybe they should make an exception in her case, and obtain her DNA with a needle and syringe. "*I want blood,*" Otis thought.

Otis looked around. They were in a rural area north of Wichita, between the towns of Valley Center and Park City.

Why did BTK put this stuff here? It occurred to him that they were standing within long walking distance of Park City, the hometown of Dolores Davis and Marine Hedge . . . two women strangled, with their phone lines cut.

Landwehr showed up a few minutes later with a police lab specialist, Patrick Cunningham. Landwehr was still hot about the conversation with Horn; he was thinking about asking District Attorney Nola Foulston if KAKE was obstructing justice. Landwehr got more irritated when detectives showed him the cigarette butts and footprints.

Landwehr glanced over at the KAKE reporters.

"Did they open the box?" Landwehr asked.

"They said they didn't, but who knows," a detective replied.

"Chris, did you touch the box?" Landwehr asked in his usual cordial tone.

None of them had touched it, but Chris Frank, knowing Landwehr had a playful streak, made a little joke. "I was tempted to open it, but I didn't have any milk to go with the cereal."

"Well, Chris," Landwehr said evenly, "if you had touched the box, I would have made sure that Nola gave you all the milk you needed in jail."

Frank smiled. He thought Landwehr was joking.

Landwehr walked back to his detectives. "If we find any indication that they opened it, there are a whole bunch of newspeople who are going to go to jail today," he said.

Otis showed him the postcard. Landwehr sent Gouge and Relph to check out the Home Depots. When they arrived at the store on North Woodlawn, they saw a KAKE truck already there. Hatteberg was inside, interviewing people ahead of the detectives.

This is why we don't like the media, Gouge thought.

In the Post Toasties box, the detectives found the usual BTK creep show: a note, "BTK'S ACRONYM LIST," and another doll, this one with a gag across the mouth and cords binding the wrists, waist, knees, and ankles. The doll was naked from the waist down, with the pubic area darkened by a marker. Rough rope connected the doll's neck to a short piece of white

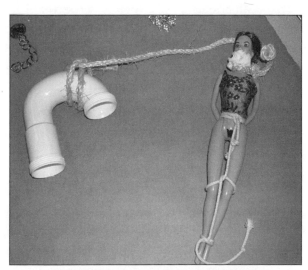

A doll representing Josie Otero was found in a Post Toasties box left by Rader leaning against a sign on Seneca Street.

plastic pipe. Landwehr recognized it as a taunting reminder of Josie Otero.

The note showed yet again that BTK fancied himself some sort of cop or secret agent. Cops love abbreviations; BTK loved them too, and had used a number of them in this note. He explained that SBT meant Sparky Big Time, or masturbation. SXF was sexual fantasy. DBS was Death By Strangulation. DTPG was Death to Pretty Girl. There were many more.

There was no reference to the other package mentioned on the postcard, and interviews and searches at the two Home Depot stores turned up nothing. Detectives asked store managers to post a notice in the employee break rooms, asking whether anyone had seen or found anything strange in recent weeks.

Otis wasn't the only person to note that the Seneca Street cereal box was found so close to Park City and to wonder whether BTK had killed two more people than the cops had acknowledged. Two days after the Seneca Street package was found, the *Eagle* published a story by Laviana and Potter pointing out the possible link between the Hedge and Davis homicides and the BTK case. They quoted former cops who said investigators had long suspected the Park City murders were related. Laviana, who had covered both homicides years before, wrote that Park City residents had gossiped about this link for years.

When Edgar Bishop saw the notice in the Home Depot break room, he came forward immediately, telling the cops about the Special K cereal box in the bed of his pickup two weeks earlier.

Bishop had thrown it away, but then he had gone on vacation—so his trash cart hadn't been taken to the curb and dumped. He still had the package.

Otis and Detective Cheryl James delivered it to the FBI lab. They saw BTK's description of how he intended to blow up his house with a propane and gasoline bomb if the cops entered it. That prompted a flip suggestion from Relph and Otis, who were still angry with the *Eagle* for showing up outside Roger Valadez's house two months before. They joked that if BTK's house really was rigged to blow up, the cops ought to invite the *Eagle* to go in first.

Landwehr smiled.

Much of the writing in the Special K box was the usual egocentric material. He liked to call himself "Rex," Latin for "king," for example. But the note labeled "COMMICATION" was intriguing:

Can I communicate with Floppy and not be traced to a computer. Be honest. Under Miscellaneous Section, 494, (Rex, it will be OK), run it for a few days in case I'm out of town-etc. I will try a floppy for a test run some time in the near future-February or March.

Was he serious?

Otis thought BTK was blowing more smoke. Gouge, Snyder, and Relph agreed. Did BTK think he could communicate with a floppy disk and not leave a trail? Was he stupid enough to think that the cops would "be honest" about whether a disk was traceable? Of course a floppy was traceable.

"He's just playing with us," Otis said.

"Maybe," Landwehr said. "But we'll try him out anyway."

He prepared to place a personal ad in the miscellaneous section of the *Eagle*'s classified ads.

"Be honest," BTK had written.

As a young cop, Landwehr had worked undercover, growing his hair to his shoulders, dressing sloppily, pretending to sell stolen goods. Landwehr had learned he was not good at undercover work because he was no good at lying. It wasn't that he was opposed to lying to criminals; he was just no good at it.

But if BTK really was asking for advice about whether a floppy disk was traceable, Landwehr intended to lie to the best of his ability.

He sent Detective Cheryl James to the *Eagle*.

James told a classified ad clerk that her name was Cyndi Johnson. She gave a fake telephone number and said that she needed to run an ad for seven consecutive days, starting immediately. The clerk charged her $76.35.

The ad began as BTK has instructed: "Rex, it will be OK. . . ."

• • •

The detectives fanned out all over town, checking UPC codes and visiting Dollar General stores to determine where BTK shopped for cereal and dolls. And the swabbing continued.

A code on the cereal box left at Home Depot showed that it came from the Leeker's grocery at 61st and North Broadway in Park City—just north of Wichita—near I-135.

Tim Potter's Marine Corps father had survived combat on Guadalcanal, Okinawa, and other Pacific islands in World War II. Potter learned that if he was patient, he could draw his father out and get him to talk about the brutality of war, along with its moments of humanity.

As a reporter, Potter made a subspecialty of writing about trauma—when murders occurred, he sought out family survivors and asked them to talk. Unlike most crime reporters, Potter seldom swore, and never told macabre jokes. He wrote with insight about tragedy, using interviews with survivors to create mini-portraits of the dead. He had often been

Landwehr communicated with BTK through the Eagle's classified section.

surprised at how willing survivors were to talk—it seemed therapeutic to them.

With the cops shutting down almost all comment about BTK, Potter had found other ways to write about the case between breaking news developments. He tried for months to get an interview with the owner of the Otero house. One day, she called him in desperation. Three days after the Seneca Street package was found, the *Eagle* published the story about her.

Her name was Buffy Lietz, and she and her husband lived at the corner of Murdock and Edgemoor. Around their little house, they had planted irises, roses, daffodils, and lilies of the valley. Potter was the first reporter she let into the tiny house. She had hung up on *America's Most Wanted* five times until she finally let them in so that they would film their segments and go away. Kids had come to her back door and pressed their faces against the glass, even before BTK had resurfaced the year before. People parked across the street and stared. Pictures of her house had appeared on the Internet. She was sick of strangers coming by. "It feels creepy," she told Potter.

She and her husband had bought the house years earlier without realizing it was a murder site. They just wanted to be left alone.

Potter felt ghoulish doing his job. He stood in the kitchen where BTK had confronted the family. L. Kelly had insisted that he must see the basement where Josie Otero had died.

When he asked Lietz if he could go down there, she said no.

The Home Depot parking lot at North Woodlawn had three security cameras. Landwehr, his detectives, and FBI agents studied the tapes until they figured out which truck in the busy lot belonged to employee Edgar Bishop. As they watched the January 8 tapes, they saw a series of images that they put together in the sequence of a story.

At first it was all blur, hundreds of vehicles pulling in and out.

But then they noticed something interesting: a vehicle circled the lot several times. At 2:37 PM, a man got out of that vehicle, approached Bishop's truck, and walked around it. It appeared that he might be writing down Bishop's tag number. Then the man appeared to put something into the truck and walk away.

They rolled the tape backward, forward, backward, forward.

They traced the man back to his own vehicle.

Backward, forward, backward, forward.

They could not make out what kind of vehicle he drove. They enhanced the video. They analyzed the slope of the hood, the slant of the windshield, the reach of the wheelbase. . . .

BTK drove a dark-colored Jeep Cherokee.

Detectives raced to the computers and checked motor vehicle records.

How many dark-colored Jeep Cherokees were there in the Wichita area?

Only twenty-five hundred.

With a few strokes on a computer keyboard, Landwehr's detectives had dramatically narrowed the suspect list.

And on the video, for the first time, they had seen a glimpse of BTK.

44

February 2005

The Big Break

On February 3, KAKE received a postcard in which BTK thanked the station "for your quick response on # 7 and 8" and thanked "the News Team for their efforts." He said to tell the police "that I receive the Newspaper Tip for a go," and promised "Test run soon."

Landwehr planned to call the bomb squad and x-ray the next package before opening it. But that raised an additional problem: If BTK's next package contained a floppy disk, would the X-ray scramble the information on it? The cops bought computer disks and checked them out. Tests showed the information would survive an X-ray.

Knowing that did little to relieve the burden Landwehr carried. At home, he and Cindy had finally brought some peace of mind to James, who had endured night terrors and slept in his parents' bed with the light on after BTK had resurfaced. His parents had convinced him that BTK was too old and too careful to stalk the child of a police lieutenant who had patrol cars cruising past the house every hour. Landwehr was trying to stay connected to the boy despite his long hours on the job. Landwehr was still losing weight, or so the chief thought; his men thought Landwehr's hair had gotten a lot grayer.

The renewed hunt had lasted ten months now. Landwehr was tired.

Rader was getting tired, too. His method of scaring people required work: write the message, being careful not to give away clues. Always wear gloves. Drive to a copy machine and copy the message. Then drive to several more locations to recopy it, often reducing the type. Recopying and trimming the edges of the paper made it harder for the cops to find which machines he used. He was tired of the driving around. He had a job and was still stalking women; it added up to time and effort. He was thinking of streamlining his tasks—which was why he had thought of the computer disk.

He used a computer at work, but he wasn't terribly computer savvy. To be careful, he had made discreet inquiries, and had asked Landwehr. He thought the cops could not trace a disk.

He enjoyed the game with Landwehr. He knew Landwehr was talking to him, and he appreciated it. In the great, grand game that they played together, they matched wits, and the bad guy always won. He wanted it to go on forever, and he suspected Landwehr did too.

For a long time, single mother Kimberly Comer had lived in fear of Park City compliance officer Dennis Rader.

She had moved to Park City a year and a half ago, and soon noticed a little red truck with tinted windows. The guy inside took Polaroids of her and her kids. She thought he might be stalking her and her roommate, Michelle McMickin. McMickin called Park City police. But when officers came, they acted as if they knew who it was—and as if they didn't care. Comer could not figure this out. Shortly after that, she actually met the guy. He was driving a white city truck and said he was the Park City compliance officer. He lectured her about belongings she had left in her carport.

Over the next several months, Rader handed Comer citations and warnings. Sometimes he put his head into her open kitchen window and looked around. He interviewed her children about her.

After she complained to Park City officials, he came more often. He claimed a 1995 Firebird she'd parked in her yard was inoperable. She got more rattled every time he talked to her. He creeped her out even after he did something nice for her kids. In early 2005, Comer's children, eleven-year-old Kelsey and nine-year-old Jordan, were playing at a park. A big black dog began to bark and chase them. Kimberly was at home two blocks away.

Rader, driving by, saw the dog chasing the children, ran into the park, scooped up the kids, and put them in his truck. He took them to their home and gave them sticker badges and his business card. He was nice, the kids said.

But then he started harassing Comer about her "inoperable" car again. At the first Park City court hearing regarding her car a few weeks later, Comer drove to the city building. She told Rader her "inoperable" vehicle was parked outside. Rader declined to go look. Instead, he put his hand on her shoulder and told her she needed to take her complaint to the next court hearing. She walked away angry. He walked away unperturbed.

He had a lot on his mind. He'd been doing a lot of writing lately.

Within days of sending that message to the cops threatening to blow them up in his lair, Rader had accepted a position with Christ Lutheran Church in northeast Wichita as president of the congregation. The church member who asked him to take that position, *Eagle* assistant photo editor Monty Davis, admired him because he was hardworking and dependable.

On February 16, a receptionist at Fox affiliate KSAS-TV found a padded envelope in the mail, gaily decorated with seven thirty-seven-cent American flag stamps. "P. J. Fox" was the name on the return address. Within a short time, the television staff was calling the cops. A crew from KWCH-TV, which produced the Fox station's newscast, took video of the contents: a gold chain and pendant, and three index cards—one of which told the cops how they should get back in touch with BTK through yet another newspaper ad. There was also a purple computer disk.

Gouge and Otis walked into the station minutes later, saw the stuff spread out on a table, and became impatient to take the items and leave. A disk! Could it be? Otis began to interview the receptionist, while Gouge talked to station managers, politely but bluntly telling them: "Do *not* broadcast any of the film you took here—and call Lieutenant Ken Landwehr before you do anything more. Do not broadcast or say anything about the disk."

They agreed. Gouge did not want these people tipping off viewers that the cops were trading messages with BTK through newspaper ads, and he didn't want it out that there was a computer disk from BTK now in police possession. If KWCH and KSAS broadcast that, the investigation would be compromised—reporters would immediately interview computer experts and BTK would learn that disks are easily traced.

The two detectives gathered up the items and left. Gouge drove. Otis pulled out his cell phone. "Get Randy Stone ready," Otis told Landwehr. "We've got a computer disk in the package." Stone was the task force's computer whiz.

The drive back to the Epic Center, where the task force was now based, took only minutes but seemed longer. Otis, talking with Gouge, was still skeptical: "He's probably deliberately done a disk where he used it at a public computer, so we'll show up and shake the place down, while he stands back and watches us."

Gouge drove to the Epic Center as fast as the law would allow. When he and Otis got there, they walked into the third-floor office where the task force gathered and gave the disk to Stone. Gouge thought the computer disk might yield a tiny clue, which would have to be matched to the name of someone driving a dark-colored Jeep Cherokee. He thought that would take a lot of time and work.

Stone loaded the disk into his computer, with Landwehr, Relph, Gouge, Otis, Snyder, Cheryl James, and FBI agent John Sullivan standing behind him. Kim Parker and Kevin O'Connor were there too, from the

Rader was president of the congregation
at Christ Lutheran Church in North Wichita.

district attorney's office. They had all learned to hold their excitement until proof arrived. Gouge thought it might take days to sort this out.

Stone quickly called up "TestA.rtf," the message BTK had created for them: It read: *"This is a test. See 3 X 5 Card for details on communication with me in the Newspaper."*

Stone then clicked onto the "properties" field of the file. And then, in plain letters, they read the name "Dennis." The screen also told them the disk had been in a computer registered to Christ Lutheran Church and had last been used at the Park City Community Public Library.

"Look at that," someone said excitedly. Was it going to be this easy?

James and Sullivan sat down at computers nearby and searched the Internet for "Christ Lutheran Church." This took only seconds. They called up the website and pointed to the name of the congregation president: Dennis Rader.

"Oh my God!" someone said.

They had a name.

Gouge, Snyder, and the rest of them looked on in amazement.

James then used ChoicePoint to get Dennis Rader's address: 6220 Independence Street, Park City.

There was the sound of scuffling feet. Stone turned from his computer and saw that all the detectives had bolted for the door.

Snyder and Relph raced north; Gouge and Otis tried to catch them, but they weren't even close. Gouge later claimed that he and Relph traded paint as they zoomed separate cars north on I-135 to Park City, but the truth was that by the time Gouge pulled his car into Dennis Rader's neighborhood, Relph was hundreds of yards ahead, and Snyder, sitting beside him, was feeling fear: Relph's driving was scary even when he wasn't on some sort of mission from God. As they rolled north, James called on a cell phone to tell them that a computer search had turned up no evidence that Rader owned a Jeep Cherokee.

They drove on, fearing another big disappointment. "Maybe BTK is setting up Dennis Rader," Snyder said.

Relph turned a corner and headed south on Independence, watching numbers fly by on the mailboxes. He saw Rader's house just as Snyder started yelling: "There's a Jeep in the driveway!"

Relph saw a black Cherokee. Snyder let out another wild yell and punched Relph in the arm again and again. Snyder yelled "Slow down!" then "Speed up!" almost in the same breath as he tried to read the Cherokee's tag number. Relph shot past the house, then slammed on the brakes, hit the gas and spun the car in a half-doughnut, tires squealing. "Shit!" Relph said, embarrassed. "So much for staying low-profile." They could not afford to tip off BTK.

It dawned on them that their car and Otis and Gouge's car were both Ford Tauruses, each carrying two men wearing suits. They might as well paint the words "COP CARS" on the sides. "Tell those guys to stay back," Relph told Snyder. Snyder called Otis and relayed the message.

"Relph is saying don't drive by the house," Otis told Gouge.

"Fuck Relph!" Gouge said. "I'm driving by—I want to see it myself."

"No, no, don't do that, man," Otis said, laughing. "You don't want to do that."

"Yeah, I do," Gouge said. But he stopped the car.

Parked half a block from Rader's house, Snyder called Landwehr to tell him about the Jeep Cherokee and ask what to do. If Landwehr gave the word, Snyder said, he would happily tear Rader's door off the hinges and pull him onto the pavement. He guessed, as he talked, that the four of them would stake out the house and wait for a lot of other cops to surround it before they went through the doors. But he thought they shouldn't wait long. *What if BTK got a tip that they were onto him? BTK might kill himself or burn his evidence if he still had it. What if there was a leak to the media now, like with the Valadez thing?*

Landwehr listened as Snyder told him about the Cherokee. "I'll get back with you," Landwehr said. And he hung up.

Otis and Gouge parked at one end of Rader's street; Relph and Snyder parked at the other. They waited and watched. Time had flown. The call from KSAS had come in the morning. It was now just after noon.

Cheryl James called again; she had found a Cherokee after all, registered to Brian Rader, Dennis's son.

They wondered if Rader was at the house. They wondered if he had a surveillance camera, and if the house was rigged to explode with propane tanks and gasoline.

"It's absolutely him," Snyder told Relph. "BTK has no idea that we saw the Home Depot tape and that we know he's got a Jeep Cherokee. So there's no way he could have set up someone else by planting the Cherokee on him. It's him!"

Relph agreed. This would be over in no time.

But when Landwehr called back, he surprised them all.

"We're going to bring you back home and plan this deal out," he told them. "We're not going to do this now."

Snyder and Relph sat in disbelief. They had BTK! After thirty-one years he was only a hundred yards away, but Landwehr told them to come home.

From the south, unmarked cars drove off the I-135 exit ramps into Park City. The cars, with two undercover cops apiece, took up positions at either end of Rader's short street. They would stay all night. Landwehr had told them to be careful; Park City had only seven thousand people. People in small towns notice strangers easily.

The detectives drove back to Wichita. On the way, as the adrenaline began to subside, Snyder talked it through with Relph. They decided that after three decades they should not hurry and risk blowing the arrest or the court case. Landwehr was making the right call.

It galled them to drive south, though.

At the task force offices back at the Epic Center, Deputy District Attorney Kevin O'Connor watched Landwehr take that call from Snyder. "I'll get back to you," Landwehr had said. Then he closed his cell phone and said something about needing to do things right.

O'Connor would never forget what happened next.

Landwehr made a little joke, poking fun at Snyder "for wanting to tear Rader's front door off its hinges."

Landwehr sat still for a moment or two.

Then he said, to those standing around him, that he would pull the task force detectives back into the office and take a long, slow approach to arresting Dennis Rader. Given the fear of leaks that had plagued the task force since Valadez, O'Connor was surprised.

But Landwehr said that he didn't want to screw up the case, that he didn't want to be wrong. He wanted the court case, if there was a court case, to be clean and solid. *It took guts to make this decision*, O'Connor thought.

Landwehr had a plan on how to be absolutely sure that Rader was BTK.

As he listened to Landwehr describe it, O'Connor began to smile.

"BTK had stalked people for thirty years," O'Connor said later. "And you know it's him, and that you can prove it. And yet Landwehr held back, because he wanted to make sure it was done right, in spite of the danger of media leaks, in spite of all the pressure. He had mentally prepared himself for this moment long before. I'm sure he'd thought it through years before: 'What if we actually find this guy? How do we arrest him? How do we prepare?' It was clear that he had already thought it through."

Gouge, Otis, Relph, and Snyder arrived at the Epic Center almost high on excitement. There were high fives and hugs and bets: surely Rader was their guy. But around them, while they celebrated, other detectives moved the case forward. Cheryl James and others were quickly amassing a pile of paper on tabletops, outlining names, addresses, phone numbers, and descriptions of relationships involving Rader's relatives, friends, coworkers, and other connections.

Landwehr now told the detectives what he had already told O'Connor and the others. He wanted to get the DNA of someone related to Rader—without tipping off Rader or his family—and see whether the family DNA was a close match to BTK. This was no surprise to the detectives. Landwehr had used this technique before, with other crimes, other men, and other families.

James had established through records that Rader had a daughter named Kerri. Landwehr said they could track down her doctors, obtain her medical files, and get a subpoena for an old Pap smear sample without her knowing it. A database search showed that Kerri Rader had gone to Kansas State University in Manhattan, two and a half hours northeast of Wichita. Ray Lundin had graduated from K-State and served as a law enforcement officer in Riley County, where Manhattan is located. He recognized one of her addresses as a residence hall. Lundin thought she might have gotten checkups at the student health center. He would go there.

Landwehr tried to sleep a little that night, in spite of the excitement ahead. He needed to put a huge arrest plan together, but he also needed to go in front of the cameras one last time and talk reassuringly to BTK.

Landwehr's plan to get the daughter's DNA touched off another vigorous debate in the district attorney's office. O'Connor was all for letting the cops obtain the DNA in secret, but Foulston, his boss, demanded to know how this did not violate Kerri Rader's privacy rights. The young woman had done nothing wrong, as far as was known. Even if taking her DNA in secret were legal, Foulston said, it was nevertheless personal, potentially embarrassing to Kerri Rader, and invasive.

"Isn't there any other way to get DNA, including from Rader himself?" Foulston asked.

"Not a good way," O'Connor replied. "That CSI stuff we see on TV . . . it doesn't work that way in real life."

"Don't bullshit me, Kevin," she told him. "Can we justify this legally? Tell me all the reasons we should do this. But then tell me all the reasons we shouldn't."

"We're trying to catch someone who has killed people," O'Connor said. "And given the evidence and the circumstances, I sure wouldn't worry about anyone suing for privacy violations."

Foulston later met with Landwehr and the task force and agreed to let them do it. But she felt sorry for Kerri Rader and wished there was another way.

At ten o'clock February 17, Landwehr walked into the fifth-floor briefing room in city hall and conducted another news conference. As usual, he kept his tone remote and formal, and his face betrayed nothing. Once again, he spoke directly to BTK:

"The Behavioral Analysis Unit of the FBI has confirmed two letters as authentic communications from BTK," he began. "The letter that was dropped in a UPS box at Second and Kansas streets in October 2004 has been authenticated. This communication contained information about

BTK that was subsequently released to the public on November 30, 2004. The FBI can confirm that it's a BTK communication, but cannot confirm the accuracy of the information he wrote about himself in the letter.

"The other communication that the FBI has confirmed is from BTK is the package that was located in December by a Wichita resident in Murdock Park. This package contained the driver's license belonging to Nancy Fox, which BTK took with him from the crime scene.

"Recent communications from BTK have included several items of jewelry. There was jewelry included in the Post Toasties box that was left on North Seneca Street . . . and in the package received yesterday by KSAS-Fox 24. The contents of yesterday's KSAS-Fox 24 communication have been sent to the FBI.

"We are in the process of determining whether or not any of this jewelry belonged to our victims."

Landwehr looked up from his printed text and addressed the cameras in a friendlier tone, as though talking to someone he knew.

"I have said before . . . that the BTK investigation is the most challenging case I have ever worked on, and that BTK would be very interesting to talk with. I still contend that this is our most challenging case, but I am very pleased with the ongoing dialogue through these letters."

In Park City, undercover cops spied on the house from a distance.

At the Epic Center offices, Landwehr and the cops frantically laid plans. Gouge heard some fancy ideas being discussed, everything from creeping up and sticking little tracking devices onto Rader's trucks to bringing in FBI surveillance planes to watch him from the heavens. They wanted Rader to lead them to his stash of evidence. They thought he might have hidden it so deep that they might never find it otherwise. But as they talked, Gouge spoke up.

"Look," he said. "We've done arrests before. We know what we're doing, so let's not get so fancy; let's do this like we've done them before."

Landwehr was thinking the same thing—they should keep it simple. No tracking devices, no eye in the sky. But they still ended up with the most complicated arrest plan any of them had ever seen. By the time the chief finalized it, they had given 215 people specific assignments, including handcuffing Rader, taking him to the county jail, collecting samples of his DNA, taking his DNA to a lab, and picking up and interviewing his relatives.

Gouge wondered how they could get it all done. Typing out search warrants with Parker by his side, he stayed up until four o'clock one morning to get all the details right.

How can we do this and keep a lid on it?

Ideally they wanted to keep the arrest out of the news until they could search his property. But when Landwehr told Chief Williams he wanted to keep Rader's arrest quiet for a couple of weeks, Williams laughed.

"You're not going to get a couple of weeks," Williams said.

"Well, can we get at least a couple of days?"

Williams smiled. "You'll be lucky to get a couple of hours before this news gets out."

On February 18, two days after police linked the disk to Rader, Lundin took a subpoena to K-State. Kerri Rader was living in Michigan, but medical records from her college years were still on file with the student health center; a Pap smear sample was at a Manhattan medical laboratory. Lundin immediately got a second subpoena, plus a court order allowing him to get the Pap smear slide from the lab. Four days later, Lundin obtained Kerri Rader's tissue sample, which had been smeared on glass and encased in resin. Lundin drove forty-five miles east to the KBI lab in the state's capital, Topeka. Before he left Manhattan, though, Lundin pointed out to every medical person he talked with that the judge had ordered all of them to stay quiet about this. They were not to call Kerri Rader or tell anyone about the search.

At 6:00 AM Sunday, February 20, a Park City woman named Deana Harris suddenly needed an ambulance. She was suffering from diabetic complications, her husband was at work, and she had no phone. She sent her eleven-year-old daughter out the door. "Call 911," she told her.

The girl ran across Independence Street. Dennis Rader answered his door and quickly showed her to his telephone. The Raders were cooking breakfast. He told her that they were getting ready for church.

The girl called 911, then ran back to her mother. The man called out to her, "I hope your mommy will be okay."

On Thursday morning, February 24, Sindey Schueler, a KBI biology supervisor in Topeka, began to extract DNA from the Pap smear.

Lundin had told her only that the task force had "a good suspect" in the BTK case and that the smear might help. Schueler had worked for the KBI since 1991 and had tested thousands of DNA samples. This one, which was at least a couple of years old, posed a challenge. Schueler had difficulty removing the thin glass cover from the slide. It took hours to chip away microscopic pieces of the resin and the glass cover. When she finally got to the tissue, she processed the material and laid the DNA pattern out on paper: a straight line broken by peaks.

Then she compared the DNA profile of the Pap smear to the DNA profile from one of the BTK crime scenes.

That week Paula Rader noticed men she didn't know sitting in cars parked down the street.

The men had long hair and sat for hours, watching passersby.

She thought they must be undercover cops. Maybe they had found a drug dealer up the street. She did not say anything to Dennis—it was nothing worth mentioning. Dennis had been busy lately, working late.

The Wichita detectives had occasionally worked seven days a week, sometimes skipping nights of sleep; but they had homes and families to go to if they wished. Ray Lundin and Larry Thomas, the two KBI agents on loan to Landwehr, had worked just as hard and had lived out of motels for the past ten months, away from home and family.

Lundin, back in Wichita on February 24, had just eaten some stuffed French toast at an IHOP and was taking a walk to burn off calories. On his cell phone, he saw that Schueler had just called him from the KBI lab. He called her back.

This is it, he thought. *What's it going to be?*

When they finished talking, Lundin thanked her and dialed Landwehr's cell phone.

• • •

Landwehr was at home helping James with his homework. He was still dressed in a suit and tie and was ready to drive back to the Epic Center. When his cell phone rang and he saw Lundin's name come up on the screen, Landwehr went into his garage and shut the door. He'd been expecting this call for a few hours now.

"This is Landwehr," he said.

Lundin, wanting to be as thorough as Schueler, began to repeat what she had said, step-by-step with all the technical jargon. Landwehr paced and listened. Finally, Lundin told him "two of the alleles didn't come in." Landwehr's heart sank. He knew that the DNA test Schueler conducted had thirteen genetic markers—alleles—for men, twelve for women. They were looking for all twelve to match between BTK and Kerri Rader.

"So it's not him," Landwehr said. He was deeply disappointed.

Lundin paused, surprised.

"No, it's *him*," Lundin said. It wasn't that those two alleles didn't match, it was that the old tissue sample didn't yield enough material to test in two areas. They were *ten for ten* on matching the parts they could test.

There was a brief silence; Landwehr took a breath.

"Sumbitch, we got him," Landwehr said. "Get your ass back here. And Ray? I'm going to buy you a big steak dinner."

He closed the cell phone, walked back in the house, and told Cindy he was going back to work.

Cindy watched his face. He smiled. Out of earshot of James, he pulled her aside.

"It's over, baby," he said.

He stayed in the house long enough to tuck his son into bed.

At her home, District Attorney Nola Foulston stared at a photograph on her computer screen and began to laugh. In the photo, Dennis Rader smiled and looked pleased with himself. A member of the task force had e-mailed it to her.

"You have no idea what's in store for you," Foulston told the photograph. Her son, fifteen-year-old Andrew Foulston, heard her start laughing loudly again. "What's up, Mom?" he asked. "Are you on crack?"

"No," she said. She couldn't tell him what was going on. So she just smiled.

At the command center, detectives cheered, smacked hands in high fives, hugged each other. But Relph suddenly wanted to be alone. Landwehr had an office, off to the side, and it was empty. Relph walked in and shut the door.

He had become convinced, over sixteen years of working murders, that God was always present and always kind.

People had suffered so much, but BTK was finished now. Relph got down on his knees. Tears began to stream down his face, and his lower lip began to tremble.

"I give thanks . . ." he began.

Rader's official portrait as Park City's compliance supervisor.

45

February 24, 2005

The Stalker Is Stalked

The cops worked deep into the night of February 24. Gouge typed nine search warrants and had O'Connor and Parker double-check them. They needed a judge to sign the warrants, but prosecutors thought news reporters might stake out Sedgwick County's criminal court judges, watching for who might be going in and out. Parker called Judge Gregory Waller and asked him to walk up the street to the task force headquarters in the Epic Center.

Janet Johnson planned how to announce the arrest to the world. She was surprised that there had been no leaks so far. Morton, the FBI profiler, was told by phone to get to Wichita from Quantico as fast as he could fly. Chief Williams had decided the best way to get BTK to confess after his arrest was to assign Landwehr and Morton to be the first interrogators.

Dan Harty and other gang officers had been swabbing people for the task force since July. It was repetitive work, and Harty was tired of it. He was startled at what Landwehr now told him: "I need you to wear a uniform tomorrow; you and Scott Moon are gonna be on the arrest team."

Landwehr said he wanted a pair of uniformed officers to start the arrest by pulling Rader over, making it look to Rader like a routine traffic stop. Landwehr wanted Harty and Moon because they'd both arrested hundreds of gangbangers, many of them armed and violent, sometimes chasing them down on foot. Landwehr was confident that his detectives could handle Rader, but he wanted Harty and Moon there, too.

A meeting at the Epic Center was hurriedly arranged to finalize plans. Landwehr, Capt. John Speer, and Deputy Chief Robert Lee found the doors locked; they waited until someone could let them in. Speer would remember the next few minutes for the rest of his life. They stood in the quiet of the parking garage, looking out on the lights of the city. Only they and a handful of other cops knew the news that the city had waited to hear for thirty-one years: BTK was going to be put in a cage. Landwehr was smiling. He and the others had never shown much affection, except with rough cop humor, but many men had hugged each other tonight. Landwehr pulled out his cigarettes and lit one.

"You know, Kenny," Lee said. "If it really is him, I'd smoke a cigarette with you." Lee had not smoked in years.

Landwehr flicked a cigarette half out of his pack and held it out to Lee. Landwehr handed another to Speer, who had quit smoking fifteen years before. Neither of the nonsmokers had a match, so Landwehr held his lighter for his two friends. Then they stood there, smoking in the silent garage.

At the meeting, the BTK detectives suddenly found themselves passed over and pissed off. The chief wanted the SWAT team, not the BTK task force, to make the arrest.

It made sense; this would be the biggest arrest the department had ever made. There was a chance that if the arrest did not come off perfectly, BTK might burn his evidence, blow up his house, kill himself, or try to take a few cops with him. The SWAT team was well-trained.

Otis fumed. There was little use in arguing. Police departments are much like military units—orders are orders.

But Otis was Otis.

"Chief, I really want to be in on that arrest."

Williams looked at him.

"Look," Otis said, "the only difference between me and the SWAT team is that a SWAT guy has a machine gun, and I don't. But you know what? I don't *need* a machine gun. We all worked this case, and we really want to do this arrest."

O'Connor thought: *Otis has got balls.*

Other detectives spoke up too. And then Landwehr. "I think these guys want to handle it, chief," he said. "And I think they ought to handle it too."

Williams nodded. "Well, no one knows BTK better than these guys."

He ordered the task force to make the arrest. Otis sat back, relieved.

Had the chief not relented, Otis would have strapped on his bulletproof vest and taken part in the arrest, anyway, hoping that body armor and a helmet would hide his identity from commanders.

Afterward, Landwehr made two calls to people he trusted. One was to Paul Holmes, the retired Ghostbuster who had served as an unofficial member of the task force. Holmes had worked hundreds of unpaid hours for the task force since BTK resurfaced. Landwehr now offered him a golden gift: Holmes could be present for the arrest.

Holmes declined.

"*What?* Oh, come on, you're gonna miss it?" Landwehr said.

Holmes had to say no. He appreciated the honor, but he was going to visit his daughter.

Landwehr also called his mother. Early on, Landwehr had asked for patrol cars to cruise past Irene's house every hour. The street officers had done their job so well that they once caught Landwehr in a moment of forgetfulness. One day he got a call from dispatchers, telling him that a white car had pulled into his mother's drive.

"Oh, shoot, that's my mother's new car," Landwehr told them. "Sorry, I forgot to tell you." He was glad officers were on top of the job.

"I can't tell you much," Landwehr told Irene now. "But I wanted to tell you, we're gonna get this guy tomorrow. It's over."

He slept well that night for the first time in eleven months.

The commanders had assigned four teams of undercover cops to Rader's surveillance. They did not watch him twenty-four hours a day . . . they left at night. And they hung back when they watched, trying not to spook him.

Rader was a creature of habit. He left for work at the same minute every day and drove home for lunch at 12:15 PM, arriving at 12:18. Like clockwork.

The commanders planned accordingly. Harty and Moon would pull behind Rader as he went home. For the traffic stop, Chief Williams loaned them his car, which was unmarked and had police lights embedded in the grill. This was convenient, because it did not look like a Wichita patrol car. The cops did not want to make Park City people suspicious.

Once Harty and Moon pulled Rader over, Gouge, Relph, Otis, Snyder, Lundin, and John Sullivan and Chuck Pritchett from the FBI would pull up and draw their weapons. Lundin was assigned to drag Rader out of his truck, with Otis backing up Lundin with a shotgun. A helicopter would provide cover overhead. A few yards behind the arrest team, Landwehr and Relph would watch from inside a car, then drive Rader downtown.

Backing the arrest team were more than two hundred people, many of them assigned to simultaneous searches. They would go to Rader's house, his church, his mother's house, his office at city hall, the library. They would confiscate Rader's city truck. The bomb unit would stand by.

There was a computer seizure team, relief teams, interview teams. Those to be interviewed included Rader and his wife, son, mother, and two brothers who lived in the area.

O'Connor asked, half jokingly, whether he could take part in the arrest. He offered to hide in a car trunk and stay out of the way. The cops smiled and said no.

They all crossed their fingers about keeping the story quiet. Otis had enjoyed a conversation earlier in the week in which he got to mislead the *Eagle* reporter who had staked out the cops at the Valadez arrest.

Tim Potter had had to cancel several vacations and long weekends with his wife as the BTK story had progressed. He called Otis at midweek, unaware that Otis was helping plan the arrest. Potter was exhausted from a string of twelve-hour days. On the phone with Otis, he said he was taking his wife to Kansas City for a long weekend. He cracked a joke, "Could you do me a favor and not arrest BTK while I'm gone?"

"Aw, man," Otis said, in a reassuring tone. "You don't have anything to worry about."

46

"Hello, Mr. Landwehr"

Landwehr and Johnson were scared to death that reporters would blow their cover. So Johnson was upset at 9:00 AM the next morning when she got a call from a Kansas City television reporter. He had heard there was going to be a BTK arrest. Was this true?

Johnson lied, telling him it was rumor. She lied again when a reporter from Wichita's KWCH-TV called. By that time, three hours before the scheduled arrest, several law enforcement agencies had spent hours staging cops into their assigned positions.

Johnson felt frantic: word was leaking out.

When she went to the daily 10:00 AM briefing for local reporters, she felt herself slipping into paranoia. The briefing went smoothly; a recitation of the crimes police had investigated the night before. She looked at her watch: two hours to go.

On a side street in Park City, two blocks from Rader's house, Officers Harty and Moon sat in Chief Williams's Chevy Impala, still amazed that they had drawn this assignment. The arrest team had come quietly into Park City, without notifying local authorities, and they were listening to their police radios. Behind them, detectives sat in other cars. Sometimes people driving past would stare.

Would Rader run, or shoot himself, or shoot at them? Whatever he did, Harty and Moon decided, they'd be ready. Moon was thirty-five and had served on the gang unit and SWAT team. Harty was twenty-eight; when he joined the force at age twenty-one he looked so youthful that Speer had called him "Altar Boy." But he was no naïf. Harty and Moon arrested gangbangers every day.

Gouge and Snyder sat behind them in one car, Lundin and Otis in another; Sullivan and Pritchett, the two FBI guys, in a third; Landwehr, Relph, and Larry Thomas in a fourth car.

Gouge pulled his car up beside Lundin and Otis. The minutes until 12:15 ticked by. Everyone wore body armor.

Otis had dozed in a recliner at home overnight but had not slept deeply. He held a 12-gauge shotgun, itching to get going. There had been times in the past eleven months when he had almost had to carry his partner to the car after Gouge suffered back spasms from the stress of work. There had been the day when Otis burst through the door of a house where the phone line had been cut, thinking he would face down BTK—but it had turned out to be some loser's scheme to keep his girl-friend from moving out. There had been weeks when Otis had looked at obituaries, hoping to find a hint that BTK might be dead. In funeral homes, Otis swabbed the nostrils of half a dozen dead men, hoping for a DNA match. He was ready for this to be over.

Something occurred to Snyder as he sat with Gouge: "Hey, who's going to cuff Rader?"

"I don't know," Gouge said. He turned to Otis in the car beside them: "Who's gonna cuff Rader?"

"It's not going to be me," Otis said. "I'm carrying this shotgun."

Snyder remembered that there were a lot of WPD cops long re-tired—Drowatzky and Cornwell and Thimmesch and Stewart and many others—who thought their failure to catch BTK had stained their careers. And now here the WPD sat amid agents from the FBI and the KBI.

"I think whoever cuffs him ought to be WPD," Snyder said.

"So do I," Gouge said.

Snyder thought for a moment.

"I think it should be you, then," Snyder said to Gouge. "You'll be the closest to Rader, and Otis will have his hands full with the shotgun."

Gouge shrugged.

Snyder smiled. "Okay," he told Gouge. "But you have to use my cuffs."

"Okay," Gouge said. Snyder handed over his cuffs.

It was 12:15. "He is on the move," a radio voice said.

In the next few moments, the undercover cop tailing Rader radioed every turn Rader made, every street he passed.

Harty looked in his rearview mirror and saw Rader, in his white city truck, driving toward them. Harty felt his heart race. He let Rader pass him; Harty did not dare look in his direction. "It's okay," Moon said. "He didn't even look at us."

Harty gunned the engine and drove up behind Rader. Moon flipped on the flashing lights embedded in the grill. Rader pulled over immediately.

What happened next took only seconds: Harty scrambled out of the car as Lundin drove up alongside and skidded to a halt at a diagonal only a couple of feet from Harty's car. Harty was suddenly trapped between cars.

Moon got out on the other side, drew his Glock, and aimed at Rader, who was getting out of his truck with an irritated look. Rader's face froze when he saw Moon wearing the distinct tan uniform of the Wichita Police Department. *He looks like his mind just went into vapor lock*, Moon thought.

Lundin drew his 9-mm pistol and moved toward Rader; but Otis, who was getting out of the passenger side, found himself trapped with Harty between the cars; he had no room to get out or aim his shotgun.

"Ray!" Otis yelled at Lundin. "You've boxed me in!"

He threw his right hip, shoulder, and 230 pounds against the door—and crunched a dent into the side of the chief's car.

"Don't move!" Moon called to Rader. "Hold your hands where I

The moment of capture—Dennis Rader is caught by the Wichita police.

can see them!" Rader stood as though frozen; Lundin, who had hesitated, now ran toward Rader.

"Get down on the ground!" Lundin ordered. He was six feet tall and weighed 225 pounds; he'd been a power weight lifter. He grabbed Rader by the back of the neck and forced him to the pavement.

Everyone else ran up now, guns drawn. Snyder's heart skipped a beat when he saw one of the two uniformed officers pull out a pair of cuffs, but Gouge moved in quickly with Snyder's cuffs, and then Snyder got there too. Snyder held his Glock in one hand and patted Rader down with the other. Harty twisted Rader's left arm behind his back; someone else pulled Rader's right arm into place; Gouge snapped Snyder's handcuffs onto Rader's wrists. Snyder looked up and suppressed a grin; Sullivan, the FBI agent, glowered down at Rader while holding a submachine gun. Sullivan would forever be known in task force lore as "Machine Gun Sully."

Snyder noticed there was none of the usual "What did I do? What's this all about?" stuff that people usually say during arrests. Rader looked resigned.

He was wearing his tan compliance officer uniform, complete with a webbed belt that held a can of pepper spray and a stick baton. One of the cops asked another, "Do you want us to take this off?"

"You can if you want," Rader said petulantly, thinking they were addressing him. They ignored him and removed the belt.

Lundin pulled Rader to his feet. Rader looked into Lundin's eyes from inches away and spoke: "Hey, would you please call my wife? She was expecting me for lunch. I assume you know where I live."

What a guilty man, Snyder thought. *He knows why we're here.*

As they propelled Rader to the back of the line of cars, Rader peered into the car that he would ride in. In the backseat he saw a man with a tanned and familiar face. The cops eased Rader into the seat.

"Hello, Mr. Landwehr," Rader said cordially.

"Hello, Mr. Rader," Landwehr replied.

Landwehr glanced at Relph, who had turned around to look as he sat at the wheel. Landwehr could see that Relph was thinking the same thing:

Rader is going to confess.

● ● ●

They had kept Park City police in the dark. The chief, Bill Ball, first realized that a police story was unfolding in his town when he saw a helicopter flying low just east of I-135. At city hall, Ball learned that Rader had been arrested. Ball saw Wichita police walk in carrying a warrant. They wanted to see Rader's office.

"Get ready for a lot of media attention," one of them said.

Landwehr and the FBI had planned a standard good-cops-bad-cops tactic: the cops who pushed Rader to the pavement were the bad cops. Landwehr and the cops taking him to the Epic Center were the good cops. They would get Rader away from the arrest scene quickly and treat him respectfully. The abrupt arrest followed by cordial courtesy was calculated to loosen his tongue. Landwehr, once an altar boy, now wanted to be Rader's confessor. There would be no made-for-TV confrontation. Landwehr had spent eleven months building a rapport with BTK. He would build on that now.

Rader complained politely that his handcuffs were too tight. Landwehr reached behind Rader and adjusted how they fit but did not loosen them. Landwehr tried to think of something friendly to say.

"A nice sunny day," he said, looking out the window. "Do you play golf?"

"No," Rader said. "I like to hunt and fish, and I'm more into gardening."

"A garden?" Landwehr said. "Well . . . you'll be planting potatoes pretty soon."

As they pulled into the Epic Center parking garage, Larry Thomas turned in the front seat and noticed that Rader was fidgety. Thomas saw why: Rader's billed cap was about to fall off his head. Rader, his hands cuffed, was tilting his head to keep the cap on.

"Can I help you with your cap?" Thomas asked.

"Yes, please."

As they walked inside, Landwehr worried about botching the interview.

February 25, 2005

The Interview

Otis and the other detectives thought that it was a mistake to assign Landwehr and Morton to interview Rader.

Interrogation is a craft requiring practice. Landwehr, their supervisor, had not interviewed a criminal in ten years. The detectives thought he was rusty and that Morton was more academic than investigator. *Rader might be dumb,* Otis thought, *or he might be clever and prepared. But it's Landwehr's case,* Otis concluded. *After twenty years, he deserves to be the first one in.*

Landwehr himself worried that he was out of practice. But the chief had already dispensed with these objections. It would feed Rader's ego to be interviewed by the commander of the BTK task force and an FBI profiler. BTK loved feeling important.

Morton had arrived from Quantico only minutes before Rader reached the Epic Center.

The two investigators got Rader a Sprite and chatted with him to get acquainted. The detectives, FBI agents, and prosecutors watched on a closed-circuit monitor from another room.

Interrogations are almost never like those on television, Landwehr would say later. The silly stuff that actors do—screaming, threatening, grabbing the perp by the throat—would ruin most investigations. In real life, most interviews start like this one did—quiet, sympathetic, and friendly, with the cops establishing trust. Landwehr wanted Rader to think that he was his best friend, his last best lifeline in working through a problem.

There is a structure to a police interview. Like a storyteller, the skilled homicide detective picks a starting point and works in a sequence: "Okay, so do you know why we are here today?" The interviewer's questions build a framework of logic and slowly herd the guy into a box. If the suspect is innocent, there's a great chance that he can explain his way out of that box. But if he's guilty, the suspect is trapped by his own lies.

After they handcuffed Rader to the table, Landwehr and Morton introduced Rader to Gouge, who carried a search warrant. Only twenty minutes had passed since Lundin had pushed Rader to the pavement. Landwehr told Rader that they wanted to swab him to collect DNA. Rader agreed, asked to see the warrant, and joked with Gouge. While defending the police after the Valadez arrest, Foulston had erroneously announced that the cops had swabbed about four thousand people since BTK had resurfaced. "I make four thousand and one?" Rader asked.

Gouge, unamused, took four swabs of the inside of Rader's cheek. Two were sent immediately to the county forensics lab; two more went to the KBI lab in Topeka. Rader was read his Miranda rights: "You have the right to remain silent. . . ."

Rader agreed to talk.

For the next three hours, as Gouge, Otis, and others watched on closed-circuit television, the dogcatcher from Park City ducked questions and talked in the third person as though "Dennis Rader" were someone else. Gouge fumed: Landwehr was letting Rader drag this out.

Rader did not ask why the police had arrested him.

Landwehr and Morton took an exceedingly long time before they asked the set-the-table question of "Do you know why we are here?" They started with tame questions: who Rader was, where he worked. At first they kept him handcuffed to the table. At one point, Rader made a boasting threat: "It's a good thing I'm cuffed."

After a while, Rader asked to go to the restroom. When they brought him back to the interview room, Landwehr left the cuffs off. It was a subtle move, meant to relax him.

Rader gave away nothing, but he seemed impressed that he was talking to Landwehr and that an FBI agent had flown to Wichita to meet him. He spoke to them as equals, noting that he too was in law enforcement. Rader seemed antsy but not nervous. He fiddled with the pens, paper, and napkins in front of him, arranging them neatly, compulsively. Landwehr was tempted to reach out and nudge a few things to mess with

Rader's head. But he did not. Gouge and Otis might think this was taking too long, but Landwehr thought patience was vital.

"Why do you think we are here?" Landwehr asked. Rader said he assumed they wanted to talk about a case.

Had he ever followed the BTK investigation?

"Yeah," Rader said, appearing unsurprised. "I've been a BTK fan for years, watching it." When they reminded Rader that they had taken his DNA, he nodded. "I assume I'm a main suspect."

Three months earlier, Roger Valadez had been angry at being suspected; Rader cracked a joke about it. His soft drink was in a fast-food cup: "Put 'BTK' on the lid," he said with a grin.

"There is no way my husband could be the man you want," Paula Rader said. "He's a good man. He's a great father. He would never hurt anyone!"

Relph felt sorry for her. She seemed kind and incapable of lying. As soon as Dennis Rader was in custody, police had rounded up his relatives.

"I'm not here to convince you of anything, Mrs. Rader," he said. "I'm just here to tell you that we have arrested your husband, and why."

Had she ever noticed anything unusual about him?

"No!"

She had followed the BTK investigation in the news. She knew that the cops had broken down Valadez's door in December—and that he was not BTK.

"You were wrong about Valadez then," she said, "and you are wrong about my husband now."

Landwehr heard later about how the detectives who watched him thought he took too long. But Landwehr had sat on the outside of many interviews, watching his own detectives—and he'd also thought that they took too long. The fact is, when you're actually doing an interview, time seems to fly.

Morton now began to get to the point. "Do you know why we came to you?" Rader demurred.

"Do you remember anything about the Otero murders?" Landwehr asked at last.

"Yes," Rader said. "Four—well, whatever was in the paper. A man and a wife, two kids. And the way the paper indicated, it was pretty—pretty brutal."

"Why do you think the Oteros were murdered?" Landwehr asked.

"Well, if you take that murder and some of the others, I would say you've got a serial killer loose."

What did he think about BTK?

The killer was like "a lone wolf," Rader said. "Kind of like a spy or something."

The beginning of the BTK media circus found the newsroom of *Wichita Eagle* nearly empty, most of the reporters at lunch. Hurst Laviana was at the vet with one of his daughters' cats when his cell phone rang.

"Something's brewing up in Park City," said his boss, L. Kelly. Not only were there a lot of WPD vehicles up there, the *Eagle* had gotten a couple of calls from Kansas City reporters who'd heard rumors of an impending BTK arrest from well-connected sources. Kelly had been in a Taco Bell drive-thru when she got the first alert.

"I'm on my way," Laviana said. He paid the vet, dropped the animal at home, then drove twenty minutes to Park City, where he found Independence blocked off at both ends of the street. Reporters and residents started to gather.

Do you know who they've arrested? Laviana asked a neighbor. "Dennis Rader," someone told him. "He's the dogcatcher."

"What do you know about him?"

"He's a complete jerk," the man said. "Everybody thinks so."

It was a nice day. People were watching the police helicopter buzz overhead. Someone pointed to a house not far from Rader's.

"That's Marine Hedge's house."

That surprised Laviana. An arrest on the same block as one of the murders? While covering the case twenty years earlier, Laviana had knocked on doors, asking about Hedge. He looked at Rader's house now and tried to remember whether he'd talked to anyone there.

By the time she got back to the newsroom, Kelly had dispatched a squad of reporters and photographers to Park City by cell phone. But she was frantically trying to reach Potter in Kansas City—he had left his cell phone in his hotel room. When he picked it up hours later, he apologized to his wife and drove immediately back to Wichita. He and many others would work the next fourteen days with no days off.

"What do you think would happen if your DNA matched BTK's DNA?" Morton asked.

Rader nodded.

"I guess that might be it then."

He thought for a moment.

"See, it's always—it's always intrigued me," Rader said. "I assume this person left something at the crime scenes that you guys could match up with DNA. But after all of these years, they still have that stuff?"

Yes, they said. They still had it.

It was time to spring the trap.

Landwehr pulled out a purple computer disk. Landwehr told Rader that this disk, sent by BTK, had pointed the cops to Rader's church and to him. Could he explain that?

"When did you type this?" Landwehr asked.

Rader looked crestfallen. "You have the answer to that right here," he said. He began to fumble around. To Landwehr's delight, he even asked for a calendar. Landwehr, poker-faced but gleeful, offered him a pen. Maybe Rader would just start writing it out.

"There's no way I can weasel out of that or lie," Rader said.

Rader asked about the law: did the death penalty apply to BTK's murders?

No.

What about prison? Rader wondered. BTK might have trouble in prison. "BTK has killed some kids and stuff."

The talking had gone on for nearly three hours—but Landwehr could tell Rader wanted to keep going.

Rader asked if he could see his pastor. "Maybe," Landwehr said. They talked some more. Rader brought up the minister again. His name was Michael Clark; could he please see him? He needed him because he was about to break down emotionally, Rader said.

"Sure," Landwehr said. "I'll go see about it." Landwehr left the room and stayed out for a few minutes, but he had no intention of bringing in someone else—especially not someone who might counsel Rader to stop talking. When Landwehr returned, Rader told him, "I really need help."

Landwehr said he could have all the help he wanted. "But first you need to talk."

Rader said he worried about how his children would take his arrest and about "Park City getting a black eye."

"What would happen to BTK's house?" Rader asked.

"We'd tear it up looking for evidence unless we know where to find the evidence," Landwehr replied.

Rader winced.

"You guys have got me. . . . How can I get out of it?"

Landwehr and Morton told him they did not see how he could get out of it.

Rader pondered the swabbing. "Isn't any way you can get out of the DNA, right?"

He sat still, his elbow propped on the tabletop, his chin resting on his upraised hand. It was the FBI profiler, Morton, who lost patience first:

"Enough, enough! You got to say it! Just say who you are!"

"I'm BTK," Rader said.

"Jesus," Otis said, watching from the other room. "It's about time."

**Landwehr and FBI profiler Bob Morton grilled Rader for three hours
before getting him to admit he was BTK.**

•   •   •

"How much money you got?"

Sam Houston, a sheriff's captain, was hearing a familiar voice on the phone: Deputy Chief Robert Lee, commander of WPD's investigations division.

"Why do you ask?"

" 'Cuz you're taking me to dinner," Lee said. "You're going to owe me a big steak dinner. The guy over here is talking about Hedge and Davis, and he's confessing."

"You're shittin' me!" Houston said. He had investigated both homicides and had come to know the families. Dee Davis's daughter was pregnant at the time of her mother's murder; Dee never got to meet the grandchild. That stuck with Houston because his wife had been pregnant then too.

Lee told Houston to come interrogate BTK.

Rader rapped repeatedly on the computer disk.

"How come you lied to me? How come you lied to me?"

"Because I was trying to catch you," Landwehr said with a laugh.

Rader seemed stunned. "You know, I thought I would pull it off and retire and have mementos; it didn't happen, you guys outsmarted me."

Rader had taken pains with the disk. "I checked the properties and the other stuff, and there was nothing there, nothing. . . . And I talked to some other people, they said, 'Oh, floppies can't be traced, floppies can't be traced.' "

He felt betrayed.

"I really thought Ken was honest when he gave me—when he gave me the signal it can't be traced."

After Landwehr left the room, O'Connor approached him. He could not imagine Landwehr would risk handing BTK a piece of original evidence like that, but he wanted to be sure.

"That disk you showed him," O'Connor asked. "Was it a dummy, or was it the real one?"

Landwehr's eyes widened.

"Do you think I'm a fucking *idiot*?" he asked, then laughed.

As they spoke, other detectives were now talking to Rader. Two at a time, they interviewed Rader about each case: the Oteros, Bright, Vian, Fox, Hedge, Wegerle, Davis. Rader greeted every detective who came to see him with an insult. He made a wisecrack about Relph's chunky build. He told Otis, "You look better on television."

"It's the makeup," Otis replied dryly.

Rader pretended to recognize Gouge: "You worked the Vian scene."

Gouge was not amused; he was in junior high school back then.

It was all just stupid, Gouge said later. The guy had murdered ten people and was going to prison, but he wanted to insult the cops in some sort of dominance ritual.

By this time, Otis was bored with Rader. He had daydreamed for years about how fascinating it would be to interview BTK. But BTK seemed to be a dork.

The cops had a huge secret to spill to the world now, and they wanted to reveal it with dignified brevity on the national stage. The rumor that BTK had been caught was on the street, the airwaves, and the Internet. They knew the national media were soon going to set up tents and camp out on the front walk of the courthouse. The cops wanted to show Wichita law enforcement in the best light.

They already had a plan for the news conference, drawn up by the chief and Johnson months before. The chief would announce BTK's arrest. Then Landwehr would announce the name of the suspect and the crimes he was accused of committing. Then they would answer a few questions.

The whole thing was to last ten minutes, tops.

But Johnson now saw that "brief and dignified" was impossible.

The cops had decided to let the politicians in.

Thomas and Lundin sat back in amazement as Rader, recounting the Otero murders, suddenly stood up, put his hands behind his back, and mocked the cries of eleven-year-old Josie Otero as Rader strangled her mother. "Momma! Momma! Momma!" Then Rader laughed—a sharp, high-pitched cackle: "Ha!"

Otis, watching on the closed circuit, found himself praying that

Rader would attack the cops in the interview room so that Otis could run in and shoot him.

Lundin told Rader to "be a man" and tell them where he'd put his trophies.

Drawing a map of the inside of his home, Rader said: "Right here is what you call a cupboard, where you put all of your dry goods. Okay, the bottom drawer, you take that out, the bottom one, you'll see a false bottom." They should look under that.

And in a closet, they'd find a large plastic tote case filled with pictures he'd cut out of newspaper inserts advertising women's and children's clothing. The slick ads were "almost like treasures to me, I've been saving these things for years."

He explained that most of his "stuff" was in his city hall office, though, "because basically what I was doing is phasing the stuff out, because I was shutting this down in about a year. If I got through it, once the story was done, I might get—I might do another hit and I might not do another hit.

"In this corner, you'll find my basic hit kit, okay? And . . . it's probably pretty incriminating. And you'll find my—my .25 auto, okay? That's another one of my backups, okay? They're in a little black bag." The attic of his home would contain "old what I call detective magazines. And

**Part of Rader's "hit kit," including duct tape, rope,
and a screwdriver, among other items.**

they all tend to be toward bondage. You know, in the fifties, they usually string up the girls. . . ."

Under the false bottom of the cupboard, investigators found Marine Hedge's wedding ring and several photos—of her body, Dolores Davis's body, and BTK himself in bondage.

The detectives interrogating Rader were startled to learn from him that the photographs of Hedge were taken inside his church.

They found bondage equipment—including come-alongs and dog collars—in a storage area attached to the back of his house and a metal shed in the backyard. Rader liked to wear the collars.

The FBI sent a team with a semitrailer load of equipment to gather and catalog evidence. It would take days.

At Rader's city hall office, they found what he called his "Mother Lode," trophies and all his original writings, in the bottom drawer of a cream-colored filing cabinet. O'Connor helped catalog and describe what they found: seven three-ring binders and more than twenty-five hanging file folders; newspaper clippings about many of the killings; drawings depicting women bound to torture machines of Rader's design; a copy of the police "wanted" poster for the Otero homicides; and computer disks that were labeled according to the chapters of BTK's "book."

Rader had stashed his original writings in his filing cabinet at Park City's city hall.

A large white three-ring binder was labeled COMMUNICATION BOOK. It held:

- A handwritten timeline of the letters and packages he sent in 2004, including the number of each communication and a brief description of it.

- The original of the Wegerle letter sent to the *Eagle* in March 2004. Taped to the sheet of white paper were the three original Polaroid photographs of Vicki's body and her driver's license. The BTK symbol was drawn in pencil.

- The original full-size version of "Death on a cold January Moring" and the original ink drawing that accompanied it.

- The full-size version of Rader's fictional "Jakey" story.

- Original Polaroid photographs depicting Rader practicing self-bondage, sometimes wearing women's clothing, makeup, and a blond wig. In several of the photos Rader was wearing the mask he later left with Dolores's body.

Rader wears undergarments from Dolores Davis and a mask over his face while hoisting himself off the ground with pulleys in one of his self-bondage pictures.

- An original version of the note in which Rader inquires whether a computer disk can be traced, along with a clipping of the ad that the police used to respond.

Among the items another binder contained:

- The original typewritten letter to KAKE in February 1978.

- Newspaper clippings about the Bright homicide and BTK's typed narrative about it.

- Newspaper clippings about the Wegerle homicide and an eleven-page account of Rader's encounter with Vicki.

- The original poem titled "Oh, Anna Why Didn't You Appear" with handwritten portions in blue ink, as well as the original blue-ink drawing depicting his unfulfilled fantasy.

- An original blue-ink drawing meant to depict Dee Davis.

- Three original Polaroid photographs showing Dee in her shallow grave, with Rader's mask on her face.

Rader wrapped himself in plastic and lay down in a shallow grave
he'd dug at Cheney Reservoir, a popular family camping spot.

- Her driver's license and Social Security card.

- Newspaper articles about her disappearance and homicide. A hand-drawn map was coded with four colors of ink to indicate the paths Rader used before and after the murder.

- The original typed letter sent to Mary Fager, along with the original ink drawing of his conception of the crime scene.

In a manila folder, they found the original "Shirley Locks" poem, protected by a plastic sleeve.

Rader kept meticulous records. Detectives knew Rader had killed ten. Reading his logbooks, they realized that he had stalked hundreds more.

It took investigators a month to digitally record all of Rader's stash—the documents and photos of everything from Rader wearing high heels to Rader hoisting himself from tree limbs with pulleys. At one point, O'Connor was shocked to find a photo of a masked body wrapped in plastic, partially buried in a shallow sandy grave.

He took it to Landwehr. "Kenny, I wonder if we've got another body here."

Landwehr was startled at first, but then looked at the photo.

"No," Landwehr said. "See that cord? Come on. He's taking his own picture with a remote trigger." Landwehr grinned at O'Connor. "Okay," he said. "This is why you are the lawyer and I'm the detective."

Rader seemed to enjoy educating detectives about his life and habits.

He was "totally a lone wolf," he said; there was never anyone else involved.

He liked bondage. "If I have sex, I would rather have the bondage. You know, I could still perform with my wife and everything, but that's the way I like to have sex. Because I like to have that person under control."

It started in childhood, he said. He once saw his grandparents butcher chickens, when he was eight, and he remembered the blood and the way the chickens hopped around after their heads were cut off, and the feeling he got as he watched.

Growing up, he knew that he thought of girls differently than his friends did. They all wanted to hold child star Annette Funicello's hand and kiss her; he wanted to tie her up and throttle her.

Over the decades, he had wanted to kill a lot more people. But he often settled for stalking them, sometimes breaking into their homes to look around, steal underwear, and pretend he was a spy.

Some women became targets when he worked part-time for the 1990 U.S. census in small towns around Kansas, others while he was on the road for the security alarm company. His farthest target lived about two hundred miles from Wichita. He had dug a grave for a northern Kansas woman he intended to kill, but she wasn't home when he came for her. In motel rooms, he put on stolen bras and panties and—using a tripod and shutter cable—took pictures of himself.

The cops debated whether to tell the people they could identify that they had almost become BTK victims. Landwehr didn't want to upset them. But he decided investigators should contact them—and make sure there were no more bodies. There were not.

Some of the targets were angry about being told they had caught the eye of a serial killer; ignorance was a blessing. None of them wanted their identities publicized.

Rader described his crimes with the same flat tone that most people reserve for recalling routine errands.

When he confronted the Otero family in their kitchen, Joe Otero struggled to make sense of it: "He said, 'My brother-in-law put you up to this.' I said, 'No, this is not a joke.' I told him I had a weapon, a .22 with the hollow points I would use. So they started to lay down. They started to lay down in the living room.

"I didn't really have real good control of the family, they were freaking out and stuff. So I bound them as best I could." He had prepared the bindings beforehand. "I already had my cords with me, and I think some of them were already tied, I mean pre-knotted."

Rader described the family as being cooperative because he used a ruse—which he inarticulately pronounced "russ."

"I just told them I was going to California; I needed money, and I needed—I needed a car. And I was going—oh, I used that on several people, I said I need food."

He tied Joe's feet to his bed to keep him from escaping. Rader had worn gloves to prevent fingerprints, but he had not bothered to wear a mask. They had seen his face. So there was no doubt what was going to happen next. "They were going down."

Rader went to his "hit kit" in the living room to get plastic bags; he returned to the bedroom.

"All hell broke loose when they found out I was going after them. I got him down, put the bag over his head. And I think I had to wrap something around it. And he went ballistic, trying to chew a hole in it or whatever."

The family's screams unnerved him. "That was a bad moment," as he recalled.

He strangled Julie until she passed out, then turned his attention to Joey—putting a bag over his head. Julie regained consciousness and "yelled at me that 'You killed my boy, you killed my boy.' And she was just going ballistic. . . . That's when I strangled her the second time."

Rader then went to the girl, who had been screaming "Momma" and crying. He strangled her, but she came back too.

"You know, I strangled dogs and cats, but I never strangled a person before. . . . Strangling is a hard way to kill a person, you know, they don't go down in a minute like they do in the movies. . . . I figured once you strangled a person, they would be done for." But if any oxygen gets in the airway, "you're going to come back. . . . You know you're being strangled, that's your torture."

At some point, he said, Joe was still moving around, "so I put the coup de grâce on him."

Rader said he then took "Little Joseph" to his bedroom and put a T-shirt under the plastic bag so he couldn't chew through it. "I set the chair to watch. . . . I think I put him on the bed and I think he rolled off and he was expired there."

Rader's first thought after watching Joey struggle and die was "Gee, you know . . . I've always had a sexual desire for younger women, so I thought Josephine would be my primary target." When he returned to the master bedroom, he saw that she had "woke up."

That's when he decided on an "encore."

"I took her down in the basement, pulled her pants down, tied her up a little bit more, found the sewer pipe." Before hanging the girl, Rader asked Josie if her daddy had a camera, because he wanted to take a picture. She said no.

The "encore" was completed, Rader explained, when he slipped the rope over her head and masturbated. He left her hanging with her toes just barely off the floor.

It wasn't enough just to kill the Oteros. He told the cops he also fantasized about enslaving them in the afterlife. In his writings he called that AFLV, short for Afterlife Concept of Victim.

Joseph Otero would be his bodyguard.

Julie Otero would bathe him and serve him in the bedroom.

Joey would be a servant and a sex toy.

Josie would be his "young maiden." He would instruct her in sex, bondage, and sadomasochism.

Thomas, needing a break, asked Rader whether he was hungry. Yes, he wanted a light dinner—a salad. He gave Lundin precise instructions about what vegetables to include, what to leave out, and what salad dressing he wanted.

And bring coffee later, Rader directed.

The guy has gall, Lundin thought. But Lundin filled his order. They wanted to keep him talking.

Snyder was next. He interviewed Rader about Kathryn and Kevin Bright.

To prepare for that hit, Rader told Snyder, he squeezed rubber balls to strengthen his hands. Detectives found such a ball with the motto "Life is good" on Rader's bedside table, next to his church usher badge.

Snyder's face must have shown his disgust.

"I'm sorry," Rader said. "I know this is a human being. But I'm a monster."

Relph interviewed Rader about Nancy Fox.

In the afterlife he fantasized about, she would be his main mistress.

To help clarify his account of her murder, Rader drew a diagram of her apartment that was detailed and accurate.

When he was a student at Riverview grade school, one of Rader's favorite subjects had been art. As BTK, he enjoyed sketching out ideas for torture chambers. One was a sealed heat box partially filled with water. He would control the heat, causing the woman inside to sweat and urinate day after day. She would drown slowly in her own fluids.

Rader didn't stop talking until nearly ten o'clock that night, and then only because the cops wanted to let him rest. He wanted to keep talking. *It was almost comical*, Relph thought.

Not as comical as what happened the next day, though.

48

February 26, 2005

"BTK Is Arrested"

Chief Williams, Landwehr, and most of the command staff had spent nearly all their lives in Wichita. They knew Wichita's virtues—a great place to raise kids, a community where neighbors treated each other like family, home to some of the brightest aeronautical engineers and most sophisticated aircraft manufacturing centers on the planet. But these virtues had never done enough to erase the nagging insecurity the natives felt about their city. Newcomers were often baffled by the way people bad-mouthed their own city. Wichitans liked the ten-minute commutes to work, the lack of congestion, and the great sunsets, but many complained openly about how there was "nothing" to do, no beach, no mountains, and (supposedly) no achievements of which to be proud. The world loved *The Wizard of Oz,* but many locals winced at references to Dorothy and Toto; they thought the movie made Kansans look like hayseeds.

The cops knew this, as they prepared to announce that they had just halted the longest serial killer reign of fear in U.S. history. They also knew that the strategy and tactics devised by Landwehr and the FBI would serve as a model of sophisticated police work, something to be studied at Quantico and elsewhere for years to come. There was a lot here for the city to be proud of.

The announcement would be broadcast worldwide, and Wichita, represented by its police force, could stand tall on a world stage. Had the cops kept the arrest announcement brief and dignified, as originally planned, it would have saved the city the public criticism that followed.

But on the day of Rader's arrest, Williams decided brevity was not possible. Williams prized generosity. He decided that he owed several people some gratitude, and he wanted them with him at the announcement. The KBI, a division of the state attorney general's office, had loaned him personnel and resources for eleven months. The FBI had been involved in the investigation for decades. Congressman Todd Tiahrt had brought him $1 million in federal money just as department administrators were getting desperate about how they were going to pay for overtime, the DNA sweep, and other expenses.

There were other considerations: Landwehr wanted to follow protocol and have Sheriff Gary Steed announce the resolution of the Hedge and Davis murders because his office had handled those cases. District Attorney Nola Foulston needed to explain the pending charges and prosecution. The mayor wanted to acknowledge the end of the city's long ordeal.

Williams decided to let them all talk.

But once the politicians got involved, the police department got into an ugly argument with some of them.

The cops intended to call the victims' families that night and tell them that BTK had finally been arrested and that they were invited to the news conference the next morning. When Johnson told this to local politicians, some of them strenuously objected. They said the families should be told nothing, because they might spill the beans to the news media—and steal the spotlight.

When word of this spread among the cops, some of them were furious: their nerves were shot from eleven months of seventy-hour weeks and the daily stress of wondering whether BTK would leave a fresh body for them to find. Some of the task force members had bonded closely with the families, who had lived with their grief for decades. The detectives called the families, one by one, and told them what was coming in the morning.

Within hours of Rader's arrest, although the police still had made no announcement, *Eagle* reporters had learned his name and occupation, that he would be charged as BTK, that the cops were pulling a truckload of evidence out of his home, that they had searched Park City city hall, the Park City library, and his church. By interviewing neighbors, searching public records, and going online, staffers began to piece together a portrait of Rader and his family and collect photographs of him. Rader looked like a different man in every photo—he was a human chameleon. That afternoon, Editor Sherry Chisenhall was surprised to receive an e-mail that claimed to include a driver's license photo, along with a note about what "the monster" looked like. Following the chain of e-mail forwarding addresses, she saw that the original sender worked for the city of Wichita. Wanting to verify that it was really Rader—the guy in this photo resembled "Monty Python" actor John Cleese with a beard; the Rader photo on Park City's website looked more like a smiling Jason Alexander from *Seinfeld*—she contacted Landwehr. To confirm that the photo was Rader, he said, he would need to see it and the e-mail thread. A limited number of people would have access to something like that. Chisenhall forwarded it to him. It was, indeed, Landwehr told her, the suspect's driver's license photo. The original sender was a detective in the Property Crimes Bureau.

Landwehr was not pleased about the leak. He told Chisenhall that as of that moment, the guy was a *former* detective—but in the end, the guy just got a talking to and apologized.

With the Valadez arrest in mind, Chisenhall again opted for caution: the *Eagle*'s Saturday, February 26, front page reported that an arrest had been made in Park City and that a BTK news conference was planned for that morning. It did not publish Rader's name, photo, or specific details of his life.

The city council auditorium filled quickly. At what should have been a joyous announcement, some of the exhausted detectives showed up in a dark and dangerous mood.

What they saw was a comedy.

Local, national, and international reporters staked out good views. CNN and MSNBC carried the news conference live. When Wichita mayor Carlos Mayans stepped forward just after 10:00 AM, he faced a crowd at city hall, and the expectation of his constituents that this would be Wichita's finest hour.

Mayans spoke for about two minutes, most of his comments platitudes: "It has been a very long journey . . . It certainly has been a challenge . . . The national spotlight has been shining upon us . . . Today I stand a proud mayor of the city of Wichita. . . ."

He was followed by Chief Williams, who briefly introduced his many fellow speakers. Then Williams spoke six words that set off a standing ovation: "The bottom line: BTK is arrested!"

But Williams didn't say what everyone was waiting to hear: the name of the suspect.

He yielded the podium to District Attorney Nola Foulston. So much for brevity. Foulston, a Democrat in a mostly Republican county, had been reelected, often by wide margins, in every election since 1988. Her detractors had long admitted she was a skilled courtroom lawyer, but they also said her skill was matched by her ego and her love of publicity. To a televison audience, a minute can seem like an eternity, which is why most TV "interviews" are sound bites of only eight to ten seconds. Foulston spoke now for a stunning nine minutes and forty-four seconds. She thanked all the politicians standing behind her, although Mayans and Williams had already done so. Then she began to talk not about BTK but about her office.

"In the last year since the reemergence of the individual, of the John Doe serial killer, I have appointed and have maintained a confident and extraordinarily qualified prosecution staff to work with law enforcement twenty-four hours a day, seven days a week."

She introduced Parker, reminding the audience of her work on the Carr case, and O'Connor, saying he was chosen for his "fighting Irish."

Chief Norman Williams announces the arrest of BTK. Behind him are (l. to r.) prosecutor Kevin O'Connor, Landwehr, Kansas Attorney General Phill Kline, District Attorney Nola Foulston, and Mayor Carlos Mayans.

She went on a good deal longer. She confirmed what Laviana had written months earlier: BTK would not face execution—he had committed all his murders during years when Kansas had no death penalty. And she noted that information restrictions would continue; court motions would be filed under seal. By the time she finished, more than half an hour had gone by since the news conference started, and the local and national audience was no closer to hearing who BTK was and why he did it.

Kansas Attorney General Phill Kline then got up and thanked the mayor and praised the law enforcement agencies represented. He promised the audience it would soon "come face-to-face with evil," but he leavened his speech with more platitudes: "The perseverance and dedication to truth and justice has made Kansas proud. On this day, the voice of justice is heard in Wichita."

Otis, sitting with the Wegerles, glanced at their faces and wondered if they were as bored and disappointed as he was. So far they had heard a lot of self-congratulation, mostly from people who had barely taken part in the BTK hunt.

Larry Welch, director of the KBI, mercifully spoke for less than a minute; then Kevin Stafford from the FBI spoke another ninety seconds.

Tiahrt stood up (for two minutes) and introduced yet another dimension to the proceedings: "The faith community in Wichita got

DA Nola Foulston speaks at the BTK press conference
while Ken Landwehr waits his turn.

together and not only prayed that that which was hidden would be revealed, but they also prayed for the families of the victims, and I know many of them are here."

Sheriff Gary Steed then came forward with real news: BTK's arrest solved the Hedge and Davis homicides, bringing BTK's murder total to ten.

And then finally, thirty-nine minutes after the news conference had opened, Landwehr was allowed to approach the microphone.

CNN had cut away nearly twenty minutes before, with a bemused CNN anchor in Atlanta telling her field correspondent in Wichita to "please get back to us if and when they have something to announce there." CNN put the news conference back on national television when Landwehr spoke.

He tried not to show it, but it pissed him off that the victims' families had been mostly ignored, and that a lot of people not on the task force had been thanked by name, some of them multiple times.

He hadn't intended to thank anyone, but now felt compelled to do so:

"I want to thank the families of the victims that gave us their trust and stood behind us," Landwehr began. "I want to thank the families of our task force who stood behind them."

Then, peering around the audience (he cracked a little joke about how nearsighted he'd become recently), Landwehr began to thank by name every cop and civilian who had worked on the task force or helped it in some tangible way. Off the top of his head, he managed to name forty-two of them—some of them twice.

"See?" he said. "I'm losing it. I want to thank everybody and their families who gave up a lot for this task force."

He took a breath.

Then Landwehr uttered what Otis took to be a subtle reprimand to the politicians standing behind him.

"I'm going to quit rambling," Landwehr said. "Let's do it. Let's do this the *right* way."

He glanced down at a sheet of paper.

"Shortly after noon yesterday afternoon, agents from the KBI, agents from the FBI, and members of the Wichita Police Department arrested Dennis Rader, fifty-nine, a white male, in Park City, Kansas, for the murders of Joseph Otero, Julie Otero, Josephine Otero,—"

At that moment, Landwehr appeared to choke up a little. He quickly recovered and continued: "Joseph Otero Jr., Kathryn Bright, Shirley Vian Relford, Nancy Fox, and Vicki Wegerle," Landwehr said. "He was arrested for the first-degree murder of all those victims. He's being held at this time at an undisclosed location. We will be approaching the district attorney's office next week, reference charges to see if charges will be filed against this individual. I thank you very much for your support."

It was over.

After thirty-one years, plus one hour and thousands of superfluous words, all of Wichita finally knew BTK's name.

One out-of-town television outfit offered a Park City police officer five hundred dollars to go to Rader's house and come back with something that said "Dennis Rader." The officer refused.

BTK's arrest is front-page news.

Sightseers arrived on Independence Street, some coming from the nearby Kansas Coliseum, where the state high school wrestling tournament was under way. When one girl in a squad of high school cheerleaders held up her cell phone camera to snap a picture of the wrong house, Police Chief Ball helpfully pointed her in the right direction.

Someone started to drag away Rader's curbside mailbox, which had his name on it. When onlookers protested, the thief dropped the box and fled.

Park City police officers directed traffic on the roads as well as the sidewalks to keep the crowds moving. Neighbors with views of the house set up impromptu businesses, selling bottled water, individual cigarettes, and good spots from which to shoot video.

The detectives continued to interview an eager Rader the day after his arrest.

Relph and the FBI's Chuck Pritchett showed Rader his drawing of Nancy Fox lying half naked and bound on her bed. As he explained the drawing, Rader suddenly apologized: he was getting an erection. Relph whisked the drawing off the table.

Over two days, Rader talked for thirty-three hours. He told Otis that he had stalked Vicki Wegerle for three weeks. He said the telephone repairman ruse he had used to talk his way into her home had also opened many other doors for him. He boasted that if an officer had stopped him for a traffic violation while he was driving Vicki's car, he would have shot him.

There should have been many more victims, Rader told the detectives. But his family and work got in the way.

He had planned to kill an eleventh victim and string her up on October 22, 2004. But when he found workers building curbs in her neighborhood, he backed off. "So what in the hell do you do?" Rader said. "You just do a backup and wait for another day. I was going to try it in the spring or fall."

After killing her, he planned to retire from killing with a last communication—a "final curtain call."

When the task force arrested Rader, he was planning to make what he called "the Vian drop"—a doll in a miniature coffin wired to look like a bomb. He'd been working on it at his city hall office the night before his arrest, telling his wife he was working late. He explained to the detectives: "I can fudge a little bit getting home late, doing BTK. It's a riot." He had a thing for dolls, he said. He would photograph their shoes; he would bind them; he would hang one and use a mirror to view it from many angles.

The twenty-plus *Eagle* reporters, photographers, and editors who came in to work the story that Saturday began to discern the outlines of the lie that Rader had made of his life. He was a church congregation president; a registered Republican voter; a longtime Boy Scout dad; a good neighbor. He'd raised two kids who were good students and good citizens; his son had just graduated from the navy's submariners school. Many of the church and Boy Scout people described Rader in the nicest terms. The *Eagle* quoted Ray Reiss, a friend of Rader's since their days at Heights High School. "It's trite to say that he's such a nice guy. Well . . . he is nice."

But the reporters also learned that he had compartmentalized his life, and in the compartment that involved wearing a uniform and working as a compliance officer, he had been deliberately cruel to people.

The *Eagle* quoted a former coworker at ADT Security Services, where Rader worked from 1974 to 1988. That was the period when Rader did most of his killing. "I don't believe the gentleman was well liked at all," said Mike Tavares. He described Rader as blunt, arrogant, and rude.

Houston, the sheriff's captain, noticed that when Rader described taking Dee Davis's body out to the bridge, he talked faster and faster, excitedly.

In Rader's writings, investigators found a journal in which Rader described how Dee pleaded with him: "Please, sir, I have children."

Investigators found photographs Rader took of himself tied up in his parents' basement. He was wearing Dee's undergarments.

Two days after Rader's arrest, Bonnie Bing's cell phone rang. It was Landwehr, sounding buoyant, telling the *Eagle*'s fashion writer that she no longer need fear BTK. In fact, he said, the letter that Cindy Carnahan had received in September was not from BTK at all. When Relph questioned him, Rader had said he never would have taken the risk of stalking a journalist. When Relph showed him a copy of the letter, Rader said that it wasn't his handiwork. Landwehr and Relph were now sure it had been written by a man from a prominent local family; he had mental problems but was harmless.

Bing was relieved.

"So why are you calling me?" she teased Landwehr. "Listen, Bud, we ain't goin' steady anymore."

Landwehr laughed. He sounded strong and happy.

He said he'd played a round of golf that morning.

Many citizens of Park City, after they got their names in the paper with a quote or two about Rader, got dozens of urgent calls from news organizations asking for more. At the *Eagle*, L. Kelly told reporters in the field to call only her cell phone; her desk phone was overwhelmed with calls from news editors and producers around the country and overseas wanting interviews. Although the reporters had been happy to give interviews about the case in the past, now their first priority had to be covering the story for local readers.

She and her boss, Tim Rogers, monitored local and national television coverage of BTK. Rogers ran across the newsroom when he saw a cable news channel reporting that Rader's daughter had turned him in: "Do we have that? Do we have that?"

"I'm checking it out," said a skeptical Kelly, dialing the phone. She called the city's biggest gossip on the case, who had sent the paper and the task force hundreds of e-mails in the past year. ("We can't control who e-mails us," Otis later said.) Kelly told Robert Beattie what she'd just seen on TV. Had he heard anything like that?

"Oh, I'm the one who told them that," he said, sounding surprised.

"Bob, do you *know that*, or have you just heard that?" Kelly asked.

"I'm just passing along everything I hear." The lawyer said he never expected the tip to be reported as fact.

Kelly next called a contact at the cable network; no, the woman said, they hadn't checked it out before putting it on the air. They had just assumed Beattie had inside information.

The network backed off the story.

• • •

Eagle reporter Suzanne Perez Tobias was in a living room surrounded by people who loved and missed Vicki Wegerle.

Vicki's husband, grown children, and others had gathered to talk over old photos, but they were waiting for Bill to get off the phone in the kitchen. Tobias was working on one of ten profiles the *Eagle* was preparing to honor the dead. In the upcoming Sunday paper, the victims would no longer be just a name, a photo, and a date of death.

"I'm sorry, Suzanne," Bill Wegerle said. "We aren't going to be able to do this today."

Bill explained that he'd gotten a call from the district attorney's office and had been told that speaking with Suzanne could jeopardize the case. He didn't want to do anything that might let Vicki's killer go free. Tobias didn't understand how talking about Vicki as a person—a beloved wife, a good mother—would have any impact on the trial, but Bill was clearly shaken. He asked Tobias to call the DA's office back to clarify what he'd been told, but it was after 6:00 PM, and no one answered. Everyone was disappointed, but the interview was over before it started.

The same thing happened to other families and reporters. Kelly fumed. Rader had confessed, the reporters were trying to portray the victims as real people, and now the burden of successful prosecution had been placed on the shoulders of their families. When Kelly received an e-mail from the DA's office saying BTK victims' families were requesting no further contact from reporters—with a list that included the Wegerles and the others who canceled interviews after getting "don't talk" phone calls—she made *that* a story.

It quoted DA spokeswoman Georgia Cole: family members had not been ordered to not talk to reporters, "We just told them the repercussions of what might happen if they did."

Three days after Rader's arrest, Laviana found an address for a George Martin, whom Laviana had heard might have known Rader in the Boy Scouts. He gave Martin's name to Wenzl, who with photographer Jaime Oppenheimer drove to Park City. Martin talked for half an hour about how good Rader was to boys in the Scouts. Wenzl thought about the knots mentioned in the 1974 Otero letter.

"I was in the Boy Scouts for about five minutes when I was a kid," he told Martin. "And all they talked about was how I needed to learn to tie knots in the Boy Scouts. Was Rader any good at tying knots and teaching knots?"

"Oh yes," Martin said. "He was one of the best teachers we had for teaching knots. All the knots, the square knot, the sheepshank, the double half hitch, the bowline knot, the taut line hitch for tying down tent poles, he knew them all. And I'll bet you he learned how to tie knots as a boy himself, in the Boy Scouts."

This was a scoop—one of America's most notorious serial killers had bound and strangled his victims using knots learned in the Boy Scouts. Wenzl asked for everything Martin could tell about Rader and knots.

Oppenheimer's cell phone rang. She interrupted Wenzl to say that they'd just been assigned to stop by the homes of Rader's in-laws and mother.

"Like anyone will open the door to us there," Wenzl said. He ignored the instructions and quizzed Martin about who else in the Park City Boy Scout troops might have known about Rader's skill with knots. Over the next half hour, editors repeatedly called Oppenheimer's phone, but Wenzl, writing down more Boy Scout names, waved off the calls.

By the time he finished with Martin, the editors were sounding frantic. Wenzl and Oppenheimer drove first to Rader's in-laws, walking up to their door as Wenzl swore about the assignment—"Nobody's going to answer the door." Oppenheimer turned on him.

"Why don't you just shut up and do your job?" she asked.

"Because I already have a great story on the knots, and this relatives thing is a goose chase," he said.

No one answered the door.

Wenzl wanted to break off and go find more Boy Scout leaders, but Oppenheimer drove to Rader's mother's house. Minutes later, they walked up to the door, with Wenzl still snapping at Oppenheimer. "If I was Rader's relative, I'd tell us to go to hell," he said. "They won't talk."

Wenzl knocked.

The door opened, and a big man with blue eyes and a thick mustache glared out at them.

"What do you want?"

"To talk to people from Dennis Rader's family," Wenzl said.

The man stepped out, shut the door behind him, and folded muscular arms across the top of his blue denim bib overalls.

"I'm his brother," the man said. "What do you want to know?"

Wenzl looked at Oppenheimer. She stifled a smile.

His name was Jeff Rader, he said. He was fifty years old, a plumber. He had never paid much attention to the BTK killings, and Dennis had never talked about them. He first knew something was up on the afternoon of February 25, when an FBI agent and two Wichita detectives interrogated him. When one of them blurted out that his brother was BTK, Jeff had laughed.

"I said, 'No *way*. You got the wrong guy.' But they just shook their heads. And one of them said, 'We're sure.' "

Jeff said Wenzl could not go in to see his mother, age seventy-nine. "It's too hard on my mother," he said. "And you'll get the dogs to yapping. But I'll talk with you for a minute."

His mother was very frail, he said. "She falls down once in a while. Doctors think she might have water on the brain."

The family never saw any sign that his brother could be a killer, he said. "My mother still can't believe it. She's still very much in denial. And so am I. But maybe, with me, acceptance is starting to creep in. I don't think my brother is BTK. But if he is—if that's the truth—then let the truth be the truth."

Cruel people had made prank calls to harass his mother, he said. "There are a lot of sick people out there. The sort who want to kick someone when they're down."

Television broadcasts had aired errors and speculation about the family, he said. No one in the family had turned in Dennis, for example. The four Rader brothers grew up with a loving mother and a tough but decent father, Jeff said. Their father, William Rader, had served as a marine and was a God-fearing man, strict but not unreasonable.

"All four boys became Boy Scouts," Jeff said. "We were a normal family. The boys all liked to be outdoors, go for hikes. We loved to hunt and fish."

There was no trouble in the family, no abuse, he said. The FBI agent had asked whether he or any of the boys had been sexually abused by their father.

"I told them no. And that's the truth."

With nine years between them, he did not spend a lot of time with his eldest brother, he said. And Dennis didn't want him around at times when they were younger. "But that was common in that an older brother never wants a younger brother around to tell on him," Jeff said. His brother was a good kid. "I wasn't," Jeff said. "I was a hell-raiser. But Dennis wasn't."

As adults, the brothers gathered with their mother at Thanksgiving, at Christmas. They enjoyed each other's company. Dennis and his wife, Paula, went to the house often to look after his mother, Jeff said. His brother often took the lead on that, driving their mother to the doctor when needed.

The family never had a clue about BTK, he repeated. He said their parents tried to teach them to be religious and to know the difference between right and wrong.

That same day, the cops stopped talking to Dennis Rader. He was devastated. He had loved it, loved talking to "Ken," loved "helping" the police, loved "working the cases."

The cops, glad to be done with him, handed him over to Sheriff

An unhappy Rader's booking photo.

Steed. Rader's first residence at the Sedgwick County jail was a small cell in the health clinic. The jail, the state's largest, had held high-profile inmates before, including Terry Nichols, one of the Oklahoma City bombing defendants. The jailers did not usually put inmates in isolation, but the staff had to improvise with Rader. They needed to evaluate where he could be safely placed.

The jailers instructed Rader to answer a questionnaire that asked about his emotional state, including whether he felt shame or embarrassment.

Yes, he wrote. *Because I got caught.*

Rader's ten murder charges once again make headlines.

June 27, 2005

Guilty Times Ten

As cops and prosecutors prepared for Rader's plea hearing in June, women wrote him marriage proposals and sent him money. Finally, he'd tapped into the romantic bad-boy mystique of serial killers Ted Bundy and John Wayne Gacy, who both married pen pals in prison. Fans wrote asking for autographs or interviews, and scholars and pseudoscholars sent queries about his psychology. Rader enthusiastically answered correspondence. People tried to sell BTK/Rader keepsakes online: code compliance documents with his signature, jailhouse letters, copies of the *Eagle* with the banner headline "BTK is arrested." He told jailers that his leg irons would fetch a thousand dollars on the memorabilia market.

A Topeka oil and gas analyst named Kris Casarona wrote long letters to Rader. She was thirty-eight and married; she often visited him in jail and wrote to him nearly every day. They insisted there was nothing to this other than the desire of a Christian woman to reach out to another person of faith.

Rader wrote to the three anchors at KAKE-TV. He clipped a photograph of Susan Peters and Jeff Herndon out of an ad in the *Eagle*, autographed it, and mailed it to them with a cheery note; he sent a color photograph of his flower garden in Park City to Peters. He drew a cartoon frog with wings on the envelope of a letter to Larry Hatteberg. He noted that he could not talk about the court case, but that he loved Hatteberg's work, especially the features called "Hatteberg's People." Perhaps Hatteberg could do a heart-warmer on the positive aspects of his life and work.

"Think about it," Rader wrote, "and I will too. . . . I will keep the door open. And if it doesn't work out—well—anyone can do a story along the line of—Animal Control–Code Enforcement—helps society out as a 'Better Home & Garden Cop.' Could be a start."

Hatteberg replied in polite but wry terms: "You mention in your letter the possibility of doing a story with a human touch about your life as the Compliance Officer in Park City. If I understand your thoughts (you might have to help me out a little here) . . . I want to be clear, I am a journalist and if I do one side . . . I need to do the other side. . . ."

Hatteberg thought they had done well covering the BTK story, though he also thought the tangle that KAKE had gotten into with the cops over the Seneca Street cereal box drop had been unnecessary. What he was angling for now was an interview with Rader. The first.

Susan Peters had broken two stories: she was the first to interview Shirley Vian's son Steve Relford, who as a little boy had let BTK into the house. Peters had also been the first to interview Kevin Bright—an encounter that brought down Landwehr's wrath. In the past several months, there had been times when Peters called the homicide section in tears begging for information about the case. At one point before Rader's arrest, she called Landwehr to tell him Kevin was in town. The KAKE staff had shown Bright some photos of men they considered potential BTK suspects and he had picked one out. Would Landwehr like to talk to Bright?

Sure, Landwehr said.

He was furious but he did not tell Peters that. Landwehr was tired of this amateur sleuthing. When Bright arrived for the meeting, Landwehr ordered the KAKE crew to stay out. After a few pleasantries, Landwehr pulled a photograph out of his shirt pocket and plopped it in front of Bright.

It was the very man whom Bright had thought might be BTK. It was also someone the cops had long ago eliminated with DNA testing. When Landwehr saw the bewilderment on Bright's face, he spoke in a cutting tone.

"Why do you think I knew which photograph it was that you were going to try to show me?" Landwehr asked. "Do you think I'm *psychic*, you dumb son of a bitch?"

Bright sat in shocked silence.

A detective spoke up. "Kenny, you're not talking to a suspect."

• • •

After his arrest, most of Rader's contact with his family was through Michael Clark, the minister of Christ Lutheran Church. He visited Rader about once a week, sometimes passing along messages. One Monday he was accompanied to the jail by one of Rader's brothers, Paul, who had secured an emergency leave from serving in Iraq.

Occasionally friends of Rader would contact the *Eagle* to defend him. And sometimes people who had their own suspects in mind, and had been frustrated by the cops' refusal to arrest them, called to insist the wrong man had been charged.

On June 27, Rader donned a cream-colored sports coat for his plea hearing. The *Eagle* and other news outlets had confirmed through inside sources that Rader had confessed, but no one except his defense attorneys knew whether he would plead guilty. What everyone was hoping for was an explanation.

Outside the courthouse, the usual tent city had sprung up, with satellite trucks and scores of journalists and television crews. Rader had the national audience he craved.

Otis and other detectives met with the victims' families one block from the courthouse. The cops positioned themselves around the group and walked them to the courthouse, past reporters. The families walked solemnly as though to a funeral, looking down at hot pavement; some held hands. The people with notepads and cameras behaved with restraint; no one asked about "feelings" or "closure."

The Internet helped build a global audience for BTK news. Even though the hearing was carried live on television, hundreds of thousands of people around the world followed proceedings through the *Eagle*'s frequent online updates. Rader immediately pleaded guilty to all ten counts of murder. But Judge Gregory Waller didn't let him leave it at that.

WALLER: "In regards to count one, please tell me in your own words what you did on the fifteenth day of January 1974, here in Sedgwick County, Kansas, that makes you believe you are guilty of murder in the first degree."

RADER: "Well, on January fifteenth, 1974, I maliciously—"

Waller interrupted. He didn't want Rader to merely parrot the charges against him.

"Mr. Rader, I need to find out more information. On that particular day, the fifteenth day of January 1974, can you tell me where you went to kill Mr. Joseph Otero?"

RADER: "Um . . . I think it's 1834 Edgemoor."

In the *Eagle* newsroom, reporters gasped: Who didn't know the Otero house was at 803 North Edgemoor? Had Rader really forgotten, or was this just an insult to the family and the authorities?

WALLER: "All right, can you tell me approximately what time of day you went there?"

RADER: "Somewhere between seven and seven thirty."

WALLER: "At this particular location, did you know these people?"

RADER: "No, that was part of what . . . I guess my what you call my fantasy. These people were selected."

WALLER: "So you were engaged in some kind of fantasy during this period of time?"

RADER: "Yes, sir."

WALLER: "Now, when you use the term *fantasy,* is this something you were doing for your personal pleasure?"

RADER: "Sexual fantasy, sir."

It was clear now that Waller wanted an explanation too . . . a detailed explanation. But it surprised even Waller that Rader gave chilling details in abundance—though he bungled his victims' names.

WALLER: "All right, what did you do to Joseph Otero?"

RADER: "Joseph Otero?"

WALLER: "Joseph Otero Sr., Mr. Otero, the father."

RADER: "I put a plastic bag over his head and then some cords and tightened it."

The exchange between Waller and Rader went on for more than an hour, with Rader's emotionless descriptions of his handiwork becoming more vivid the more he talked. The judge led Rader into a detailed description of all ten murders and a public revelation about what happened after he strangled Marine Hedge with his hands.

RADER: "Since I was still in the sexual fantasy, I went ahead and stripped her. I am not for sure if I tied her up at that point in time, but anyway she was nude. I put her on a blanket, went through her purse and personal items in the house. I figured out how I was going to get her out of there. Eventually, I moved her to the trunk of the car—the trunk of her car—and took the car over to Christ Lutheran Church, this was the older church, and took some pictures of her."

The pastor, sitting behind Rader in the gallery, grimaced. District Attorney Nola Foulston turned toward *Eagle* legal affairs reporter Ron Sylvester and, with eyes wide, mouthed the words: "In the church!"

At one point, trying to remember the details of Dee Davis's murder, Rader rolled his eyes upward and made noises that the court transcriber tried to describe:

RADER: "I took her out of her car . . . this gets complicated, then the stuff I had—clothes, guns, whatever—I took that to another spot in her car, dumped that off. Okay, then took her car back to her house, left that . . . let me think, now [makes popping noise with his mouth several times]."

Landwehr, looking embarrassed, turned to Relph and Otis and spoke in a stage whisper as though addressing Rader: "Jesus, you stupid son of a bitch, can you look any goddamned stupider? You'll make anybody watching think that *anybody* could have caught you anytime."

Relph and Otis stifled their laughter, but they were embarrassed too.

The cops, with Otis taking the point position, escorted the families out of the courthouse. This time they were surrounded by cameras and a more aggressive attitude.

"How do you feel?" reporters asked. "How do you feel?"

The families said nothing.

Landwehr walked with them.

"Any comment, Lieutenant?" someone asked.

"Not now, thanks," he said.

A few steps away, Steve Relford walked slowly, staring straight ahead.

As a little boy, he had let Rader into his home, then cried in the bathroom as Rader pulled a bag over his mother's head. He had spent most of his life since then drifting, getting high, and getting tattooed with human skulls.

He had made several threats against Rader. The cops had lectured him, and now he was trying to stay silent.

"How do you feel?"

"Fine," Relford said. He kept walking, his face turning red.

"Do you feel you have closure?"

"No."

50

July 2, 2005

Demons Within Me

KAKE's newsroom phones would not accept collect calls, so all three of the station's anchors had included their home numbers in letters asking Rader to talk to them.

By the time he wrote to Rader, Larry Hatteberg had spent thirty-one years on the story. He had been twenty-nine when he filmed the scene outside the Otero house in 1974. He was fifty-nine when he helped report BTK's return in 2004.

For years, he'd worked on his three-minute "Hatteberg's People" vignettes from his home office. He liked solitude and owned better camera and editing equipment than KAKE had in the studio. Still, he wasn't prepared when his phone rang at 10:20 AM on Saturday, July 2, summoning him from drinking a tall Americano from Starbucks on his back deck. On the phone he heard a computer asking whether he would accept a collect call from the Sedgwick County jail. He said yes. Then a voice spoke.

"This is Dennis L. Rader."

Hatteberg was suddenly nervous. This was the first BTK news media interview. Hatteberg had left most of his notes at KAKE, he didn't have his recording equipment hooked up, and he was feeling small terrors about saying something stupid to a serial killer, like "good to hear from you" or "thanks for calling."

So Hatteberg took a risk. He asked Rader to hang up and call back in a few minutes, giving Hatteberg time to hook up his recorder. Rader agreed, and in the moments that followed Hatteberg agonized over whether he'd lost the interview. But Rader did call back; he seemed eager to talk.

In the measured, warm voice that Rader had heard coming from his television for decades, Hatteberg asked about the recitation of BTK crimes in court five days earlier: "It seemed that you were incredibly cold about it, and you were talking about it the same as you would be talking about items at a grocery store. Can you talk about that?"

For about thirty seconds, Rader rambled in the odd tangent-upon-tangent way he had at the hearing, then settled down.

"I was totally unprepared for what the court asked me. I was a little shocked that the defense didn't step up to tap me on the shoulder to say 'Let's reconsider this,' or approach the bench.

"I basically just shot from the hip. I realized that was very cold and everything, but I just wanted to get the facts out just as quick as I could, try not to get too emotionally involved. If I sat down and actually—somebody sits with me in a room and we start talking about the cases, I get pretty emotional about it. Even right now it cracks my voice a little bit."

But his voice was not cracking.

"It's been a very trying and hard thing for me."

Then the man who had written in 1978 "How many do I have to Kill before I get a name in the paper or some national attention" told Hatteberg: "I think the bottom line is I want the people of Sedgwick County and the United States and the world to know that I am a serial killer.

"There are some things you can learn from this. I'm not trying to profit from it. I'm going to pay for it with a life sentence."

Hatteberg asked, "Do you have any remorse over the killings?"

"Yes, I do. . . . I fault Factor X," Rader said, a reference to his 1978 letter. "I have no idea. I'm very compartmentalized. I can live a normal life, quickly switch from one gear to the next. I guess that's why I survived so well in those thirty-one years; very compartmentalized. I can wear many hats. I can switch gears very rapidly. I can become emotionally involved; I can become cold at it. That's something maybe I will finally figure out, if I ever figure it out; it's a mystery."

Hatteberg asked how he felt about killing children, noting that "a lot of people just shake their head . . . particularly when you had children of your own."

"I think in the long run it was a sexual fantasy, the children. If you really look at it they were more of an offshoot, the action of going toward the crime, not so much the crime; the crime afterward was more of a—I guess you call it—a high for me. . . . There was probably some sexual fantasy in that. More of it was tended toward the adult persons; the kids just happened to be there, I think. That didn't work, with the adults; Josephine was probably the only one that I really expressed that sexual fantasy."

Rader then said he hoped Hatteberg would be able to edit their conversation before broadcast so it would not shock the community too much.

This baffled Hatteberg. How could anything be more shocking than Rader's crimes?

"Can you talk about Factor X a little more? When you wrote to us in the seventies, you said that it was Factor X that made you kill. Can you describe what that is?"

Rader noted that sometimes armed robbers shoot people because they are afraid of getting caught. But what drove him was "a really, really deep subject" that a telephone conversation couldn't adequately address. "I just know it's a dark side of me. It kind of controls me. I personally think it's—I know it's not very Christian, but I actually think it's demons within me."

Hatteberg offered Rader another chance to take responsibility for his actions: "What would you want to tell the families at this point? The families who have been hurt so much."

Rader responded like a project manager: "In the sentencing, it's going to be very remorseful—very apologetic to them. I'll be working on that. That's part of the thing that I and the defense has been working on, is the speech prepared for that. I have a lot of bad thoughts come about that: how can a guy like me—a church member, raised a family—go out and do those sorts of things? The only thing I can figure out is I'm compartmentalized; somewhere in my body I can just do those sorts of things and go back to a normal life. Which is unbelievable. . . . I looked in Mr. Fox's eyes on TV once, the tears in his eyes. I could be in the same shoes. I feel for them. I know they don't understand that, but I do."

When BTK began communicating in March 2004 after decades of silence, a lot of Wichitans speculated that he wanted to be caught. When

Hatteberg asked about that, Rader said: "No, I was not planning on being caught. I just played cat and mouse too long with the police, and they finally figured it out."

"Were you going to kill again?"

"No. Although I did set some things up for the police and place a couple of spins on it, but I was pretty well shutting things down."

That didn't match what authorities had said after Rader's arrest.

"So you were not going to kill again; you had no projects in the works?"

Rader was coy.

"Well, yes and no. That's a secret. There was probably one more, I was really thinking about it, but I was beginning to slow down agewise, my thinking process, so it probably would have never went; probably more of an ego thing to tell them that that was going to go. . . ."

"Had you picked the person?"

"Yes . . . there was one already picked out."

"Do you know her name?"

"No, not at this time. No no no, I'll never release that. I don't want them to get upset."

Interesting; he was concerned about her feelings.

"Do you have any feeling for the people that you killed?"

"Oh yes, I thought I said that earlier; I went through that a little. I saw Mr. Fox—you talking about the victims? Oh yes, I do. I have a lot of feelings for them; they were a—I guess they were more—more of an achievement or an object. . . . They were actually just an object to me."

Prodded to talk about that, Rader said, "When I was in grade school I started having some problems."

"What kind of problems were they?"

"Sexual fantasies; probably more than normal. You got to remember puberty—all males probably go through some kind of sexual fantasies. It was probably weirder than other people. . . . I think somewhere along the line, I knew probably by the time I was in the eighth grade, or a freshman in high school, I knew I had some abnormal fantasies. But they exploded on January 15, 1974. That's when the ball came loose. . . .

"I'll have a long time to figure it out," Rader concluded. "Many more years."

•   •   •

Rader invited Hatteberg and anchor Jeff Herndon to see him two days later, the Fourth of July, at the Sedgwick County jail. They weren't allowed to take a camera, but they took notes. They asked Rader why he resurfaced when he could have gotten away with murder.

The spark was reading Hurst Laviana's thirtieth-anniversary BTK story in the *Eagle* in January 2004. Laviana had interviewed a lawyer who was working on a book about the murders, and Rader explained that it bothered him that someone else was writing his story.

He said his wife knew nothing. He had never told anyone about BTK before his arrest; he never would have told anyone.

He was not worried about prison. "It can't be that bad." In jail all the inmates did was sit around and learn how to commit crimes—how to rob a bank, how to start a fire. "Crime 101," he called it.

Had he ever posted a message on the online BTK discussion boards? No, Rader said. He was afraid it would be traceable.

"Did you ever have an accomplice?" Hatteberg asked. Charlie Otero, who had come to court from New Mexico for the plea hearing, had said that he thought there was no way Rader could have killed his father without help.

Rader hesitated.

No, he said.

"But I did have a little friend with me."

The friend, he said, was an imaginary frog he had named "Batter." In recent days he had drawn the smiling, winged cartoon frog on envelopes containing his correspondence. As Rader talked, Hatteberg understood him to mean that Batter was the demon within.

51

July 11, 2005

Auction Bizarro

It was a tiny dwelling, only 960 square feet, a 1954 ranch-style home where he and Paula had raised their two children, where he had plotted murders and stored trophies. His crimes had cost Paula her breadwinner and her home. She wanted to sell the house.

Tim Potter talked the auctioneer, Lonny McCurdy, into letting him take a tour of the empty house a few days before the sale. Potter wanted an exclusive story; McCurdy wanted more bidders.

When Potter saw the dust outline of the bed on the hardwood floor of the main bedroom, he realized he was looking at the spot where BTK had slept and planned and daydreamed.

In the bathroom, Potter pondered his own reflection in the mirror, then eased open the medicine cabinet door. This was intimate territory. There were two clippings from the *Eagle*'s feature section taped inside: tips on how to tell if you have a cold or the flu.

For the auction, the *Eagle* sent two photographers, plus Potter, Hurst Laviana, and a young reporter named Brent Wistrom, working his first full shift of night cops. Also present were the *New York Times,* the *Los Angeles Times,* the *National Enquirer, People* magazine, *Inside Edition,* network, cable, and local TV photographers with their power cords and satellite trucks—all rubbing elbows with home-buyers, the curious, and the just plain nosy.

Police blocked off the street and kept the public away from the property. Some walked up anyway and snapped pictures.

Michelle Borin-Devuono, a strip club owner well known to Wichitans from her wry and seductive ads on late-night local television, walked into Rader's house with a real estate agent and her muscular, tattooed husband, former Wichita Thunder hockey player Len "Devo" Devuono.

She and other bidders gathered around the auctioneer in the backyard. Some bid via cell phone. One couple held a video camera and traded off cradling their Chihuahua.

Park City Police Chief Bill Ball took a picture of his officers monitoring Rader's backyard. They in turn took a picture of him. Ball then aimed a camera at the reporters and photographers. "Turnabout's fair play, right?" he said.

Many of the neighbors had put up yellow tape and "Keep out" signs in their yards. In the months since Rader's arrest, news and film crews from as far away as Denmark had knocked on their doors.

McCurdy reminded the bidders that the stove, refrigerator, dishwasher, dryer, and washing machine would stay with the house.

"Think of the rental potential this has," he exclaimed.

He noted it was conveniently located only a few hundred yards from I-135.

"Park City is a city on the move," he declared.

He did not mention BTK.

The strip club owner had the winning bid of ninety thousand dollars—thirty-three thousand dollars above the appraised value.

"I'm a real estate investor," she told Potter later. "I'd like to see all the proceeds go to Mrs. Rader and help her family out. I've worked very hard all my life to get where I'm at today. I couldn't even imagine what she is going through. This is the least I can do." But Paula Rader would not soon see any of the proceeds. Families of BTK's victims sued to seize the "extra" thirty-three thousand dollars that they argued was the fruit of her husband's notoriety. During the legal battle, the buyer backed out.

After the auction ended, Laviana found himself alone in BTK's backyard, listening to Wayne Newton singing through the auctioneer's loudspeakers:

"Danke schoen, darling, danke schoen. Thank you for all the joy and pain. . . ."

August 17–19, 2005

The Monster Is Banished

For Rader's sentencing in August, District Attorney Nola Foulston thought detailed testimony in the national spotlight was in order.

Many Wichitans, including some defense attorneys, criticized this decision. Rader had confessed and accepted his fate. Why go to the expense of such a hearing? Why put all the sordid details on television, where they would shock the victims' families and needlessly embarrass Rader's innocent wife and children? Was Foulston grandstanding?

Prosecutor Kevin O'Connor despised the backroom gossip. For one thing, Foulston had asked every one of BTK's victim families whether they had any problem with her putting on the evidence. None objected.

Rader fails to convince people of his remorse during his sentencing hearing.

For another thing, O'Connor said, "If we had wanted to grandstand, the best way to do that would have been to call a press conference and stand there and talk, just the DA, and hold forth for hours in front of the cameras. But that's not what Nola did."

People needed to hear from the cops about what they knew, she decided. Otherwise, the only full public explanation of BTK's crimes would have come from Rader himself, at his plea hearing. Although Rader's account to the judge had been detailed and horrifying, he minimized the torture.

O'Connor said there was one other reason to proceed. Foulston had long experience with victims of crime. She'd kept that promise, made years before, to handle some murder trials herself, in spite of the work it took to supervise more than fifty assistant prosecutors. She knew how therapeutic it was for victims' family members to personally confront a killer at his moment of justice. "It is almost like a way for the family to say 'You didn't get away with it,' " O'Connor said.

There were other advantages, some of them dark. Otis knew enough about Rader now to know that he feared for his life in prison and wanted inmates to think that they were about to meet a big, bad serial killer—a

Wichita police detective Dana Gouge presents toys found in the Vian bathroom during Rader's sentencing hearing.

dangerous man who should be taken seriously. Otis also knew what convicts thought of child molesters and guys who liked to dress in women's clothing. He hoped all the inmates planned to watch Rader's sentencing on television.

In the hearing, held over two days, Foulston asked the detectives to go into gruesome detail about each murder from the witness stand. "I was so sick of the arrogance he had shown at his plea hearing," she said later. "Much of what we did in the sentencing was deliberately designed to break down his arrogance by showing publicly who he really was."

Ray Lundin of the KBI told how Rader had mocked Josie Otero during his confession. Dana Gouge pulled on rubber gloves and held up the toys that BTK had tossed into the bathroom to occupy Shirley Vian's children while he strangled her. Foulston, O'Connor, and Prosecutor Kim Parker showed photographs Rader had taken of himself in bondage, wearing a stolen bra and slip.

Otis tried to get Rader to make eye contact with him as he described Rader confessing to Vicki Wegerle's murder, but Rader avoided his glare, glancing up only to peek at photos of her body when they flashed on the courtroom screen.

Some of what Foulston and the cops did in the courtroom was

Sedgwick County Sherrif's Office Capt. Sam Houston holds up the mask Rader left by Dolores Davis's body.

designed to mess with Rader's head. Foulston wanted to send him to prison as a psychologically shaken man. She had pondered how to do this, and Landwehr's vivid descriptions of what an anal-retentive neat freak Rader was gave her an idea about how to do it.

When Landwehr took the stand, Foulston approached him with a bag full of Rader's cutouts of women on index cards that Rader had neatly bound with rubber bands. She dumped them out, undid the rubber bands, and deliberately made a mess of the pile pawing through it. Rader, watching this angrily from the defense table, threw his pen on the floor. But Foulston found her own surprise in the pile: she picked up one of the hundreds of cards at random, turned it over, and read the name "Nola" on the back.

Startled, she showed it to Landwehr in the witness chair.

"Did you realize this was in this pile?" she whispered.

"No," Landwehr whispered back in surprise. They had both examined the photos in preparation for the hearing and had missed it.

The next day, after hearing statements from victims' family members, Waller sentenced Rader to ten consecutive life sentences, one for each murder. Rader, by now sixty, would not be eligible for parole until well past his one-hundredth birthday.

Rader had prepared for this. One day, as deputies were moving Rader

**Wichita police detective Tim Relph unfolds the nightgown
found beside the body of Nancy Fox.**

in leg chains to another part of the jail, Rader began to jog in place. He said he was exercising so that he would not enter prison as a weakling. And though he had been heterosexual all his life, he was now considering alternatives. Homosexuality might be interesting in prison, he told the cops.

Before dawn the morning after the sentencing, deputies took Rader on the thirty-minute drive from Wichita to the El Dorado Correctional Facility. Rader was dressed in a red jumpsuit and slip-on sandals, shackled at ankles, wrists, and waist.

Sheriff Gary Steed, who years before had investigated the murder of Dolores Davis, assigned himself and two deputies to make the drive.

On the way, they heard a news station play a recording of accusing voices from the previous day's sentencing:

"I'm Carmen Julie Otero Montoya," the Oteros' daughter had told Rader in the courtroom. "Although we have never met, you have seen my face before. It is the same face you murdered over thirty years ago—the face of my mother, Julie Otero. She showed me how to love, to be a good person, to accept others as they are, and, most of all, to face your fears. I'm sure you saw that in her face as she fought to live. My mother against your gun. You are such a *coward.* . . ."

**Wichita police detective Kelly Otis tries to make eye contact
with Rader during the sentencing hearing.**

She described every family member, starting with her playful father.

"I'm sure you could feel his love for his family as you took away his last breath. You are such a coward."

Her sister, Josie.

"It's amazing to me that you could be so cruel to a sweet, beautiful child."

Joey, forever nine years old.

"His name was Joey, *not* 'Junior,' but I guess it really doesn't matter to you. . . . A man with a gun against a little boy. You are definitely a coward. . . .

"Just recently I realized that I could not remember my mother's voice. It was a painful discovery, but as I put my thoughts on paper it comes to me—I am my mother's voice. And I know we've been heard."

The judge allowed representatives from all seven families to talk. In the car with Steed, Rader listened to their voices as he looked at green pastures rolling by. Steed wondered how Rader was handling this. Some of the people making statements the day before had cried; some had denounced Rader venomously, including Dee Davis's son, Jeff, a former sheriff's officer:

"I have determined that for the sake of our innocent victims and their loving families and friends with us here today, for me this will be a day of

**Wichita police detective Clint Snyder holds the knife
Rader used to stab Kathy Bright eleven times.**

celebration, not retribution. If my focus were hatred, I would stare you down and call you a demon from hell who defiles this court at the very sight of its cancerous presence. . . . If I were spiteful, I would remind you that it is only fitting that a twisted, narcissistic psychopath, obsessed with public attention, will soon have his world reduced to an isolated solitary existence in an eighty-square-foot cell, doomed to languish away the rest of your miserable life, alone."

In the car, Rader lowered his head and took off his glasses with his cuffed hands. He glanced at Steed, who saw tears in Rader's eyes.

Rader had made a lame attempt during the hearing to apologize, but no one had taken it seriously. Some of the families of his victims had not even heard it; to express their contempt they left the courtroom before he started what would become known in Wichita as "the Golden Globes speech." Rambling on for more than twenty minutes, Rader had thanked nearly every person in the courtroom and every person he'd met in jail, as though he were taking a final bow.

He noted traits he had in common with the people he killed: military service, schooling, hobbies, pet ownership. And he spoke wistfully of his "relationship" with the cops.

Rader's final steps before entering El Dorado Correctional Facility to serve ten consecutive life sentences for first-degree murder.

"I felt like I did have a rapport with the law enforcement people during the confession," he said. "I almost felt like they were my buddies. At one time I asked about LaMunyon maybe coming in and having a cup of coffee with me."

Steed wondered: was Rader sorry, or was he sorry only for himself, that it was over, that soon he would find himself alone in a cell, while the media moved on to other stories?

Rader pointed out to Steed how green the pastures looked. Steed agreed. Kansas was usually bone-dry in August, the grass a rusty brown, but rain had brought the land to life. The world looked fresh and new.

Rader looked at the prairie, luminous at dawn. Steed realized this might be BTK's last look at the countryside and the big Kansas sky. Rader would be housed alongside death row inmates, kept in a cell for twenty-three hours a day.

When they reached the prison entrance, Rader got out and, for a moment, did a quirky-looking stretch to adjust his back.

He shuffled to the prison door, squinting into the rising sun, surrounded by fences topped with loops of concertina wire.

He went in.

Epilogue

It remained for the living to ponder two questions: why did Dennis Rader do it, and why did it take thirty-one years to catch him?

The detectives who researched the records and interviewed his family and friends found no broken home in his past, no evidence of abuse in his childhood, none of the clichéd explanations for deviant behavior. The fact is, some people kill for no reason, and many people from broken or alcoholic or single-parent homes turn out well. The most disturbing thing childhood friends told the *Eagle* about Rader as a boy was that he had no use for humor. None of them knew about his inner life and the secret hobbies that he began nurturing when he was young.

Rader himself, talking frankly with the detectives during his thirty-three-hour interrogation, said there was nothing in his family or his past that made him what he was. He argued that his own explanation—that there was a demon within, a monster that controlled him, "Factor X" as he sometimes called it—was the only one that made sense. How else do you explain a man who made many friends but strangled people, who lovingly raised two children but murdered children?

Hearing this, Landwehr and his homicide detectives rolled their eyes. They know, because they talk to murderers all the time, that the character of many of them seems to be shaped by a cold-blooded egocentrism. It's all about them; it's always someone else's fault; it's always the fault of "factors"—such as how they were raised, or that they were drunk and not in their right minds when they killed the baby. Most murderers have some similar sort of jailhouse justification for refusing to accept responsibility for their acts. The cops hear these excuses from killers so much that the excuses bore them. In the end, Rader may have garnered more publicity than most killers, but to the ears of his interrogators, his justifications did not sound unique or interesting at all.

So why did he do it? Why is it that one Boy Scout grows up to become a serial killer, while other Boy Scouts like Kenny Landwehr, Kelly Otis, and Dana Gouge grow up to become the investigators who hunt him down and put him in a cage? Landwehr said it boils down to this: we all make choices. Rader made his—and ten people died.

In an interview he gave to a state-paid psychologist evaluating him immediately after his guilty plea, Rader talked about motivation: "I don't think it was actually the person that I was after, I think it was the dream. I know that's not really nice to say about a person, but they were basically an object. . . . I had more satisfaction building up to it and afterwards than I did the actual killing of the person."

Detective Tim Relph pointed out that Rader began to plan how to lie to everyone around him long before the Otero murders. Rader made it clear that even in the air force, years before he murdered the Oteros, he was training himself to break into buildings, stalk women, and develop ruses to talk his way into their homes. When he returned to Kansas, he used his family, school, work, hobbies, volunteering, and church to create a cover story for who he really was.

There was a time when Relph thought there was a good chance that Rader was a Jekyll and Hyde, living a painful and psychologically divided life. But then Relph interviewed Rader, and it became clear to him that there was no remorse, and little division in Rader's mind. "People will think ninety percent of him is Dennis Rader and ten percent is BTK," he told us, "but it's the other way around."

Detective Clint Snyder went further: Rader is the closest thing Snyder has ever seen to a human being without a soul. "You don't see that very often, even among murderers," Snyder said. "Some murderers still show signs of being human and caring for others."

Tony Ruark, one of the psychologists who was brought into the BTK case in the late 1970s, thinks that the task force detectives' analysis is not quite satisfactory.

"Something really did happen to Rader early in life to make him the way he is. I wish I could be the one to find it," Ruark said. "I do believe the detectives when they say that there was no child abuse in his past, no broken home, no sexual abuse. And like the detectives, I don't think there is a 'Factor X' explanation, as Rader called it. There is nothing mystical about what happened to him. There is no demon within.

"Still, when I read Rader's comments, I did not take it the way the detectives did. I don't think Rader meant what he said to be an excuse. I've seen other sexually deviant people say similar things, and when they blame their behavior on a 'Factor X,' they are usually just trying to put a label or a name to this incredible drive they feel to perform deviant acts. I think that's what Rader intended—to try to put a name on the drive that possessed him."

Ruark is also certain that if Rader was honest in his answers to psychologists, "eventually we would find something that had happened to him, probably early in childhood. Now, you need to understand that whatever it was, it doesn't necessarily have to be something big or traumatic—or even *relevant* to the rest of us. It might be an encounter or an event that the detectives and the rest of us might consider irrelevant and inconsequential, and I'm pretty sure it would be something that happened not from outside but within Rader's own mind. But I am fairly sure we would find something, and I am sure that what we would find would be some sort of childhood event that Rader immediately associated with feelings of sexuality. Somehow, very early on, Rader encountered an event where he immediately linked sexual pleasure with watching a living creature suffer and die. And after that first encounter, Rader probably began to work very hard to nurture those feelings. He began to go out of his way as a child to create situations in which he could play out the dominance and torture to increase his sexual pleasure."

Ruark was startled by the numerous sexually deviant fetishes Rader has, the intensity of feeling he has for them, and the incredible amount of work Rader was willing to do to satisfy them.

"I've treated people with sexual fetishes before, but I've never seen anyone like this guy, where there were so many fetishes, and where they so dominated his life: the cross-dressing, the trolling for females, the slick ad photographs he carried with him at all times, the filing system, the note taking, the enormous effort he put into burying himself while wearing a mask, and photographing himself with a remote camera."

Ruark said he's sure of one other thing: "These drives don't just appear by magic. No one ever lives a normal life and then wakes up one day and decides: 'Hey, I think I'll go become a sexually deviant serial killer.' "

Besides the violent sexual fetishes, the dominant characteristic of Rader's psyche is his ego. Landwehr had pondered BTK's ego as early as 1984, when the Ghostbusters first thought to turn it against him.

Rader's ego demands acknowledgment; he daydreams about being mysterious, like James Bond, but he craves the notoriety attached to Jack the Ripper, Son of Sam, Ted Bundy, and his other heroes.

In that June 27, 2005, interview with the psychologist immediately after detailing ten murders for Judge Waller, Rader sat in front of a camera and said, "I feel pretty good. It's kind of like a big burden that was lifted off my shoulders. On the other hand, I feel like I'm—kind of like I'm a star right now."

Before Landwehr and the FBI plotted out their faux news conferences in 2004, they had pondered how the news media have changed since 1974 and how those changes might prove useful. They knew that BTK did not merely crave headlines, he craved *national* headlines.

"In 1974 and in 1978, when he first wrote to us, he was still not national news, no matter how bad he was; he was still just a Wichita story," Landwehr told us. "He saw that, so he didn't communicate enough with us back then to trip himself up.

"But in 2004, with the Internet and cable television covering crime like they do, he finally became national news, and that played to his ego, and that really got him going. There were only five communications from BTK years ago. But there were—what?—eleven communications from BTK in eleven months in '04 and '05? And in the last one he made that mistake, and that's how we finally got him."

Some of the cops, including Landwehr, were surprised when they finally got a good look at BTK. They had assumed he would be smarter. Back in the 1970s, some cops had theorized that BTK was a criminal mastermind who disguised his intellect with crippled sentence syntax and intentional typographical errors. The timing of the "Shirley Locks" poem appeared to be connected to a contest in *Games* magazine. Local Mensa members fussed over that possible connection for years, convinced that BTK was brilliant. But it had just been a coincidence of timing.

After talking to Rader for hours at a time, the detectives concluded BTK was more lucky and stupid than smart.

And he reinforced that conclusion when he stood before the judge and the cameras on sentencing day and compared himself favorably with the people he murdered.

"Joseph Otero," Rader said. "He was a husband, I was a husband. . . . Josephine—she would have been a lot like my daughter at that age. Played with her Barbie dolls. She liked to write poetry. I like to write poetry. She liked to draw. I like to draw. . . ."

But if he is stupid, how come a police force full of smart cops took three decades to put him in cuffs?

"The Keystone Kops," Rader called them in that post-plea talk with the psychologist. "They had thirty-some years to break it, and they couldn't do it. The taxpayers who are paying the money for Sedgwick County, they really need to have . . . a sharper bunch."

Rader wasn't the only person who questioned the cops' competence. There was plenty of grousing around Wichita.

By November 2005, nine months after he pointed his Glock at Rader, Scott Moon had been promoted to detective and was working in the Exploited & Missing Child Unit. He was bench-pressing weights at the downtown YMCA one day when he overheard a group of lawyers gossiping and laughing about the BTK case. Wasn't that news conference announcing Rader's arrest an embarrassment? All those cops just seemed to *love* patting themselves on the back. And after all, the cops didn't do much of anything. They weren't smart enough to catch him until the guy turned himself in. BTK was probably laughing at them.

Moon dropped his weights on the rack and walked toward the lawyers, his adrenaline pumping.

"I helped arrest him that day," he said. "And if you ask me, he looked pretty damned embarrassed about it."

Moon was ready to talk some more, but the lawyers looked down at the floor.

Few people knew the full story of what Landwehr and his detectives had done, or how cleverly he had played Rader. After the arrest, Landwehr told us the strategy that caught Rader—playing to his ego and enticing him to communicate until he made a mistake—was suggested by the FBI's Bob Morton.

But Holmes and Dotson, Landwehr's fellow Ghostbusters, scoffed at this, pointing out that the Ghostbusters had decided as early as 1985 to do that very thing, should BTK resurface. Landwehr and Dotson had talked endlessly and with some anguish about BTK in the decades after the Ghostbusters broke up. Landwehr had rehearsed what he would do: use the media, play to his ego, trip him up.

Yes, FBI behavioral specialists were involved, Holmes said. "The FBI did help shape it with us. But we came up with the idea long ago. And Kenny carried it out."

But why would Landwehr say, as he did after the arrest, that the strategy was the FBI's idea?

"Because Kenny's not stupid," Holmes said. "What's he gonna do? Invite the FBI into his case, then listen to their ideas, and then call a press conference after the capture and take full personal credit for the strategy and the glory? He's too smart for that. He's still working homicide cases, he still needs the FBI, and they really did help shape the strategy. But that's typical Kenny, to give them all the credit. He doesn't give a damn about taking credit."

O'Connor pointed out several acts that combined wisdom with restraint, including the way Landwehr coolly took that call from Snyder, telling him they'd found the black Jeep Cherokee at the home of BTK. Landwehr had decided immediately to pull back the detectives and risk the long, slow but strategic route to Rader's arrest. Landwehr had, almost in the next breath, begun to propose how to verify Rader's DNA signature by obtaining the Pap smear DNA of his daughter.

O'Connor thought one of the most ingenious—and courageous—things Landwehr did took place many years before BTK resurfaced. "In the late 1980s and early 1990s, when DNA testing became more of a scientific possibility, Landwehr refused the temptation to test the DNA material in the BTK case. Had he tested it then, he would have used up the samples that they had." They wouldn't have yielded nearly the amount of genetic information they did once the tests became more sophisticated.

And they wouldn't have been nearly as useful in eliminating suspects and proving Rader was BTK.

"It was a really smart move," O'Connor said. "And it was typical of Landwehr; he was playing a long game with BTK long before BTK came back."

The arrest was such a relief to Landwehr that he was willing to listen to any amount of criticism over why it took so long, knowing that it no longer mattered.

His detectives knew—and did not care—that some people would refuse to accept the best explanation: when people kill randomly, they often get away with it. That's why Ted Bundy got away with perhaps thirty-six or more murders before they caught him. Jeffrey Dahmer nearly got away with seventeen. Richard Ramirez, the Night Stalker, killed fourteen. Wayne Williams in Atlanta may have killed as many as twenty-four. John Wayne Gacy killed thirty-three.

Most murders occur for explainable reasons—money, power, revenge, jealousy. Most killers kill someone they know. The cops can usually connect the dots and find the killer.

Detective Otis told us he would have bet his job that once BTK's identity was known, he'd find a connection among the victims—however small. But there was none.

And though Rader made mistakes, he was careful to never leave fingerprints, to always wear gloves, and wipe down vehicles. Above all, he kept his mouth shut. The DNA technology that finally nailed the case—it did not exist when BTK was killing people and leaving his semen at murder scenes. When the CSI guys preserved the fluid they found in the Oteros' basement, they couldn't foresee how it would be used thirty years later. And even when genetic science had caught up to the evidence, it didn't directly lead to his capture.

But how do you explain that to critics? How do you convince people of this when week after week they watch fictional cops use fictionalized science to get instantaneous results on television?

Landwehr decided soon after Rader's arrest to avoid being apologetic or thin-skinned.

"What happened, happened," he said. "The fact is, we never would have caught him had he never resurfaced. He'd gotten away with it; he'd gotten away with murder.

"We had put together, with the help of the best FBI experts, all those lists with thousands of names of potential suspects," Landwehr said, "and he wasn't on most of them." Like tens of thousands of other Wichitans, Rader had worked for Coleman for a short time; it was a coincidence that Julie Otero and the Brights also had worked there later. He was in the air force during the Vietnam era but didn't cross paths with Joe Otero. He was a Wichita State student when its enrollment was about fourteen thousand.

"When you pick out a hunting area as he did, and never leave any evidence behind, there's a good chance you're going to get away with it," Landwehr said. "He left no witnesses, or the witnesses he left, all they could really tell us was that BTK was 'a white male.' "

Once the cops caught Rader and saw example after example of how stupid he was, it embarrassed them.

Landwehr asked Rader about the strange string of characters at the top of his letter to the *Eagle* in March 2004—the Wegerle message. Rader had stenciled *GBSOAP7-TNLTRDEITBSFAV14*.

Rader looked at Landwehr as though the commander of the BTK task force were the stupidest man on earth. It's a code! Rader said. A German fractional code he had learned in the air force! Rader said this as though explaining that the sun rose in the east.

What did the code mean? Landwehr asked. He told Rader the FBI cryptologists could not figure it out.

It meant "Let Beattie know for his book," Rader said. Hurst Laviana had quoted the lawyer in his January 2004 BTK story. Rader was clearly baffled at how the cops could have missed the meaning of that coded message.

But when Landwehr asked Rader to re-create how he had formulated the message into code, Rader tried—and could not do it. He could not make any more sense out of the stenciling than the cops could.

The year 2005 was a good one for Landwehr. On April 9, only forty-three days after the biggest arrest of his career, he pulled a four-iron out of his golf bag on the 585-yard thirteenth hole of the Tex Consolver golf course in west Wichita. Landwehr scored a double eagle—two shots on a par five. His buddies Bob Ebenkamp, Mike Razook, and Steve Schulte looked on and cheered. In some ways, Landwehr would cherish that far more than the "Hello, Mr. Landwehr" moment.

Chief Norman Williams named Landwehr Wichita's police officer of the year for 2005. At one of the official gatherings to celebrate this, Landwehr stood patiently as a city staffer pinned a flower to his lapel. Then he leaned against a wall to wait for the ceremony, looking tired and uncomfortable.

"Nice flower," someone said.

"Yeah," Landwehr deadpanned. "But I wonder, does wearing it on the left lapel somehow signify that I'm gay?"

When the ceremony began, as Landwehr stepped up to speak, someone in the small room took his picture with one of those point-and-shoot cameras. The rasping rewind noise was so loud that several heads turned to look at the embarrassed photographer, who was trying to look small in her chair.

It was Irene Landwehr, eighty-five years old, sitting with Kenny's wife and son.

He was now semifamous, if only briefly, and was appearing, with his detectives, in nationally televised cable news documentaries. Women fawned over him at speaking engagements; he would look at the floor in embarrassment, leaving them talking to the top of his graying head.

There would be a made-for-television movie, in which Gregg Henry played Rader, and Robert Forster, looking like Landwehr, played a composite cop with a different name. CBS released it in October 2005 after crash-producing it in six months. People in Wichita made fun of the highly fictionalized account in part because the pseudo-Landwehr had the invaluable help of an attractive female detective, played by Michael Michele, even though the primary detectives on the BTK task force were guys who looked like linebackers gone to seed.

"That's all I need," Landwehr said when Tim Potter told him about the fictional female. "Cindy will kick my ass."

He looked forward to the time when the people from the news networks finally stopped shining lights on him and clipping tiny microphones to his shirt. To the time when he could relax and have a smoke and play golf and sleep at night without having to hunt BTK in his dreams.

At El Dorado Correctional Facility, Rader sits in his eight-by-ten cell, sometimes in boxer shorts with his hairy back exposed. Most of the time he wears a two-piece uniform—chocolate-brown scrubs—with a white T-shirt and blue slip-on shoes.

His cell is furnished with a metal desk, a metal stool bolted to the floor, a combination toilet-sink-water fountain, and a concrete bed covered with a two-inch slab of foam.

In the mornings he splashes water on himself from the metal sink. He gets to take a shower nearly every other day.

He spends a lot of time talking on the phone in his cell, mostly to Kris Casarona, the Topeka woman who befriended him in jail.

Rader never leaves his cell without wearing restraints. Guards pass his food trays through a hinged slot called a "bean hole." Other inmates call him "child molester." Landwehr thinks Rader probably would not survive if he were ever put into the general prison population; someone would kill him.

Although Rader can leave his cell an hour a day for a walk in one of

Rader's official prison mug shot at El Dorado Correctional Facility.

the fenced enclosures in the yard, he often declines to go. The enclosures resemble dog runs, with fencing overhead. Each enclosure has a chin-up bar. There are about twenty such pens in the yard. Each pen is limited to one prisoner at a time, but the inmates can yell at each other from pen to pen. It gets loud in the yard.

His neighbors include the Carr brothers, who killed those four people in the snow.

Inmates sometimes communicate by sending things from cell to cell using dental floss. They call it fishing. They shove notes, called "kites," under doors. Some have tried to get autographs from Rader, hoping to sell them. He got in trouble not long after his arrival for trying to smuggle a letter out by tucking it into an envelope addressed to someone else—but all his mail is screened, so it didn't work. Since then, his good behavior has earned him the right to purchase pencils, paper, and "handicrafts" at the commissary; watch television; and listen to the radio. The prosecutors—as well as many other Wichitans—were outraged when the *Eagle* broke the story about Rader's living conditions and perks. District Attorney Foulston had argued that Rader could look at just about anything and find it sexually stimulating, and Judge Waller had recommended to prison officials that Rader not be given access to anything that could fuel his violent sexual fantasies. But the warden determined that Rader would be treated much like other inmates in his classification; he can earn rewards and lose privileges based on his behavior in prison.

Rader's view consists of a vertical slit window at the back of his cell. From there he can see food service workers and corrections officers coming and going at shift changes.

Rader's phone conversations with Casarona often start with him voicing hope that his ex-wife and children will communicate.

Someday they will, Casarona tells him.

I'm never going to be able to hold Paula again, he tells her.

To his surprise, Landwehr missed the chase.

"As with a car chase, your adrenaline is pumping, and when it's over—well, it didn't feel good when it was going on—but for eleven months, we were challenged like no other. We were never bored. Not that going back to the regular stuff is all that boring, but . . . I had to adjust to it after it ended.

"But over time, I realized something: there's a lot of stuff that can happen, and maybe they won't be as famous as this one. But there are still a lot of bad people out there; you are still gonna see people doing harm to kids out there, and it's your job to stop them. There are still going to be serial killers out there. And maybe the next one will start tomorrow, and this one, unlike Rader, will be leaving new bodies for us to find. And that will be a lot worse to endure than what we had to go through with Rader."

Landwehr spent more time with his family after Rader's arrest. They went to Hawaii for a few days. He took Cindy to Las Vegas to see a singer she'd spent thirty years swooning over: Barry Manilow.

At night, on his back porch, he could look at the moon and the stars moving slowly over the tops of tall trees. The crickets sang, and he listened.

His wife and his son had done much to settle him down. Gone were the days when he regularly got hammered in bars or got drunk alone. James demanded that he quit smoking too. "Don't you know smoking causes lung cancer?" Landwehr kept smoking, out of sight of his son.

He thought about what to do with the rest of his life. He refused to take the test to become a captain. For one thing, he had no advanced degree; for another, he did not want to give up command of the homicide section.

"Don't make him move," Cindy Landwehr told Chief Williams one day. "He'd be miserable."

He was in his early fifties. He had no plans to retire. "Where would I go to work?" he said with a shrug. "I don't have a lot of skills."

A year after Rader's arrest, people were still coming up to him once or twice a week to thank him. When he and Cindy went out to eat, groups at other tables stole glances, pointing and whispering.

"I can't take you anywhere," Cindy teased him.

Several people urged him to write a book. He turned these suggestions away, "at least for now." He agreed to help the *Eagle* with this book because he thought his hometown deserved to know the real story of the investigation.

But there was one nine-year-old boy who was not shy about shining a light on him.

Before Rader's arrest, Kenny and Cindy had explained to James what his father's role was in hunting BTK.

His job, he told James, was to help his detectives catch the bad guy. James was terrified at the risk his father was taking, but Landwehr told him repeatedly that he had plenty of help, not only from Otis, Gouge, Relph, and Snyder, but from Chief Williams, Capt. John Speer, Capt. Randy Landen, Deputy Chief Robert Lee, and hundreds of other Wichita cops.

"The KBI is helping," he told James. "The FBI is helping."

"The FBI and the KBI?" James asked.

"Yes," Landwehr said.

"Aren't those guys like real secret agents?" James asked.

"Yes," Landwehr said. "I have a lot of help."

That conversation seemed to settle James's fears.

After Rader's arrest, much to Landwehr's embarrassment, James began to talk to strangers in Wal-Marts and grocery stores; James would see them looking at his father, recognizing him. James began to walk right up to these people and tell them that his father was the cop who had caught BTK.

This was mortifying to Landwehr, who had played a team role in a group that included dozens of people who had done clever things and had worked long days for months.

Landwehr pleaded with James not to say that he had caught BTK, or to at least tell a better version of what happened.

After a few such talks, the boy finally got it right. He would walk up to people staring at his father. He would introduce himself.

"My name is James Landwehr," he would tell them. "And my father is Lieutenant Ken Landwehr. And he caught BTK."

And then he would add one more line:

"He had a lot of help."

Acknowledgments

We are grateful that the police officers who hunted and caught BTK trusted us to tell their side of the story. Special thanks to Ken, Cindy, James, and Irene Landwehr; Dana Gouge; Kelly and Netta Otis; Tim Relph, and Clint Snyder. They gave us interviews lasting many hours. Ken and Cindy Landwehr, Gouge, Otis, Relph, and Snyder also fact-checked the manuscript, eliminated errors, and dispelled several fascinating myths that had attached themselves to the BTK story over thirty-one years.

We appreciate the time given to us by the victims' families, who spoke with us and other *Eagle* reporters despite their continuing sorrow. We interviewed Kevin Bright, Jeff Davis, Dale Fox, Kevin Fox, Georgia Mason, Beverly Plapp, Charlie Otero, and Steven Relford.

This book would have been lacking without the help of the investigators mentioned above, as well as the following members of law enforcement:

Current and former members of the Wichita Police Department: Chief Norman Williams, Jack Bruce, Gary Caldwell, Bob Cocking, Bill Cornwell, Paul Dotson, Bernie Drowatzky, Raymond Fletcher, Floyd Hannon, Raymond Hartley, Dan Harty, Darrell Haynes, Paul Holmes, Cheryl James, Janet Johnson, Robert Lee, Randy Landen, Richard LaMunyon, Scott Moon, Arlyn Smith, John Speer, Randy Stone, Bobby Stout, and Joe Thomas.

From the Sedgwick County Sheriff's Office: Sheriff Gary Steed and Sam Houston.

From the Kansas Bureau of Investigation: Director Larry Welch, Ray Lundin, Sindey Schueler, and Larry Thomas.

From the Federal Bureau of Investigation: former profilers Roy Hazelwood, Gregg McCrary, and Robert Ressler.

From the Kansas Department of Corrections: Frances Breyne and Bill Miskell.

From the Sedgwick County District Attorney's Office: District Attorney Nola Foulston, Kevin O'Connor, Kim Parker, Aaron Smith, and Georgia Cole.

Current and former employees of KAKE-TV were our competitors on the daily BTK story but opened their notebooks to us for this book. Thanks to Larry Hatteberg, Ron Loewen, Glen Horn, Dave Grant, Chris Frank, Jeff Herndon, Cindy Martin, and Susan Peters.

We are indebted to many other sources, including Jeff Rader, Tony Ruark, Roger Valadez, Emery Goad, Robert Beattie, Emil Bergquist, Jeff Carrs, Karin Clark, Kimberly Comer, Jan Elliott, Thelma Elliott, Troy Griggs, Misty King, George Martin, Bob Monroe, Ray Reisz, Olivia Reynolds, Karin Rodriquez, Keith Sanborn, Jim Wainscott, Jack Whitson, Brian Withrow, the meteorologists at the National Weather Service's Wichita office, and several other people who asked to not be named.

We did much of our own reporting but had the benefit of work by current and former employees of the *Eagle* as the story unfolded over thirty-one years. Ken Stephens and Bill Hirschman, who led the newspaper's BTK investigations decades ago, kept their own files throughout the years and donated them to us when we started this book. In 2004 and 2005, virtually everyone in our newsroom was called into play to help with the newspaper's coverage of the BTK story. Special thanks to the following current and former members of the *Eagle*'s staff: Theresa Johnson, Jean Hays, Marcia Werts, Les Anderson, Deb Bagby, Lori O'Toole Buselt, Jeff Butts, Brian Corn, Bob Curtright, Monty Davis, Glenda Elliott, Stan Finger, Larry Fish, Tanya Foxx, Josh Funk, Jerri Gean, Deb Gruver, Travis Heying, Carolyn Hytche, Dion Lefler, Abe Levy, Teri Levy, Fred Mann, Mark McCormick, Kevin McGrath, Lisa McLendon, Davis "Buzz" Merritt, Denise Neil, Jaime Oppenheimer, Deb Phillips, Connie Pickler, Bo Rader, Jerry Ratts, Carrie Rengers, Joe Rodriguez, Michael Roehrman, Tim Rogers, Casey Scott, Tom Shine, Alice Sky, Paul Soutar, Craig Stock, Dana Strongin, Ron Sylvester, Rick Thames, Suzanne Perez Tobias, Randy Tobias, Lon Teter, Jeff Tuttle, Katherine Leal Unmuth, Dan Voorhis, Ronda Voorhis, Van Williams, and Brent Wistrom. Chuck Potter copyedited the book for the *Eagle*.

Dan Close was a consultant and manuscript assistant. Jillian Cohan read the manuscript.

Wichita Eagle editor Sherry Chisenhall detached us from other duties, some for more than a year, to work on this book; that sacrifice is deeply appreciated. Her thoughtful reading of the manuscript reminded us again of why she deserves the title in front of her name.

This book would not have been possible without the support of *Wichita Eagle* publisher Lou Heldman. His backing made it possible for us to spend the time and effort necessary to produce this account. In addition, Lou agreed at the start of this project to donate a significant portion of the book's proceeds to help build and maintain the Sedgwick County Law Enforcement Memorial, which will honor Wichita-area officers who have died in the line of duty.

Early on, fellow journalists and authors Teresa Riordan and Ron Suskind gave us encouragement and advice on getting published.

Many thanks to our agent, Mary Tahan, who loved this book from the beginning, believed in us, and guided us at every step. Once Harper-Collins senior editor Doug Grad got his hands on the proposal, he would not let go, for which we are most grateful.

And finally, we'd like to thank our own families, who put up with us—and without us—throughout the reporting and writing. Their love means much to us. Thank you.

ROY WENZL, TIM POTTER, PROJECT LEADER L. KELLY, AND HURST LAVIANA

Index